Getting
the Picture

Getting
the Picture

The Ekphrastic Principle
in Twentieth-Century
Spanish Poetry

Margaret H. Persin

Lewisburg
Bucknell University Press
London: Associated University Presses

Associated University Presses
440 Forsgate Drive
Cranbury, NJ 08512

Associated University Presses
16 Barter Street
London WC1A 2AH, England

Associated University Presses
P.O. Box 338, Port Credit
Mississauga, Ontario
Canada L5G 4L8

The paper used in this publication meets the requirements of the American National Standard for Permanence of Paper for Printed Library Materials Z39.48–1984.

Library of Congress Cataloging-in-Publication Data

Persin, Margaret Helen, 1948–
    Getting the picture : the ekphrastic principle in twentieth
-century Spanish poetry / Margaret H. Persin.
        p.   cm.
    Includes bibliographical references (p.   ) and index.
    ISBN 0-8387-5335-3 (alk. paper)
    1. Spanish poetry—20th century—History and criticism.
2. Ekphrasis.
PQ6085.P37   1997
861'.609—dc21   96-44360
                                                 CIP

Dedicated to the memory of my beloved aunt,

Margaret Halaburda Adames

1912–1973

Caminante, son tus huellas
el camino, y nada más;
caminante, no hay camino,
se hace camino al andar.
Al andar se hace camino,
y al volver la vista atrás
se ve la senda que nunca
se ha de volver a pisar.
Caminante, no hay camino,
sino estelas en la mar.

—Antonio Machado, *Campos de Castilla*

[Traveler, your footprints are
the road, and nothing more;
Traveler, there is no road,
the road is made by walking.
By walking the road is made,
and upon looking back
one sees the path that never
shall be trod on again.
Traveler, there is no road,
only wakes upon the sea.]

¡Oh mi voz condecorada
con la insignia marinera:
sobre el corazón un ancla,
y sobre el ancla una estrella,
y sobre la estrella el viento,
y sobre el viento la vela!

—Rafael Alberti, *Marinero en tierra*

[Oh my voice decorated
with the marine insignia:
above my heart an anchor,
and above the anchor a star,
and above the star the wind,
and above the wind the sail!]

Contents

Acknowledgments

Acknowledgments

THE journey that one takes in the writing of a book leads to many choices, ideas, people, and destinations, not to mention a few dead ends. In my own journey toward the completion of this project I have been inspired by the light that my beloved aunt bequeathed to me. It was in her modest library that as a little girl I first pored over books on poetry and art, and banged out simple words on an ancient typewriter. To her this book is dedicated.

The evolution of my ideas has been influenced by many very generous people. First and foremost, I would like to thank all of the poets who graciously gave me permission to cite their poetry. Among my colleagues are Andrew P. Debicki, whose keen readings of chapter versions have been ever insightful and probing and whose encouragement has been unflagging; W. J. T. Mitchell, who very magnanimously shared with me a chapter of his *Picture Theory* (1994) previous to its publication; Mary Lee Bretz, whose indispensable intellectual dialogue with me on ekphrasis forced me to continually question my presuppositions and readings, and to improve my presentation; and all the other members of my wonderful department at Rutgers University, most especially Tom Stephens, Carl Kirschner, Carlos Narváez, Phyllis Zatlin, Susana Rotker, Tomás Eloy Martínez, Frank Dauster, Mary Gossy, Gerard Aching, Marcy Schwartz, and Jorge Marcone, who faithfully participated in our "brown-bag lunches," listened to me, asked me questions, commented on my work, and learned more about ekphrasis than they ever bargained for. Special thanks also go out to Martha LaFollette Miller, John C. Wilcox, and Sharon Keefe Ugalde, for gently having given me constructive criticism on the manuscript and moral support when I hit some rough spots. I am also very grateful to my graduate students, most especially Mary Makris, Carys Evans Corrales, Marcia Pauls, María Inés Zaldívar, Eduardo Chirinos, José García, and Enrique Yepes, who have participated in my Spanish poetry seminars and who have been a sounding board for the evolution of my ideas on ekphrasis. Debbie and Duane Clause and Herb and Ronnie Segars gave me friendship and days on the ocean when I needed to be recentered; Audrey Augustynowicz shared her wisdom with me; Jim McClellan could always make me laugh; and Eleni Bourodimos not only transcribed for me the Greek words in this book, but also taught me how to dance like Zorba.

I also wish to acknowledge Rutgers University, most especially the Faculty of Arts and Sciences and Rutgers College, whose support and aid in many different forms were indispensable to the development and completion of this project. The FASP leave that I was granted in 1991 gave me the time and space to do the required reading and to think through my project, and the new computer facilitated the writing process. And finally, special thanks to both Rutgers University's Research Council and the Program for Cultural Cooperation Between Spain's Ministry of Culture and United States' Universities, which provided subvention support to Associated University Presses for the publication of this study.

The illustration found in chapter 5 and my reading of the Valente poem that accompanies it are dedicated to Casey and O'Malley.

Parts of the following chapters of this book were previously published, at times in different form:

Sections of chapter 1 and 4 appeared in *Novísimos, Postnovísimos, Clásicos: La poesía de los 80 en España*, edited by Biruté Ciplijauskaité.

Chapter 2 was published previously in *Hispania*, the journal of the American Association of Teachers of Spanish and Portuguese, vol. 72 (1989): 919–26.

Chapter 3 (an early version) appeared in *Siglo XX / 20th Century* 3, nos. 1–2 (1985–86): 11–15.

Section of chapter 4 appeared in *Monographic Review / Revista Monográfica* 6 (1990): 93–104.

Section of chapter 5 appeared in *Anales de la literatura española contemporánea* 12, no. 3 (1987): 273–90.

Section of chapter 6 appeared in *Siglo XX / 20th Century* 12, nos. 1–2 (1994): 171–82.

Section of chapter 7 appeared in *Studies in Twentieth-Century Literature* 16 (1992): 109–26.

My deepest thanks to the editors of these journals and of *Novísimos* for permission to include materials published by them.

1
Get the Picture?

Mᴜᴄʜ current critical debate centers around the concepts of textual indeterminacy, the decentering of the sign, and by extension, the self-referential text. All have as a principal focus the problem of the Word and its (in)ability to communicate Truth by means of its semantic as well as its ideological structures. A demonstration of this polemical confrontation between Truth and the artist's always failed attempts to express it can be found nowhere more clearly exemplified than in the case of ekphrastic literature, where the writer in her/his role as the reader of another text, has to confront the naming and breaking of artistic limits of various genres, literary as well as visual. In the current study, I wish to undertake a probing look at how Spanish poets of the twentieth century read visual art and write texts that utilize the discursive strategy known as *ekphrasis*, and in turn, how their poetic texts presuppose certain theoretical, ideological, and discursive issues for the reader. As a result of the poets' reading practices, those visual works "read" by them are inscribed in their poetry, and in a variety of ways. This analysis, I hope, will shed light on the poets' own particular and distinctive stance toward many primary issues, such as textuality, representation, language, literature, and art in general, to name only a few. And in turn, poetic texts of this type also bring to the forefront a series of issues which bear directly upon the reading—and writing—process, and reveal a poet's choices, propensities, and philosophical as well as ideological postures that perhaps could only be surmised in a less explicit fashion from a reading of texts that are not ekphrastic.

What is the basis for this technique, why does it hold so much interest for Spanish poetry of the twentieth century, and what does it have to do with the nuanced differences between the representations supposedly based upon objective reality—mimesis—and others that call that mode into question? In the studies

13

that follow on individual poets, I hope to offer answers to these substantive questions, and to thus establish a conceptual as well as a cultural framework. I propose to take a look at how Spanish poets of the twentieth century approach the verbal-visual connection, in the hope of discovering not only their rationale for attempting to approximate one discourse through another, but also to gain insight into the undecidable nature of the Word, also into the reading and writing process, as exemplified in the poet's attempt to represent a plastic/visual art object within the frame of literature.

DEFINITIONS

Ekphrasis as a literary technique is surely not new. It has been defined in various ways and from various perspectives, and has been utilized from the classical period to the present day. A conventional definition of *ekphrasis* is to be found in the *Oxford English Dictionary*, which states that it derives from the ancient Greek έ'κφράσις, and is "a plain declaration, description or interpretation of a thing" (*Oxford English Dictionary*, 831). From a theoretical and critical perspective, it would be well to also consider other more specific definitions of the term, for the concepts and implications that they suggest in regard to the relationship of the visual to the verbal arts.

Many critics have noted the presence, through its evocation, of visual art in the verbal context, beginning with the earliest examples hearkening from antiquity, and including the oft-cited example of Homer's description of Achilles' shield in the *Iliad*.[1] Horace, in the first century before the common era, put forth his well-known yet enigmatic and various interpreted dictum in regard to the relationship of painting to poetry "Ut pictura poesis," invariably translated into English by the phrase "as is painting so is poetry." This dictum gave rise to several interpretations and misinterpretations of the visual/verbal dialectic throughout the ages. Gotthold Ephraim Lessing, in the eighteenth century, rejected resoundingly what he considered to be a contrived connection between literature and the plastic arts. In his *Laokoön: An Essay on the Limits of Painting and Poetry* (1766), he repudiated the possibility of comparing visual and verbal art, since the visual is based on a perception of the spatial aspects of a work, while the verbal depends on language's basic and inherent temporality. More recently, art critics, whether contemplating the verbal or visual work of art, have been inclined to reject Lessing's position, in order to defend the viability of a verbal/visual connection. Joseph Frank, in his seminal three-part essay, "Spatial Form in Modern Literature" (1945) argues that a verbal text may indeed take on a spatial quality through such techniques as juxtaposition and simultaneity. He cites many examples drawn from modern literature, such as Djuna Barnes, T. S. Eliot, James Joyce, Ezra Pound, and Marcel Proust, as writers who had indeed overcome the seemingly irreconcilable differences in artistic discourse, and who had succeeded in communicating spatial relationships traditionally associated with visual art, through a verbal medium.

Another contemporary critic, Murray Krieger, in his "Ekphrastic Principle and the Still Movement of Poetry; or *Laokoön* Revisited," returns to the oft-studied "Ode on a Grecian Urn" by John Keats, and cites Leo Spitzer's perspicacity in observing that through the power of metaphor, literature, in a very real sense, becomes the object of its desire, the plastic work of art. By its verbal structures a literary text has the capacity to emulate the spatial configurations of visual art. But there is a beautiful paradox involved in this transformation, since "The object of imitation, as spatial work, becomes the metaphor for the temporal work which seeks to capture it in that temporality" (Krieger 1967, 107). The literary art piece uses the spatial art object as a metaphor to represent itself, the temporal work of art. In addition to the ode by Keats, other examples of ekphrasis that he mentions are T. S. Eliot's wheel and Chinese jar. For Krieger, the ultimate irony in ekphrastic art is that it "retains its essential nature as a time-art even as its words, by reaching the stillness by way of pattern, seek to appropriate sculpture's plasticity as well. There is, after all, then, a sense in which literature, as a time-art, does have special time-space powers. Through pattern, through context, it has the unique power to celebrate time's movement as well as to arrest it, to arrest it in the very act of celebrating it" (Ibid., 125). In Krieger's subsequent *Ekphrasis: The Illusion of the Natural Sign* the author presents a diachronic overview of the "still movement" of ekphrasis, and centers his definition upon the idea that ekphrasis becomes "a general principle of poetics, asserted by every poem in the assertion of its integrity" (Krieger 1992, 284).[2]

Emilie L. Bergmann, in her study on ekphrasis in *Art Inscribed: Essays on Ekphrasis in Spanish Golden Age Poetry*, once again cites Leo Spitzer and his early study of Keats's "Ode on a

Grecian Urn," where Spitzer, corroborating the *Oxford Classical Dictionary*, defined ekphrasis from a specifically artistic perspective as "the poetic description of a pictorial or sculptural work of art" (Bergmann 1979, 1). But as she notes, this reference in a verbal text to visual art has been in usage only since the fourth century (Ibid.). Previously, ekphrasis in purely rhetorical terms had referred solely to description, in its most general usage. Bergmann further comments that ekphrasis originally had served as what she terms a solely "descriptive digression," and that there existed a separate literary tradition in which "descriptions of painting and sculpture served an allegorical or symbolic function" (Ibid.). It was only much later that the term ekphrasis combined these two functions. Bergmann takes issue with the stance of Jean H. Hagstrum, who prefers to separate the merely iconic value of a visual description from a verbal text which gives "voice and language to the otherwise mute art object" (Hagstrum, 1958, 18 n. 34). This bestowal of voice and language may be accomplished in a variety of ways, such as through *prosopopoeia*, apostrophe, emblem, or inscription. For Hagstrom evidence of voice and language of the mute art object must appear on the superficial level of the verbal text. Hagstrom thus limits the ekphrastic strategy to a very narrow range of verbal texts, and prefers to trace the origin of the term *ekphrasis* to the Greek ἐκφράζειν meaning "to speak forth," or "to digress" (Ibid., 2). Bergmann, for her part, prefers the etymology of *ekphrasis* as "to report in detail" or "to elaborate upon," thus maintaining allegiance to a much broader definition of the term. For Bergmann, ekphrasis includes the two techniques described by Hagstrom, rather than only one.

In her recent work, *The Art of Interference: Stressed Readings in Verbal and Visual Texts*, Mary Ann Caws refer to ekphrastic works, "interartistic translations," as "stressed readings"; "the problematics of address and translation of ideas and forms, of relation and involvement, lead to a reading situation I am calling *stressful, a term I insist upon taking as positive*" (Caws 1989, 3) [Caws's italics]. Caws selectively refines her definition of stress, in order to take advantage of the play present in the term's accepted meanings:

> I mean first, of course, in the sense of a certain anxiety relating to the projects both of comparison and of the expression of that comparison: to *relate* occasions stress. Secondly, as in metric stress, it is an accent placed on certain details in particular, sometimes in a

recurring pattern. Lastly, there is the stress of a "stressed" metal, where the trying moment proves some sort of endurance. Such stress is indeed *trying*, since, in its translation from one domain to the next, the accent and the positive energy discharged by the problematics of address encounter each other in a struggle at once vivifying, vitalizing, and agonistic. (Ibid.)

In the case of the visual image that is evoked in a verbal work of art, it would seem that all the definitions posed by Caws for the term *stress* would indeed apply. The play of the various definitions of stress inserts into the ekphrastic text the very anxiety, lilting yet uncertain lyricism, and breaking points that lead to the possibility of the simultaneous presence/absence of the alien text, the alien other of the visual artwork. The ekphrastic text responds to the interartistic challenge, since there is a basic and underlying tension between the various art forms that vie for expression through, and/or in spite, of the linguistic medium.

For many critics, the problem of visual art in literature presents an insoluble conundrum, that is, how is the artist to express in linear or temporal terms that which is spatial? Or, as Diane Chaffee states, "how do writers create spatial form in language which, by nature is linear?" (Chaffee 1984, 312). And while acknowledging the difficulty inherent in the juxtaposition of these two very different types of discourse, Chaffee delineates several specific techniques through which the writer may indeed attempt to get beyond the seemingly irreconcilable dichotomy of time and space. She establishes her definition of ekphrasis as "the verbal description of either an actual or make-believe work of art" (Ibid.). For Chaffee, this coming together of two disparate art forms represents a transformation of a visual art form into another which is verbal in nature, thus bringing about a confrontation between time and space, between word and vision, within one sensorial experience. In her study of ekphrasis in Hispanic literature, Chaffee draws her examples from such authors as Lope de Vega, Cervantes, and Borges. She demonstrates through specific examples such devices as interruption of the story line, juxtaposition, simultaneity, spatial progression in time, and digression that stops a narrative flow, all techniques that encourage the reader to experience this confrontation between time and space.

The definition of ekphrasis that I utilize in this study is broadly based, borrows from, and is dependent upon previously debated conceptual parameters. I therefore term as *ekphrastic* a poetic text that makes reference to a visual work of art, whether real or imagined, canonized or uncanonized, and thus allows that art object, in truth the object of (artistic) desire, to "speak for itself" within the problematically ruptured framework of the poetic text. This art object's ability to speak for itself is dependent upon the intertextual status of its problematic presence in the verbal text as well as the status of the reader. The ekphrastic text, by its very nature, reveals in an explicit fashion the writer's/reader's experience that Robert Scholes refers to as the "surrender of sovereignty," where there are exchanges of "power and pleasure" (Scholes 1989, 108–9). Furthermore, I will include in this broadly viewed framework a poetic text which refers to the oeuvre of a particularly named artist: this type of text may not make reference to a specific art work, but rather attempts to capture the essence of, or pay homage to, an artist's style by means of, for example, description, selective detail, transgression of boundaries, sequencing, or a host of other suggestive strategies.

In order to consider ekphrasis within the context of Spanish poetry written in the twentieth century, one must note that it becomes necessary to widen and broaden the definition of the arts that has held sway, namely as those products of artistic inspiration which find their source in the nine Muses of classical mythology.[3] For in the Spanish poetry produced in this era, the arts are represented by not only painting, sculpture, architecture, history, comedy, tragedy, and music—the art forms canonized by classical tradition—but also by other uncanonized forms such as television, cinematography, photography, commercial and consumer advertising, comics, posters, and soap operas, all examples of mass culture and mass media. These uncanonized embodiments of the ekphrastic principle make their raucous presence known more deliberately and emphatically in the Franco and post-Franco era, a detail that must be taken into account from the perspective of ideology, which will be discussed in the next section. Contemporary Spanish poets have a propensity to push the limit for the conventional definition of the arts. If one considers all the visually perceived art forms, both canonized and uncanonized, that exist and clamor for the attention of the I/eye in the current age, then it is not illogical to consider that these art forms will come in contact with one another; influence one another; and reflect the realities, desires, infelicities, prejudices, and presuppositions of their cultural, social, artistic, and political context. As Marcia Lou Pauls comments, examples of ekphrasis are to be found that embrace, often

in a brazen, impudent, and insolent fashion, marginalized forms
of artistic expression. These include all manner of

> graphic arts, such as typeset, printing, binding, etching, and engrav-
> ing, as well as the iconography of everyday things, the banal images
> often depicted in Pop Art. Here one recalls visual design associated
> with written documents such as telegrams, stamps, postcards, tick-
> ets, timetables, street signs, menus, obituaries, product lables, maps
> and a plethora of other modern graphic forms whose meaning de-
> pends as heavily on the visual codes at work in them as on their
> linguistic content (Pauls, 5).

Thus, "the traditional arts" find themselves in the company of
others that simultaneously do and do not "speak the same language," not only with each other, but also with the text that
attempts to frame them as well as the reader of the hybrid text.[4]
This reader's presuppositions about textuality are constantly being put into question because of the iconoclastic nature and the
politics of rupture that define the modern and postmodern
ekphrastic text. Indeed, precisely because of the impudence and
insolence of the marginalized forms, it is the poetic text that gets
framed, since it must fit or adapt itself to the presence of the
Other. The poetic text also gets framed in the sense that evidence
is falsified in order to impute guilt. The poetic text seems to
deliver the goods, but the art object never really does appear.

In the first chapter of his *Protocols of Reading* entitled "Reading: An Intertextual Activity" Scholes asserts that "Reading has
two faces, looks in two directions. One direction is back, toward
the source and original context of the signs we are deciphering.
The other direction is forward, based on the textual situation of
the person doing the reading. It is because reading is almost
always an affair of at least two times, two places, and two con-
sciousnesses that interpretation is the endlessly fascinating, difficult, and important matter that it is" (Scholes, 1989, 7). I would
assert that the ekphrastic text doubles the process and the fascination, since the reader of the literary text must read and interpret the reading process of the writer, who, in turn reads
and interprets a visual text. The act of reading is inscribed upon
the ekphrastic text and serves as its basic and very obvious
presupposition.

I believe that Scholes's suggested protocol may be carried yet
a step further, since in reading the poet reading another text, we
too as readers have the opportunity to get a glimpse of how *we*
read and are read by a poet's reading of that other text. The reader

"reads" the choices that each poet has made in regard to the varied media discourses evoked in the poetic text, and in the process becomes conscious of which aesthetic ideals have been chosen, favored, and valued, and conversely, which have been rejected and/or repressed. Similarly, the reader must determine what type of relationship exists between the I/eye of the poetic text and that of the visual work of art. The poet's point of view concerning the art object—sensory, philosophical, ideological—enters into dialogue with that of the reader.[5] This type of text, the ekphrastic one, by its very nature, reveals the complexities of textuality (and doubles them), and makes explicit, indeed celebrates and problematizes, the concepts of sign, representation, and reference, the relationship between one text and another, the creator and the created, language and mind, sender and receiver, sign(s) and system(s), inside and outside, presence and absence, seeing and saying, Self and Other.[6] As Scholes comments, "In reading we find ourselves, to be sure, but only through the language of the Other, whose existence we must respect" (Scholes 1989, 50). This comment about the reading process is doubly illuminating as well as doubly vexing, since it may be applied to the poet reading a text of visual art, as well as to the reader of the poetic text, who reads the poet reading that other visual work, whose discourse is the alien Other within the literary, linguistic one.

The Problem of Discourse

The prime focus of the encounter and confrontation between or among various art forms and their means of communication, whether verbal, visual, or a combination of the two, is that of the problem of discourse. How is it that one can speak of one art form in terms of another? How is it that each poet confronts and appraises the rapprochement of one form of art with another? It is precisely in this rapprochement and in the poet's attitude toward it that one may observe that poet's originality and creativity: s/he appears to allow the alien Other to speak for itself. This alien Other both is and is not within the literary text's frame, since its presence has been evoked via language in the literary text, but that very presence projects and defines itself by means of its difference from that same literary text. In her *Salome and the Dance of Writing: Portraits of Mimesis in Literature*, Françoise Meltzer refers only to portraiture but the same could be said of the evocation of any visually perceived and verbally evoked art object: "That which ruptures the limits of the text is the portrait itself, with its solid frame refusing all synthesis. As such, the portrait is radical otherness in the text" (Meltzer 1987, 46). Each poet develops a method and a reply to that which may seem like a dead end or at least a supposedly insurmountable barrier, namely, the evocation of an alien discourse within and by means of another (and an Other). By taking possession of another form and by nominally declaring sovereignty over that art object, the poet attempts to preempt its authority. But it is interesting to note that in this preemption of jurisdiction (jurisdiction: law + to point out in words, thus, the administration of authority and justice) the poet admits if only implicitly that poetic discourse in and of itself is no longer viable or at least not totally self-sufficient, and no longer serves the specific artistic needs demanded by that poet's view of reality, originality, and creativity. In this manner, the poet is thus obliged to search beyond the traditional limits of the discourse of lyric poetry, and ultimately must surrender in part to the authority of the visually perceived art object. In exploring this "un-"limited option, paradoxically, the poet inscribes in the text not only the tradition against which s/he is reacting, but also a new tradition, which calls for a more flexible definition of poetry. Broader avenues are opened in regard to structure, discursive strategies, perspectives, and voices which have been gleaned from the other alien art forms.

The inside/outside polarity serves in regard to the reader's function as well. Because of the strong mimetic tradition of literary description, the reader is drawn into the poetic text and asked to imagine the visual work of art "as if" it were visible to the naked eye.[7] Thus, the poet draws the reader into the poetic text, but at the same time demands that the reader perceive the visual artwork as an outwardly observed object. The reader is lured into and framed by the text, once again from two different perspectives. The poetic text insists upon the reader's being constantly aware of the evocation of an exterior art object; the reader is enclosed in a border that separates the verbal from the visual. The reader is pulled in, in order to be left out. But this difference involves a "frame-up," since there is a falsifying of evidence, in that the visual art object is not really present after all; the writer has framed only a forgery, a copy, a simulacrum of the desired object. Thus, the poet, the reader, the poetic text, and the visual art object may all ruefully declare, "I've been had! I've been framed!" The text, whatever its nature, gets framed in the sense that evidence is falsified. A crime has been committed, but only circumstantial evidence and Derridean traces remain. The poetic text pulls off a sting, seems to deliver the goods, but the art object presented is a brilliant fake, a "true" copy that faithfully and subversively evokes the presence/absence of the desired Other.

In considering the attempt to represent one artistic medium within another, there are certain theoretical issues that come to the fore as paramount, and must be considered from the point of view of the role of the reader, discursive practice, and the underlying ideological stance that they presuppose. The reader's process of reception and interpretation are dependent upon and mirror those of the poet. We, as readers, read the poet reading another text. It seems to me that we catch the poet red-handed (or is it "read/eyed"?) at an exquisite moment of self-revelation in a double(-crossed) act of reception *and* response to a visual art object. There is a special type of dialogue in the ekphrastic text between the visual art object and the poetic text that frames it; the function of the reader, then, is to interpret and frame the poet's reading of not only this other artistic text but also of how the poet reads art, culture, and their individual and/or combined roles in society. Poet and reader attempt to participate in the economy of both power and pleasure as well as surrender and sovereignty of the reading process. I would assert that through the ekphrastic text the poet demonstrates *both* surrender and sovereignty in that, on the one hand, s/he submits to the vision of another in her/his own text, and on the other, dominates that vision by controlling how it is represented through the medium of language. The "exchange of power and pleasure" posited by Scholes must be extended in regard to the ekphrastic text, since we as readers are witnesses to the poet's exchange of power and pleasure with a visual text, which in turn contributes to our own exchange, based upon our own experience of the poet's hybrid texts. And finally, this "power and pleasure" can be viewed from yet another perspective. Caws alludes to Roland Barthes's "eroticization of the text" (Caws, 4), as a further elucidation of this concept of pleasure, which for Caws is double in the ekphrastic text, since it is a double text, both verbal and visual. So, for the reader it may very well be at minimum a ménage à trois, in which poet, reader, and text(s) participate in a mutual and very erotic exchange of power and pleasure from a variety of perspectives. The "bedroom scene" becomes even more complicated, crowded, and saturnalian, when one considers that the artistic space of the ekphrastic text is also peopled by the presence of the visual artists to which the verbal text makes reference. And in turn, texts of this type also bring to the forefront a series of issues that bear directly upon the reading—and writing—process, and reveal a poet's choices, propensities, and philosophical postures that perhaps could only be surmised in a less explicit fashion from a reading of texts that are not ekphrastic.

The first of many issues raised by the confrontation of verbal with visual art in regard to discursive practice is that of intertextuality, either the broader view espoused by Jonathan Culler and Julia Kristeva, or the narrower view held by Harold Bloom. Ekphrasis is a special case of intertextuality, in that a verbal text permits entry via the sign system of language and via the process of description of a plastic work of art that is visually perceived. The poet attempts first to place in juxtaposition two very distinct codes which proceed from two very different media, and then to communicate one via the other. And as Claus Clüver rather humorously comments, "an ekphrastic poem can be variously related to the work on which it is based: as an interpretation, a meditation, a commentary, a critique, an imitation, a countercreation, and other things besides, at times perhaps motivated by a Bloomian anxiety of influence, although painters do not often occupy the place of fathers that poets need to kill" (Clüver 1989, 69). The poet recognizes the iconic value of the visual work to which s/he has recourse and the code of the other artist whose work is reflected in the poetic text. Just as the visual artist enters into the "sense of the process of constant interferences, constant modifications, and constant transformations" (Pleynet 1984, 39), so too the poet. And in attempting to "swerve away from" (Bloom 1973, 14) the precursor artist who has been identified as a source, the poet attempts to attain her/his own manner and style of originality and creativity, but has to do it in such a way that the art object of another medium is effectively communicated through the alien discourse of language. In regard to painting, Marcelin Pleynet views this process as "a more or less conscious elucidation of a culture's antagonisms and contradictions" (Pleynet 1984, 38); the same could be said, I propose, for the intertextual power of ekphrastic poetry. The poet's choice of a certain art object of a certain artistic discourse speaks of not only the poet's aesthetic ideals, antagonisms, and contradictions, but of the cultural milieu that s/he represents as well.

The second issue that must be considered in this confrontation between twentieth-century poetry written in Spanish and the visual arts is that that Gustavo Pérez Firmat names as liminality: "the liminal entity is one that in a given situation takes up a position of eccentricity, one that occupies the periphery in relation to a contextually determined center" (Pérez Firmat 1986, xiv). The poetic works to be considered here tempt (and [at]tempt to go beyond) the limits of poetic discourse. Paradoxically, the central focus of this poetry is its marginality. What does a poem or a collection of poems wish to communicate when it attempts to be or represent an Other, be it painting, sculpture, cinema, comic, billboard, or something else? As Pérez Firmat states, this type of text is therefore constituted by a productive tension between restraint and mobility, order and disorder, tradition and treason" (Ibid., xviii). This tension may be seen in all of what would be termed modern literature, from the explosion of the avant-garde movement at the beginning of the twentieth century, to the contemporary postmodern iconoclastic art forms.[8]

Continuing this same line of thought in regard to liminality, one must confront questions and issues pertinent to genre, the literary canon, and the very definition of the text. If a text exhibits liminality as a central, defining characteristic, can this text be included in good faith within a traditional canon? In short, what precisely defines the limit(s), and who is the gatekeeper? (In this particular case, I use the term gatekeeper, with its patriarchal overtones, for a specific purpose.) Ekphrastic texts reveal the play of limits, the conventions, and their rupture that continually question the stability of that very canon.

Related to the issue of genre is that of gender, whether in regard to the role of the artist (the poet or the painter) or the reader. As several critics have already noted, ekphrastic literature must confront the issue of gender, because the I/eye of the text traditionally has been male; the so-called male gaze defines the sensory as well as the philosophical point of view of the art piece, and decides the erotic value as well. A male viewer looks upon a passive and mute object of beauty, very often represented by a female body. The male critic W. J. T. Mitchell proposes that the tradition of the male gaze finds a female permutation "in the frequent occurrence of the heroine or female narrator as painter or keen-sighted viewer, a "seeing" as opposed to a "speaking" subject, a dweller in space rather than time" (Mitchell 1989, 97).

For her part, the feminist critic Dale M. Bauer applies the Bakhtinian concepts of heteroglossia and dialogism to the problem of female narrative practices in order to dismantle the tradition of the male gaze. She proposes to "read the woman's voice—

excluded or silenced by dominant linguistic or narrative strategies—back *into* the dialogue in order to reconstruct the process
by which she was read out in the first place" (Bauer 1988, 4).
Spanish women poets of the twentieth century enter into dialogue with the traditional patriarchal canon, but assert their
presence by finding their own voice, even in the silence imposed
by that very canon through the surveillant male gaze. Inexorably
the issue of gender will lead once again to the reader, whether
male or female. Jonathan Culler, in the chapter on "Reading as a
Woman," in his *On Deconstruction (1982)* identifies three separate moments in the reading process, whereby a reader (whether
male or female) may become aware of the gender-related presuppositions that inform the reading process. It would seem that in
regard to the issue of gender, there becomes obvious an underlying dialectical tension that is in the final analysis irreconcilable
between the traditional limits imposed on the text by the canon
and the rupture of those limits by an ekphrastic text whose artist
(poet or painter) is female. The liminal text both inscribes and
casts out the canonically defined one; and the gender-related
issue of the gaze, whether that of the artist (visual or verbal) or
the reader, bring explicitly to the surface the basic Otherness of
representation, an unwanted presence that forces the viewer to
acknowledge the mutability of the sign.[9] This idea of liminality
brings us in a necessary and irremediable fashion once again to
the issue of discourse, as we saw before. In ekphrastic poetry, the
poet calls attention to the inadequacy of the poetic endeavor by
attempting to transform a discourse taken from another medium.
Thus, the "borrowing" of a discourse from an iconic representation becomes symbolic, and represents poetry and all art's failure—in any medium—to grasp reality, truth, and eternal beauty
within its artistic boundaries. And in so doing, the poetic text
is able to speak of itself and of its (in)ability to communicate
that which is both exterior and interior to the creative process.
The poet pays lip service to the iconicity of her/his text and that
of the visual artist whose work is evoked in the verbal/linguistic
discursive code. S/he attains, through linguistic means and only
to a certain degree, a like representation of the visual artist's
perception of reality. Wendy Steiner notes in *The Colors of Rhetoric* that "the attempt to overreach the boundaries between one
art and another is thus an attempt to dispel (or at least mask) the
boundary between art and life, between sign and thing, between
writing and dialogue" (Steiner 1984, 5). From Steiner's perspective, the "as if" of representational art, whether verbal or visual,

hides the illusion and the delusion. Steiner further comments that "art as mirror claims to reveal what is "truly" there" (Ibid., 7). But I would hold that in ekphrastic poetry, the poet as well as the reader is continually reminded of the frame, and the intrusion of one art form upon another, thus emphasizing in a direct manner the self-referentiality of this particular type of text. The poet, in making reference to yet another art form, insures that the receiver of the text is aware that the text(s) is/are only a paltry approximation of reality, a different combination of ever-changing signs in an endless concatenation that never can grasp that object that it desires to represent.[10]

Another perspective that proves to be useful in the appraisal of ekphrastic poetry is that offered by the Russian theorist, Mikhail N. Bakhtin. His concepts of *heteroglossia* and *dialogism* insert a dynamic element into this meeting of discourses that takes place between the verbal and the visual arts. Although in his Bakhtin essay "Discourse in the Novel," *The Dialogic Imagination* Bakhtin rejects the poetic genre because of what he views as its stultified petrification and the univocality of its structures, I believe that the poetry of the twentieth century, with its use of multiple perspectives, speakers, tones, and registers effectively answers and puts to rest his objections. Surely, Spanish poetry of this century has surpassed the restrictions and traditional limitations signaled by Bakhtin in his time, namely, those of unity, singularity, and monovocality of the poetic voice. In the current age, the poetic text enthusiastically enters into dialogue with other texts, whether within the canon or not. And this intertextual dialogue is played out very convincingly within the parameters of the texts that use ekphrasis as a major discursive strategy. The dialogism signaled by Bakhtin manifests itself in ekphrastic poetry in the art object's "speaking for itself" within the frame of linguistic and literary discourse. Thus, in another fashion, the ekphrastic text is able to enter into dialogue with its cultural context, to bring to the surface once again the issue of self-referentiality, and to offer up for consideration not only its own mode of discourse and its systems and methods of communication, but also those of the "other" work of art to which it refers. The Bakhtinian concepts of heteroglossia and dialogism inexorably lead to the issue of Self versus Other. One critic sees all of Bakhtin's work as a unified whole which confronts this basic dialectic. As Michael Holquist comments, "The suggestion of Bakhtin's total *oeuvre*, conceived as a single utterance, is that our ultimate act of authorship results in the text which we call our self" (Morson 1986, 67). This in turn leads to questions of text as self, and the relation of self to society.

Also, from this same perspective, it would be well to consider the concept of the frame, as well as that of the incursion of another alien text within the poetic text. Susan Stewart makes the cogent observation that "It is an old argument in aesthetics that it is not the picture that makes art art, but the frame and the frame's implicit message 'This is art'. The frame focuses our attention not upon content alone, but upon the organization of content and the relationship between content and its surroundings" (Stewart 1978, 21). But what of the case of the ekphrastic poem, where the poet attempts to permit the entry of another text of a different medium into the poetic one, and also attempts to use poetic discourse to represent that alien Other? That Other invades and breaks the boundaries of the verbal representation, but does it in such a fashion so as to utilize the discourse of the alien host. Where does the frame of the poetic text begin and/or end in relation to the frame of the other artistic text? Is there closure of one or the other of the texts that are before the reader's eyes, in either a literal (i.e., typographical) or symbolic sense? Or is the door (frame?) forever ajar to permit the entrance and/or escape of one text into the other/Other? As Theo D'haen comments, these texts "alert their audience to the fact that reality is preframed by society just as much as art is" (D'haen 1989, 436). The observer's perception of the work of art as well as reality is colored by the frame that surrounds it. And this frame is the supporting ideology that motivates artistic discourse as well as the notions of value in art and society as a whole.

And with this mention of the Other, there springs up another even more unsettling issue. As J. Hillis Miller comments in his essay "The Critic as Host,"

> The previous text is both the ground of the new one and the something the new poem must annihilate by incorporating it, turning it into ghostly insubstantiality, so that the new poem may perform its possible-impossible task of becoming its own ground. The new poem both needs the old texts and must destroy them. It is both parasitical on them, feeding ungraciously on their substance, and at the same time it is the sinister host which unmans them by inviting them into its home, as the Green Knight invites Gawain. Each previous link in the chain, in its turn, played the same role, as host and parasite, in relation to its predecessors. (Bloom et al. 1979, 225)

Although Miller bases his analysis on two texts whose shared medium is the verbal, as much could be said for the ekphrastic poem. In other words, the central focus of the ekphrastic poem is constantly shifting, for the poet as well as for the reader. The precursor visual text necessarily must (dis)appear in a continual ebb and flow of presence and absence, in order to give way to a "new" text, one that is verbal in nature. This focus cannot remain solely on the verbal text, which must permit the visual referent to be conjured up by the verbal discourse. There is a dialogue in two different languages between these texts of differing discursive modes, and more importantly, on the waxing and waning of the distinct planes of reference and in the slipperiness of the sign, which once again leads to a metatextual perspective. The centrality of a text of this type is its marginality: the focus ultimately becomes centered on the indeterminacy of the text (which text?), paradoxically, in the act of creating, re-creating, consecrating, and desecrating one form of artistic representation within another, and imposing one discourse upon another, one act of reference upon another. And could it be that, as Miller suggests, the parasitical relationship of one artistic text to another bespeaks the parodical analogy that one is to find in the relationship of critic to artistic text? In other words, we as readers enter into the mise-en-abyme of the ekphrastic poem, and by our illusory presence seemingly sustain yet another link in the unreliable representation of an ungraspable reality. Our Otherness also opens and closes the frame(s) of the ekphrastic poem.

Ultimately, the issue that comes to the forefront in the consideration of ekphrastic poetry is that of ideology. As Mitchell points out, the issue of how image relates to text always and invariably leads to ideological considerations (Mitchell 1986, 1–4).[11] Ekphrastic art is common to all epochs. But what is interesting to note is the particular way in which image is represented in any given text. This, in turn, will give an indication of how a particular period approaches and deals with representation, sign, and value in general terms. And from a particularly aesthetic perspective, the simultaneity of verbal text and visual image speaks not only about the topic at hand, but also about the sign's value and authenticity within the framework of art and literature, and how culture and society feel about the two, either separately or together. Or as Steiner puts it in regard to the painting-literature analogy, "the interartistic comparison inevitably reveals the aesthetic norms of the period during which the question is asked. To answer the question is to define or at least

describe one's contemporary aesthetics, and this is the value
of entering once again the history of analogical insight—and
disappointment—that characterizes the painting-literature connection" (Steiner 1989, 18).

All that has been previously considered in this discussion of
the ekphrastic poem—the questions of discourse, or rather, the
confrontation of discourses; the problematic nature of representation (whether verbal or visual) and its (dis)connection to the
world outside the text; intertextuality; liminality; heteroglossia
and dialogism; genre; gender; the literary canon; and the final
consideration of ideology—all these paths ultimately lead to a
consideration of the metapoetic dimension of the ekphrastic
poem. The poet, in reflecting and reflecting upon another text
alien to yet seemingly made present by poetic discourse per se,
invariably throws light upon the simultaneous generating and
destructive process of artistic creation, in whatever the artistic
medium. In regard to what he terms as "intersemiotic transpositions," Clüver comments that ekphrastic texts "are always read
also as texts about text making that show us possibilities and
limitations inherent in the two sign systems, alert us to the signifying power of syntactical and other structural devices available
in each, and make us aware of differences in aesthetic codes and
in sociocodes, especially governing depiction and description"
(Clüver, 70). In this manner, the "new" text (and I place the word
"new" in a privileged but suspect position) is a repository of
other texts and also a discreet as well as a discrete commentary
upon the coexisting success and failure of poetic discourse. From
my perspective there is a basic and overriding indeterminacy in
the reading of an ekphrastic poem, a skepticism in regard to the
power of the text to signify as an organic whole, a stubborn refusal to closure.[12] In this invasive, wounding encounter between
the verbal and the visual, that that comes into clear focus is
the equivocation of the textual message and of its method of
representation. The "dual coding" that is and is not one effectively subverts the possibility of a univocal reading of the text.
Ekphrasis offers itself up as the trope of tropes, a most effective
manner for a poet to express the Otherness that is ultimately all
art, all language, the reading process, the sign itself, and ultimately, our relationship to our environment, the ambivalent,
powerful yet subversive give-and-take between Self and Other.
By having recourse to another discourse alien to verbal communication (but using verbal communication to evoke that very
alien discourse), the poet is able to underscore the prison house

that is language, and the (in)ability of the WORD to communicate Truth by means of its structures.

Thus, I believe that ekphrasis as a discursive strategy becomes a prime metaphor of the Word's enigmatic and transparent Otherness. The sign is eternally and continually inhabited by an Other whose presence is marked by absence and is in constant oscillation, an Other whose presence is defined and deferred by the rupture of frames, limits, and Oneness. The presence of the Other symbolizes the sign that is continually in play. And as Mitchell comments, this Otherness is manifested in many ways, including but not limited to sexuality and gender difference, "the historical difference between the archaic and the modern, the alienation between the human and its own commodities, the conflict between a stable social order, and the monstrous revolutionary "Others" that threaten it, the gap between a historical epic obsessed with war, and a vision of the ordinary, nonhistorical order of human life that provides a framework for a critique of that historical struggle" (Mitchell 1994, 31–32).[13] In the final analysis, then, the figure of ekphrasis comes to represent art's questioning stance faced with Otherness. How is it that art never, ever achieves possession of the object of its desire, the exterior reality that it forever seeks? Ekphrasis attempts to represent that uneasy relationship between art and the resolutely ungraspable, and to celebrate that Otherness. Ekphrasis embodies the textual wound, the inevitable opening where the alien Other is the place, the vehicle, the barrier, the cure to penetration and (im)perfect (re)presentation. And this welcome yet alien Other, marginal by nature, comes to occupy the central locus of (un)certain signification.

THE EKPHRASTIC PRINCIPLE IN TWENTIETH-CENTURY SPANISH POETRY

At this juncture, it would be well to return to the question that was posited at the beginning, namely, what does ekphrasis have to do with twentieth-century Spanish poetry, and why would it be beneficial to take a look at differing examples of its occurrence? What I propose with all of this is the following: each writer approaches the relation of verbal and visual art from a distinct perspective. Ekphrasis, as it has been variously defined, is most decidedly NOT a new invention of twentieth-century Spanish poets. But shades and nuances of this evocative relationship are demonstrated to change with each writer. Thus, by taking a look at the specific manifestations of this trope of tropes, one may be able to acquire some insight into the stance of the poet in regard to a variety of relationships. In terms of Bakhtin, one could speak of the relationship between Self and Other, between text and society. In the jagged and visible needlework where there is an attempt on the part of each poet to represent and patch together different types of discourse from other media, we as readers attain a vision of the writers' and text's (and texts') presuppositions; we are able to see the particulars of the creative process as well as the ideological resonances of each poet's cultural context, to which that text and those texts respond. In each and every epoch one may find examples of ekphrastic literature; but that that is of interest, in my opinion, is the particular manner in which the image confronts the verbal text, and vice versa, and comes to be a marginal yet central part of that verbal text. The melding of the verbal and the visual—and the underlying presuppositions of this uneasy aggregation—points to ideological considerations of the particular literary period, the culture and the society which act as its foundation and backdrop.

I believe that this preamble will suffice, wherein the major theoretical issues of ekphrastic poetry have been presented. I will leave for the succeeding chapters an in-depth discussion of specific texts drawn from twentieth-century Spanish poetry. Chapter 2 on the poetry of Manuel Machado initiates this look at ekphrasis within the twentieth-century Spanish context, and establishes the framework for the consideration of its complex issues and contextualizations in succeeding chapters. Machado's ekphrastic poetic texts are straightforward and yet very unsettling, since they pose questions that lead to the heart of representation, power, truth, and value. Chapter 3 of this study singles out the ekphrastic poetry of Rafael Alberti, in order to explore the time/space relationship not only in regard to the painting/ poetry dialectic, but also to consider the means that the poet has at his disposal to (re)present in verbal form the two competing models of visual representation utilized by Picasso, namely, the Renaissance fixed-point perspective, and the multiperspectival one preferred by modernism. Thus, the poet confronts time from an aesthetic, historical perspective as well, since his attempt to tame and enclose two different responses to the time/space conundrum through his poetry frames his vision and debt to the visual artist. The ekphrastic poetry of Gloria Fuertes and Carmen Martín Gaite are considered in chapter 4, in order to contemplate the issue of not only ekphrastic liminality, but also of canonical liminality as well. These two poets call into question the frames and limits of poetry from various perspectives, and also point to the concept of the artistic gaze, the implicit I/eye of the artistic text whether visual or verbal. In chapter 5, the poetry of Jaime Gil de Biedma and José Angel Valente focalizes the concept of framing, and how the gaze of the poetic I/eye views not only that which is inside/outside the frame of the poetic and visual texts, but also how ekphrastic poems lead to metapoetic readings. The gaze reveals the theme of each individual poetic text, as well as the frame's coding devices and strategies. Thus, self-referentiality and ideology support and subvert the poetic text's overt message of oneness. Chapter 6 utilizes the poetry of María Victoria Atencia and Ana Rossetti as a point of departure to consider how the concept of the gaze motivates the two female poets to put into practice female "double vision" and "double voicing," so as to circumvent the silencing effect of the surveillant male gaze operant within conventional examples of patriarchal canonicity. And finally, chapter 7 addresses the verbal/visual text combination which uses the filmic media as the basis for ekphrasis in the poetry of Pere Gimferrer and Jenaro Talens. These two poets decenter authorship and authority in a postmodern turn, and in the process call for a new definition of ekphrasis itself. In a self-reflective manner, the specific poetic texts of Gimferrer and Talens comment upon the ideology of poetic form and content, art, and literature in general, and their relationship to the larger cultural context.

The choices I have made concerning the poets and their specific texts were based on the issues of clarity, applicability, and originality of method, and demonstrate most convincingly what Meltzer terms the "point of danger: the moment when the text risks annihilation by the power of representation itself, of which the text is but one facet" (Meltzer, 215). I believe that each of the poetic texts considered here illustrates in exemplary fashion yet another stance in regard to the verbal/visual artistic connection, and gives voice and visual substance to art's unique confrontation with not only modern and contemporary Spanish culture and society, but with the broader European context as well.

2

How Manuel Machado Did (Not) Get the Picture

A central strategy of representation and of its problematization found in Manuel Machado's verse is that of ekphrasis. This trope remains a constant throughout the years of his poetic production, from his earliest collections that began to appear in the waning years of the nineteenth century to the ones published nearer to his death in 1947. The poet's transmutation of other artistic media into verbal form permitted him to not only enrich the scope of his discursive ploys and plays, but also to confront the core issue of artistic truth in a unique fashion. For as will be demonstrated in the consideration of representative Machado texts, the poet's manipulation of the ekphrastic trope reveals his unremitting fascination with the time/space and inner/outer dialectics; this fascination, in turn leads him to grapple with the issues of artistic value, representation, and referentiality within the enigmatic signifying process.

Although very well received in his lifetime, the poetry of Manuel Machado has been unfavorably compared since his death with that of his younger brother Antonio. Thus, in recent years it has not received the critical attention that it deserves. In light of contemporary developments in literary theory and criticism, it would be wise to take another, closer look at the older Machado's verse from the perspective of representation and referentiality, in order to discover new insights and to be better able to place it within the context of twentieth-century poetry both of the Spanish generation of '98 and beyond. By analyzing particular components of Manuel Machado's style, it is hoped that the reader will be able to understand how his verse represents a link between the Spanish peninsular tradition of his epoch and that of the Latin American "modernistas" as well as the modernists of other European nations.[1]

Machado's verse, in a paradoxical turn, articulates a healthy skepticism in regard to art's capacity, in whatever the format or medium, to objectively grasp and then enunciate a reality that refers to something other than itself: he "puts into words" the impossibility of doing just that. This uncanny (sub)version of linguistic truth prudently leads to the consideration of self-referentiality as a defining attribute of the signifying process. In Machado's poetry, he imbues the technique of ekphrasis with the power to throw light not only upon a specific work of art supposedly outside the poetic text, but also upon textuality as a general theoretical construct. Machado's poetic text reveals something of itself, "speaks for itself," and speaks to the issue of its own composition, and by extension, to all artistic composition. The poet presents to his readers seeming verbal descriptions of other artworks, but his texts at the same time problematize representation, whether verbal or visual, by underscoring the idea that representations are "representations," and therefore are not equivalent to objective reality. He wields his strategies of composition so as to herald the presence of the other artworks, but also destabilizes the lines of demarcation—both keeping in and keeping out—between allusion and illusion.

The ekphrastic poetry of Machado is in consonance with that of other poets of his and subsequent generations who had been schooled in the classical tradition.[2] One only has to think of Miguel de Unamuno's *El Cristo de Velázquez (The Christ of Velázquez)* or Rafael Alberti's *A la pintura (To Painting)* or *Los 8 nombres de Picasso y no digo más que lo que no digo (The 8 Names of Picasso and I Do Not Say More Than I Do Not Say)*. All of these poets were well aware of the ekphrastic tradition in Spanish letters, and continued with an artistic mode that was favored by authors of the Golden Age.[3] The portrait poem of Machado that first comes to mind and indeed reminds the reader of this Golden Age tradition is his famous and often studied "Felipe IV" ("Phillip IV"),[4] which first appeared in March 1901, and was later included in his second published collection of verse, *Alma (Soul)*, which appeared in 1902. (See color plates.) This poem is to be found within the grouping aptly entitled "Museo" ("Museum"):*

---

*Author's note: So that this book will be accessible to readers in sundry fields of humanistic interest, I have provided translations for those sections cited in Spanish. I have opted for an accurate if literal translation of the poetic texts, with verse divisions indicted by a slash, and stanzas by a double slash. Moreover, in poetry by male writers I have utilized the convention of a pre-

Nadie más cortesano ni pulido
que nuestro rey Felipe, que Dios guarde,
siempre de negro hasta los pies vestido.

Es pálida su tez como la tarde,
cansado el oro de su pelo undoso,
y de sus ojos, el azul, cobarde.

Sobre su augusto pecho generoso
ni joyeles perturban ni cadenas
el negro terciopelo silencioso.

Y, en vez de cetro real, sostiene apenas,
con desmayo galán, un guante de ante
la blanca mano de azuladas venas.
(Machado 1902, I:45–46)

(No one more courtly nor polished / than our King Phillip, may God keep him, / always dressed in black down to his feet. // His complexion is pale as the afternoon, / the gold of his wavy hair tired, and cowardly the azure tint of his eyes. // Upon his august and generous chest / neither jewels nor chains disturb / the black, silent velvet. // And, instead of a royal scepter, it barely holds, / with gallant dismay, a kid glove / the white hand with azured veins.)

There is something very disquieting about this text, which is presumably based on a Velázquez portrait of the Spanish Hapsburg monarch. First, the text cannot be pinned down to one specific meaning. For example, does the speaker in Machado's text intend to praise or criticize his subject? What is the subject of his text, the painting by Velázquez, King Felipe IV himself, or something else? And how is the reader to interpret such ambiguous expressions as "Nadie más cortesano ni pulido / que nuestro rey Felipe" ("No one more courtly or polished / than our King Phillip") or "que Dios guarde" ("may God keep him")?[5] Are they to be taken at face value, or are they meant to be ironic? The speaker does not give a solid clue. Gustav Siebenmann has already commented that textual indeterminacy is a salient feature

sumed male lyric voice, and with poetry by women, a female lyric voice. Where there is an ungendered poetic "I" and voice, my renderings also are ungendered. My translations of the poetic texts are not meant to re-create the poem's aesthetic effect, but rather to be an aid to those readers not familiar or only slightly familiar with Spanish. Unless otherwise noted, all translations are my own.

of all of Machado's poetry, and not merely the portrait poems (Siebenmann 1973, 96–97). The reader is sure to notice that the poetic speaker's choice of detail is deviously indeterminate. For example, in the first tercet the speaker specifically mentions the monarch's feet, a body part that is ambivalent at best (Cirlot 1962, 106) and is not normally associated with sovereignty. And in the second tercet the speaker further muddles the message by obliquely suggesting a decadent cast to the monarch's representation, thus giving credence to Machado's "modernista" tendencies: "Es pálida su tez como la tarde" ("His complexion is pale as the afternoon"), the king's golden hair is "cansado" ("tired"), and the blue tone of his eyes is "cobarde" ("cowardly"). Similarly, in the final tercet the speaker utilizes the expression "desmayo galán" ("gallant dismay") to suggest a limp-wristed vision of "la blanca mano de azuladas venas" ("the white hand with azured veins"). The adjective "azuladas" ("azured") of course reminds the reader of that color's association with "cobarde" ("cowardly") of the second tercet.

This particular portrait poem is disquieting for yet another reason. Strangely enough, it does not coincide with any one known portrait of Felipe IV by the painter Velázquez; rather, it seems to be a composite of that of the king and that of his brother, "el Infante don Carlos" ("Prince Charles"). In the third stanza the speaker points out the absence of any sort of jeweled embellishment, which seems to repeat the details of the Velázquez portrait of Felipe IV (number 1181, Prado). But in stanza 4, the famous "guante de ante" ("kid glove") described by the speaker belongs not to Felipe IV but to Velázquez's portrait of don Carlos (number 1188, Prado).[6] (See color plates.)

Much critical ink has been spilled trying to formulate a theory on how and why Machado could have been so "mistaken," to rationalize away the reasons for such a glaring inaccuracy, and to speculate on which one of Velázquez's portraits of the king this poem is really about.[7] But I think that this critical focus is off the mark. Needless to say, the question that keeps coming to mind is: "Why did Machado opt to paint a portrait in words of a portrait in oil that does not in fact exist?" The poet himself makes reference to his supposed inconsistency in this portrait poem, and in others that will appear in subsequent collections. He states: "En una palabra, yo pinto esos cuadros tal como se dan y con todo lo que evocan en mi espíritu; no como están en el Museo, teniendo muy bien cuidado de cometer ciertas inexactitudes, que son del todo necesarias a mi intento" ("In a word,

I *paint* those portraits just as they are given and with all they evoke in my spirit; not as they are in the museum, keeping in mind to commit certain inaccuracies, which are totally necessary to my intention" [Machado's italics]) (Carballo Picazo 1967, 108). My reason in mentioning Machado's own words in regard to his "inexactitudes" ("inaccuracies") is not to fall into the trap of authorial intent, but merely to signal that there is more to these poems than meets (or doesn't meet) the eye. The poet's words give a clear signal that he himself had in mind more than one reading. I believe that Machado's inaccuracies are pivotal in that they are the specific meeting place where two different discourses attempt to coincide, and that they are the entryway to the reader's gaining a view of how Machado experiences that which Robert Scholes referred to as the play of "surrender and sovereignty" and "the exchanges of power and pleasure" in the reading and writing process. Machado implicitly makes reference to the seeming presence of another artistic discourse within that of poetry, but does so in a way that problematizes the very issue of representation. The poet simultaneously surrenders to, and has sovereignty over, Velázquez's version(s) of representation, and is both inside and outside his own reading process. On the one hand, he attempts to mimic in linguistic fashion an iconic representation of the royal figure. But on the other hand, he slyly winks to his own reader with the glaring inaccuracy of his text in regard to the visual representation.

One possible answer to the puzzling question regarding Machado's "inexactitudes" is this. These portrait poems of Machado are more than mere representations of an historical figure who in turn has been depicted on a piece of canvas or are products of a visual artist's imagination. Because of their surface inaccuracies Machado consistently draws attention to the problem of artistic representation in general and discourse in particular: his portrait poems, indeed all art in general, do not and cannot grasp reality in their essence. And this, I think, is the key to Machado's use of the ekphrastic principle in his verse. To say it in another way, Machado's ekphrastic poems are about not only the other art forms they describe, but also about the difficulty of making any art form coincide with something outside itself, with outward reality, and concomitantly, they are also about the questionable value of art as representation. In speaking of his portrait poems, the poet himself stated: "He procurado la síntesis de los sentimientos de la época y del pintor; la significación y el estado del arte en todo tiempo; la evocación del espíritu de los tiempos;

la sensación producida hoy en nosotros" ("I have endeavored to synthesize the sentiments of the epoch and the painter; the meaning and the state of art at all times; the evocation of the spirit of art of the times; the sensation produced in us") (Carballo Picazo, 108). This citation is especially significant because in it the poet does not speak of the success or failure in representing objective reality, but rather of art's process, effect, and value, not only on the producer, that is to say the artist, but also on the receiver, either contemporary to the artist or chronologically removed from the artist's era. In this manner, Machado underlines the unbreakable bond that he sees between the artistic text and its historical context, whether at the moment of the art object's unveiling or of its subsequent receptions. But he also problematizes this uncertain system of signification by constantly pointing to art's simultaneous success and failure in its unending attempt to represent. The poet unceasingly reminds his readers that his own readings of the visual art objects are correct and true, but only to a certain point. It is then left to us, his readers, to continue the logarithm (or is it logo-rhythm?) of our own signifying calculations and calculating signification.

Norman Bryson, in his *Vision and Painting*, comments that "To understand the painting as sign, we have to forget the proscenic surface of the image and think behind it: not to an original perception in which the surface is luminously bathed, but to the body whose activity—for the painter as for the viewer—is always and only a transformation of material signs" (Bryson 1983, 171). This last key phrase, "transformation of material signs," applies as well to the poetry of Machado. The poet attempts to place in juxtaposition two different codes that come into conflict. The poet pays lip service to the iconicity of his work and that of the painter; he attains to a certain degree a like representation of the painter's perception of reality. As Wendy Steiner notes in *The Colors of Rhetoric*, "the attempt to overreach the boundaries between one art and another is thus an attempt to dispel (or at least mask) the boundary between art and life, between sign and thing, between writing and dialogue" (Steiner 1984, 5). W. J. T. Mitchell refers to this moment as that of "ekphrastic hope," where the writer leads the reader to believe that the impossibility of reproducing one discourse in another can be overcome, that through imagination, metaphor, and the magic of language, the reader can actually "see" the work of art (Mitchell 1994, 152–53).

The poet calls attention to the futility of the painter's and of his own endeavors by intentionally including an inaccuracy.

Thus, the iconic becomes at once the symbolic, of both the painter and the poet's failure to grasp reality, truth, and eternal beauty within codified artistic boundaries. Steiner further comments that "art as mirror claims to reveal what is 'truly' there" (Steiner 1984, 7). But Machado's verbal studies of other art forms explicitly and implicitly point out that what is "there" is only an illusion; his obvious inaccuracies perhaps can be viewed as a celebratory metaphor of art's simultaneous success and failure at mediation between reality and the viewer's inevitable distortion of that reality. The reader is then left to ponder a most vexing issue. Given that the poetic speaker has pointed out to the reader that the painter's representation of reality may be just an illusion, then this same reader will have to face the possibility that the poet's representation, stated in linguistic terms, may indeed be an illusion as well.

Returning to "Felipe IV," the detail of the limp-wristed hand that grasps the "guante de ante" could be interpreted as a metaphor of both Velázquez and Machado's representation of power. In the Velázquez portrait of Don Carlos, the Infante holds a glove in the right hand, and in the left, a broad-brimmed hat. The right arm is more in the foreground and hangs flaccidly at the prince's side. The left arm is bent slightly, and a gloved left hand holds a hat, which is turned so that the viewer may see within the crown (and metaphorically, within the "Crown"). The hat as well as the right glove are empty. Traditionally, both glove and hat have been utilized to represent power and its exercise, whether manual, royal, or intellectual (Cirlot). Don Carlos "manifests'* [*L. manus "hand" + festus "to be bold," "to make apparent to the senses"] the outward signs of power and privilege, but since he is the king's brother, his power is only apparent rather than actual. For Velázquez, royal power was not in the hand(s) of Don Carlos, but of Felipe IV. Thus, it is logical that both the glove and hat of Don Carlos are empty.

For Machado, the description of Felipe IV's hand holding the empty glove occurs at a pivotal moment in the text, since the poem closes with this telling detail. But in another sense, it is at this juncture that the poem opens itself to subversion and undecidability. How is the reader to interpret this problematic metaphor of power? It may well be the place where the reader experiences Machado's own exchange of power and pleasure with the text that he had been reading, namely, the portrait(s) painted by Velázquez. The empty glove is polysemic, and reveals more in its emptiness than it covers, in spite of or perhaps because of the emphatic absence to which the speaker calls attention. The empty glove breaks the frame of the mimetic representation of Velázquez's "Felipe IV," and causes the reader of the text to consider other avenues of signification. Aside from the fact that the detail of the hand holding the glove proceeds from Velázquez's portrait of Don Carlos rather than of the king, the image of the hand and glove also posits another facet of Machado's uncanny meditation on the problematic nature of representation. The hand, especially the right one and a royal one at that, suggests power and control. Machado emphasizes the absence of this function by specifying that the royal, lily-white, and blue-blood hand holds "en vez de cetro real" ("instead of a royal scepter") the common (i.e., shared, usual, and less-than-royal) symbol of power, the glove. As Mary Ann Caws notes, the hand may generally connote the possibility of a handshake, with an implication of "agreement, understanding and correspondence" (Caws 1989, 36). But here in this portrait poem, that which the hand holds is an elegant but very empty glove. This lack thus puts into question the agreement, understanding, and correspondence to which Caws refers. On one level, the empty glove may point to Machado's opinion of the king, the Hapsburg line, or royalty in general. But from another perspective, this conspicuous detail also illuminates the duplicitous nature of power, whether royal or artistic. Just as a monarch commands with the movement of a hand, so too the artist, whether visual or verbal. (Or is it through sleight of hand???) The artistic representation is based on the image, which may well be a mirage. As Caws points out when speaking of the power of imagery in general, representation "has become a mere glove of itself, the empty outside gesture and what it weighs on. . . . [I]f what we are accepting is that the outside counts as the inside truth it sheathes, then is not the representative cover of what represents—i.e., the glove on the hand, in its sheathed or veiled pointing, in its designation as in its creative power—to be taken as the true representation because it reveals?" (Ibid.) Implicitly then, that which Machado's empty and (un)common glove (dis)covers is art's questionable power, its failed success and successful failure. It faithfully represents its unfaithful delineation. The representation of the absence of power is present and made manifest throughout the poem not only in the problematic empty glove, but also in the use of negation, in the speaker's emphasis on the lack of jewelry and royal scepter, and in the silent velvet of the king's royal robes. As Caws remarks, "Nothing weighs in it, but much weighs upon it" (Ibid.).

Other texts from succeeding collections—*Museo (Museum)* (1907) and *Apolo. Teatro pictórico (Apollo. Pictorial Theater)* (1911), may now be more easily contextualized, bearing in mind Machado's use of ekphrasis as both a discursive strategy and a metaphor of the difficulty of representation. In both of these collections the ekphrastic principle is the focal point around which the poet organizes his implicit meditation on the value and purpose of art, and the concomitant dependencies that he sees among its many manifestations, styles, and postures. The structural arrangement of *Museo* is a case in point. This collection is composed of four subsections whose headings recall four different styles and epochs of representational art, namely, "Primitivos" ("Primitives"), "Renacimiento" ("Renaissance"), "Siglo de Oro" ("Golden Age"), and "Figulinas" ("[clay] Figurines"), and thus attempts to faithfully transliterate the structured and chronologically ordered encounter of a visitor to a museum gallery into a linguistic approximation. The first poem of the "Primitivos" is entitled "Alvar-fáñez. Retrato" ("Alvar-fáñez. Portrait") (II: 11–12); in it the speaker recounts the exploits of the Cid's right-hand man, based on the details disclosed in the Spanish national epic. Here the art form alluded to is oral as well as visual. The reader is very likely to relate the name "Alvar-fáñez" to the famous supporting character in the Spanish national epic, a poem of oral tradition, but the word "retrato" ("portrait") suggests a visual perception. The speaker juxtaposes modes of discourse drawn from two distinct media, namely, epic (oral) poetry and representational portraiture. Moreover, these discursive codes/modes are in conflict, since the oral text is less stable and allows more flexibility in its (re)presentation* [*presentation, re presentation, and representation) than the visual one. Like the poem about Felipe IV discussed earlier, this text poses for the reader a similar representational conundrum. Does the "retrato" referred to in the title indicate that the poem is about Alvar-fáñez himself; is it about how his story is told in the *Poema de Myo Cid (Poem of My Cid);* does it refer to an imagined oil portrait hanging in a dusty, obscure corner of a seldom visited museum; or perhaps does it attempt to represent and frame all of these representations?

The poetic text is ambiguous, and once again the speaker does not offer to the reader an easy solution for the decoding of the various modes of discourse. For example, the first two lines of the verse state "Muy leal y valiente es lo que fué Minaya, / por eso dél se dice su claro nombre, y basta" ("Very loyal and valiant is what Minaya was, / thus of him only his clear name is stated, and it is enough"). At first glance these lines, verbal rather than visual, seem to depict Minaya himself; but the reader actually "sees" him through the curtain of his relationship to others ("muy leal") ("very loyal") or his actions ("valiente") ("valiant"), and ultimately through the otherness that is language itself, "dél se dice" ("of him it is stated"). In addition, the reader is distracted by a lyric voice that intercedes to offer his second-hand description ("se dice") ("is stated"), which calls attention to Minaya as a purely linguistic sign ("Su claro nombre") ("his clear name"), and which uses a discourse alien to twentieth-century standards of the Spanish language. In the second strophe, several of these same techniques are repeated. One reads of his relationship to the Cid and to his function as ambassador to the court of Alfonso; ultimately the reader is quoted the very words of the loyal vassal himself, "Ganó a Valencia el Cid, Señor, y os la regala" ("The Cid won Valencia, [my] Lord, and he bequeaths it to you"), spoken by Minaya to the king. In this manner, the speaker underscores the oral origins of this written text, yet by naming it a "retrato" encourages the reader to break the frame of that discourse as well, to envision it as a portrait of visual proportions. And in so doing, as Theo D'haen comments in his general article on the multivalent possibilities of framing, "the constant frame shifting opens up structural blanks for the reader to fill in. At least part of this filling in will be involved with gauging the very act of textual framing itself, and what it entails for the reader's own relation to the texts in question and the worlds they picture to him or her" (D'haen 1989, 432).

The poem ends with

> . . . Deste buen caballero aquí el decir se acaba
> de Minaya Alvar-fáñez quien quiere saber más,
> lea el grande poema que fizo Per Abat
> de Rodrigo Ruy Díaz Myo Cid, el de Vivar.
>
> (Machado 1907, II: 12)

(. . . Of this good knight here the telling is done / of Minaya Alfar-fáñez whoever wants to know more, / read the great poem that Per Abat made / about Rodrigo Ruy Díaz My Cid, he of Vivar.)

The poet calls attention to the work of art as a set of conventions and modes of discourse: he purposefully conjures up for the

reader the linguistic codes of the intertext in his use of vocabulary, namely, "deste" ("of this"), "el grande poema" ("the great
poem"), "fizo" ("he made"), and "Myo Cid" ("My Cid") all archaic forms alien to twentieth-century Spanish discourse.[8] The
speaker also calls attention to the ambiguity of his own text and
of its modes of discourse by referring the reader to yet another
text. Implicitly, this speaker points to the text, any text, as inexact
in the art of representation, and prone to modifications in the
process of its transmission from one artist to another, one medium to another. The ephemeral reality of his vision is based
upon that of another artistic representation, to which he directs
his reader, "Lea el grande poema que fizo Per Abat" ("Read the
great poem that Per Abat made"). The frame of the speaker's
vision is firmly in place, since it is enclosed in turn by yet another frame, that of the intertext of the *Poema de Myo Cid (Poem
of My Cid)* (Madrid: Espasa Calpe, 1929). But the reader must be
aware that the Machado poem continually makes reference to
the process of representation and of the difficulty that the artist,
whether verbal or visual, encounters in making art coincide
with something outside itself. So, in a very real sense, this poem
speaks about various forms of textuality, and the means of representation that are at the disposal of the artist, whether verbal or
visual. Concomitantly, the speaker points to the responsibility of
the viewer/reader in the creative process by signaling the role of
the receiver in the evolution of artistic forms. Both the pleasure
and power of this particular text are based upon the knowledge
of a previous text, and upon how the receiver—"juglar" ("trouba-
dor"), audience, scribe, poet, reader, painter, viewer—utilizes
that text in the creation of a new one, within a frame that will
surely be broken in a creative and original fashion once again,
at a future point in time. The speaker of this poetic text invites
the reader to continue the process forward—by going back to a
previous frame—with his command, "quien quiera saber más /
lea el grande poema que fizo Per Abat" ("whoever wants to know
more / read the great poem that Per Abat made").

In another poem of *Museo*, entitled "Las Concepciones de Murillo" ("The Conceptions of Murillo") (2. 41–42), and contained
in the subsection "Siglo de Oro" ("Golden Age"), the poet utilizes the classical discourse of a well-structured sonnet to speak
of Murillo's various renderings of the Virgin Mary. In the body
of the text, he places his focus on only one of the paintings, in
spite of his having referred to a plurality in the title as well
as in the opening line of verse, "De las dos Concepciones, la

morena. . . ." ("Of the two Conceptions, the dark one. . . ."). In this fashion there is suggested an explicit comparison between two works, while the poem provides only an implicit one. It is left to the reader to fill in the blanks, to recall, and even perhaps to seek out both the painting described in the poem as well as the other whose treatment is lacking on the surface level of the text. But once again, the absence that the poet signals fails as icon even as it succeeds as symbol, fails on the mimetic level while it succeeds on the semiotic level. For in the absence of the second Murillo painting Machado has found expression for the silence of art and for its uncanny ability to focus on itself as well as something exterior to itself. The poet creates for the reader a significant and signifying gap, framed by the description of one of the Murillo paintings, whose presence is known only by allusion/illusion. The linguistic description of the painting is not the painting itself. Similarly, with the use of ellipsis, the poet creates a space for a description of the other painting by Murillo, but allows the reader the option of filling in that frame, or allowing it to stand as it is, empty and full at the same time. The presence of the Other is made manifest by reference to its absence. Machado resolutely breaks the frame of his own text by the acknowledgment that he concedes to the other of "las dos Concepciones" ("the two Conceptions").

This twentieth-century poetic text does not repeat the failure to capture reality's essence that was evinced in Murillo's work: Machado's poem fails in its own original way. Furthermore, "Las Concepciones de Murillo" can also be interpreted as a play on words that is consonant with the ekphrastic principle under discussion here. Aside from referring to the two paintings, the text evokes the two images formulated by any artist, one a mental image and the other given concrete form. But *both* of these images, the concrete and the theoretical, are misreadings of the reality that is ungraspable by any art form. Thus, by extension, the poet is trapped between his own "dos concepciones" ("two conceptions"), and so too is the reader. It is an unending process of imperfect reflection upon/of art, as meditation, mediation, and reduplication. The fact that there are two or more "concepciones" ("conceptions") of the same reality underscores the failure of art.

The title of *Apolo. Teatro pictórico* is especially significant to the theme and artistic process being examined here, in that it once again draws attention to the multifaceted relationship among the arts, and moreover to the arts as mask. *Teatro pictór-*

ico makes reference to the play (in all senses of the word) of images that is art. And in regard to Apollo, Machado himself explained his reasoning behind the title: "Mi libro se llama así porque, no siendo ninguna de las nueve musas la deidad inspiradora de la pintura y siendo Apolo, en la mitología, el padre de todas ellas, me pareció que el título cuadraba perfectamente en la índole de mi producción. Por eso se llama *Apolo*" ("My book is so named because, there being none of the nine muses the inspiring goddess of painting and Apollo being in mythology the father of all arts, it seemed to me that the title suited perfectly the nature of my production. Thus, my book is named *Apolo*") (Carballo Picazo, 101). Under the aegis of Apollo, the father of all arts, Machado makes reference to painting, poetry, and drama, three distinct aspects of artistic representation.

This collection consists of twenty-five sonnets, which are divided into several distinct groups and headed by the names of famous Western European painters or schools of art. These headings include "Sandro Botticelli," "Leonardo da Vinci," "Rubéns," "Rembrandt," and "Greco," and echo the organization already seen in *Museo*. One could imagine a visit to an art gallery that would repeat approximately the same chronological trajectory. But in virtually all of the poems the poet points out to the reader the conventions of several types of discourse that make representational art possible. He emphasizes as he has done in the previously considered texts that the poem is a purely linguistic construct, a sign system that is agreed upon by poet and reader, just as the painting is a covenant between artist and public. Each system has a codified preestablished set of rules and well-defined parameters. Consider, for example, Fra Angelico's "Annunciation" ("Anunciation"). In the original painting, the joyousness of the angel's task in communicating the divine message to Mary is enclosed and framed by arches and vaulting,[9] with depth provided by an angled (and "angel-ed". . .) view into an interior room. This segment occupies the right two-thirds of the painting. The expulsion of Adam and Eve from the Garden of Eden takes up the left third of the visual text; its forlorn message of exile and alienation is the counterpoint to the painting's affirmative message, and also lends chronological, biblical narrativity to the work as a whole.

Machado's poetic evocation of the painting, *"La anunciación"* (2: 51–52), proceeds from the subsection entitled "Beato Angélico" ("Blessed Angelico"). In his artistic creation, Machado deletes the scene depicting Adam and Eve, replacing it with a portrayal of the painter in the act of painting Mary's encounter with the angel, a version that is once again "inaccurate," at odds with Fra Angelico's creation in tempera. But from a different perspective, Machado does indeed remain true to the friar's model. By displacing and replacing Adam and Eve with Fra Angelico in his text, the poet underscores the idea that the artistic creation is a process as well as a finished product, a process in which a specific artist must participate, utilizing preestablished artistic conventions. Fra Angelico does not appear in his own painting, but is placed within the frame of Machado's representation of his work. Symbolically, the painter takes on the role first of God the Creator, and then of Adam and Eve, by serving as a catalyst for later events, by giving birth to a new creation, one made in his/their own image. In presenting the painter producing his version of reality, the poet implicitly encourages the reader to continue with the analogy. Just as Adam and Eve created the possibility of narrativity in the text of the salvation script, so the painter through painting, so the poet through poetry, and the reader through yet another version of the text, in an open-ended series of approximations to concrete reality. Each sender and each receiver enters into this concatenation of the creative process, and each are privy to the conventions of discourse of each artistic text. In his poem, Machado simultaneously celebrates and violates the concept of the frame holding in and keeping out the process of art's concatenation and narrativity. The poet lays bare how the narrativity of an artistic work functions, and how the creator of any work in a very real sense is both inside *and* outside the frame, and frame of reference of the text. Thus, Machado's poem takes on the role of "announcing" art's unending design, and the relationship among text(s), frame(s), creator(s), and receiver(s).

Another example is to be found in the sonnet that celebrates Leonardo da Vinci's "Giocconda" (2. 63–64). The speaker describes Mona Lisa's enigmatic smile as well as that of the enigmatic and ambiguous "nosotros" ("we"), the unspecified receivers of both the visual and verbal texts: ". . . Y nosotros también, eternamente, / llevamos en el alma su sonrisa" (". . . And we also, eternally, / carry in our souls her smile"). It is significant to note that this reference to "nosotros" appears in exactly the middle of the sonnet, in lines 7 to 8. In this fashion the receivers are encouraged to be both inside (literally and metaphorically) and outside the frame of the text, or rather, the *texts*. "Nosotros" will be the observers of the painting, and thus privy to its modes of discourse, and also will be the readers of the poem, and therefore knowledgeable in its conventions. This sonnet's two tercets contain five questions, presumably to be pondered by the receivers, whether the viewers of the painting or readers of the poem. The enigma that the speaker alludes to by way of his questioning posture refers not only to the subject of Leonardo's painting but also to the greater issue of art as a form of communication and how the viewer is a witness as well as a participant in the artistic process, simultaneously inside and outside the frame of the text.

The poem "Carlos V" ("Charles V") (2. 67–68) memorializes a painting by Titian which represents the Hapsburg emperor on horseback. This painting is most probably the portrait entitled *Charles V on Horseback at Muhlberg* housed in the Prado Museum. The poetic text utilizes yet another technique to stress the poet's concern with the question of art and how it refers to not only the exterior world but also to itself. Structurally, Machado uses once again the classical sonnet form, and faithfully describes the emperor as represented by the painter Titian. The poet attempts to reproduce in linguistic terms the representation of the visual artist's work by using enjambment and end-line ellipsis. The reader's eye is thus able to take in with easy verbal flow, parallel to the visual one where the observer's eye takes in all the aspects of the painting, the totality of the richly detailed and precise description of the imposing monarch. In the two quatrains Machado attempts to include not only the outward visual manifestations of the monarch's sovereignty, such as the "plata y oro" ("silver and gold"), "la soberbia armadura" ("the proud armor"), and the royal purple of his plume, but other telling characteristics as well. For example, the poet provides geographic clues as to the source of various accoutrements: "El que en Milán nieló de plata y oro" ("He who in Milán made fine inlays of silver and gold"), "en Toledo este arnés" ("in Toledo this harness"), and "la remota playa de oro y de sol de Moctezuma" ("the remote beach of gold and sun of Moctezuma"). The reader in this manner is reminded of the geographic expanse of Carlos V's hegemony. The overall impact of this verbal representation is similar to the gallery visitor's experience, upon viewing the larger-than-life portrait of the imposing monarch. There is a sense of grandeur, harmony, synchrony, strength, and cohesiveness.

The first of the two tercets states:

Todo es de este hombre gris, barba de acero,
carnoso labio socarrón y duros
ojos de lobo audaz, que, lanza en mano

(Machado 1907, II:67)

(All is of this gray man, beard of steel, / fleshy cunning lip and hard / eyes of a daring wolf, who, lance in hand)

Here the speaker focuses on the man rather than on the monarch, but at the same time aggrandizes the person by concentrating on aspects of his outward appearance—rather than the mere trappings of power—that are telling in their manly value, sensuality, and forcefulness: "barba de acero" ("beard of steel"), "carnoso labio" ("fleshy lip"), and "duros ojos de lobo audaz" ("hard eyes of a daring wolf"). The poetic text ends with

recorre su dominio, el Mundo entero,
con resonantes pasos, y seguros.
En este punto lo pintó el Tiziano.

(Ibid., II:68)

(he roams his domain, the entire world, / with resounding steps, and sure ones. / At this point Titian painted it [him].)

Carlos V is present in a very active sense, brought to life in spite of the strictures of time, space, and the artistic conventions of both painting and poetry: "recorre su dominio, el Mundo entero" ("he roams his domain, the entire world"). The speaker underscores this active presence with the verb "recorre" ("he roams") as well as the adjective "resonantes" ("resounding") that distantly recalls the verb "resonar" ("to resound"), and also subtly plays upon the space/time difference between painting/sight ("recorre" / "he roams") and poetry/orality ("resonantes" / "resounding"). With this emphasis on the active status of Carlos V, it would seem that the speaker is attempting to override the static nature of the art object, whether painting or poetry. Alas, the thirteenth verse of the sonnet ends abruptly, at which point the speaker intercedes to remind the reader that the text has not captured objective reality after all, but only another artist's conception of it. The speaker calls attention to the fact that this representation is an approximation of another, namely, that of the artist Titian, who created a portrait (it) of Carlos V (him). It should be noted that in the painting's display in the Prado Museum, the painter's authorship is plainly visible to the gallery visitor's eye. It appears on a neatly lettered placard at the base of the painting. Here the poet mimes the visual format in the organization of his own text, placing the "signature" at the foot of his creation, precisely at the bottom, in the last line of verse. But in a sense, this signature is a forgery, since the poetic speaker makes reference to the visual artist's authorship at the base of *his* work of art: "En este punto lo pintó el Tiziano" ("At this point Titian painted it [him]"). Just as in the case of the problematic glove of the poem entitled "Felipe IV", here the poet signals a pivotal moment where there is both closure and aperture, both surrender and sovereignty in the reading process, where the frames of the two texts (don't quite) elide. Machado has surrendered the sovereignty of his text to the painter Titian, but in another sense has sovereignty over Titian's rendering of Carlos V in his sovereign splendor, given that the poet "recorre su dominio" ("roams his domain"), that of the visual artist. He has the power to pick and choose how he wishes to represent Titian's masterpiece in his own work. But just as Titian's signature is a forgery in the poet's text, so too the poet's, in the counterfeiting* [*to counterfeit: pp. of *contrefaire*, "to make in opposition, thus to make an imitation, so as to defraud or deceive."] of the visual artist's work.

With this act of forgery in the problematic signature, the poet calls attention to the painting as a deceptive/defective product, and also implicitly communicates that the literary product is a forgery as well, a mere approximation to the visual one, thus a forgery of a forgery. The poet implicitly suggests that the visual and verbal representations are mere approximations of objective reality. Just as the empty glove of "Felipe IV" is full of signification, here the forgery is honest rather than deceptive. It signifies the truthful representation (of art's fraudulence) as well as representational truth. By insisting upon Titian's signature, the poet points to the existence of the frame that separates art from reality. The conventions of discourse needed by the receiver for the recognition of that frame and the appreciation of the visual and verbal texts—and for the intertextual relationships between the two—are a mutually agreed upon system that can never totally grasp an object exterior to itself. Thus once again the poet subtly indicates that there is more than meets the eye; these poems based upon silent portraits speak of not only the products of the artistic process but of the process itself. The viewer is caught up in the process of artistic reception and appreciation of both painting and poem. But it must be remembered that the whole question of aesthetic truth and value rests firmly on the premise of codes and conventions. Art—whatever its form—is good, valuable, and valid only by social contract; it is a part of reality valuable in its own right, but it is only approximate in its representation of that reality and in its truthfulness concerning that reality.

These are but a few examples from Machado's poetry that serve to underscore the complex and enigmatic relationship between poet and painter, poet and reader, sign and thing, art and life, representation and reality. I believe that Machado's use of the ekphrastic principle is a vehicle to communicate about a much larger issue, namely, artistic creation in general and the questions that it posits about representation, reality, value, and artistic truth. Thus, even though Machado's pen describes the work of disparate artists—individual or collective, verbal or visual—it may be very convincingly argued that the overriding concern that propels all of Machado's poetic production is his basic skepticism yet celebration of art and of its questionable ability to grasp objective reality and truth in its essence. These poems may be read from a variety of perspectives, but it is clear that the poet offers to the reader a specific challenge to go beyond the mimetic possibility of interpreting them as mere transmutations into linguistic form of works of art exterior to the poetic text. The trope of ekphrasis is both an allusion and an illusion, and as such contributes to the simultaneous success and failure of the signifying process, thus emphasizing its own self-referential power.

We have seen in this chapter how in his portrait poems Manuel Machado talks not only about visual art and its processes, but about representation and artistic truth in general. Keeping this in mind, it is now much easier to reconcile what would on the surface appear to be seemingly unrelated results of artistic experimentation in the trajectory of Machado's development as a poet.[10] As has been demonstrated here, his earlier works show an affinity with the Latin American "modernistas," with their propensity toward the adaptation of techniques from the other arts such as painting and music (Celma Valero and Blasco Pascual 1981, 119). Machado himself makes reference to this connection in the series of essays that he published under the title of *La guerra literaria* (*The Literary War*) (1914). But I think that his concern goes beyond the mere transposition of one art form to another. In the collections considered here and in those that he was to produce when he had decided definitively to turn away from the "modernista" sphere, Machado continues to grapple with the troubling issue of representation—be it of Self or Other—and how the artist must attempt the impossible, namely, to capture reality with a preestablished set of codes.

One need only consider such famous titles as his "Adelfos" (*Alma*), or "Retrato" ("Portrait") and "Yo, poeta decadente" ("I, Decadent Poet") from (*El mal poema [The Bad Poem]*, 1909) to see the common denominator that appears in different guises throughout his entire career. Another clear example is to be found in *Canciones y dedicatorias (Songs and Dedications)* (1915), where the poet uses as a pretext (and "pre-text") the works of other writers to produce his own text. For example in the poem "A Rubén Darío" ("To Rubén Darío") Machado plays upon the dialectic of presence and absence that inhabits not only Machado's text about Rubén Darío, but also the works of that New World poet as well: "Como cuando viajabas, maestro, estás ausente, / y llena está de ti la soledad, que espera / tu retorno" ("As when you traveled, teacher, you are absent, / and solitude is full of you, which awaits / your return"). But in so doing, the issues of artistic creativity, intertextuality, and representation are brought sharply into focus. With *Cante hondo (Deep Song)* (1916) and *Sevilla y otros poemas (Seville and Other Poems)* (1918), Machado superimposes the rhythms and ambience of his native Andalusia upon his verse. But once again, he insures that the reader will be aware that his text is only a description of reality, and not reality itself. For example, the poet himself includes a prose prologue to explain his derived art form, in this way establishing a particular type of frame for the portrait that he offers of his native soil, his artistic interpretation of reality. In *Ars moriendi (Art of Dying)* (1921), he reproduces a representation of himself in the text entitled "El poeta de "Adelfos" dice, al fin. . . ." ("The poet of 'Adelphos' says, at the end. . . ."). This poem echoes and reflects [upon] an earlier version of the Self that had appeared in a poem entitled "Adelphos" from *Alma*, but is in counterpoint to that earlier image. While the earlier "Adelfos" is stated in sensual, affirmative terms, the latter poem utilizes the vocabulary and cadences of a more pessimistic view of life and death. Ultimately the two poetic texts serve both as the frame and the portrait of the poet and his poetry. Poet and poem become (as) one; Self is and is not the Other. Likewise, this same technique of reduplication is used in "Nuevo autorretrato" ("New Self-Portrait") of the collection *Phoenix. Nuevas canciones* (1935), which recalls an earlier attempt at self-representation, "Retrato." In all of these cases the poet places the focus of his attention on representation, and how one medium or another, one artist or another, one discourse or another, addresses the issues of art versus life, art in life, art and life. And all echo Machado's earlier concerns in regard to representation and to its truthful fraudulence and fraudulent truth, as seen in his *Alma, Museo, and Apolo. Teatro pictórico.* Other examples could be mentioned, but the pattern is clear.

This brief foray into Manuel Machado's work can in no way do justice to his creativity or to his imagination. But it is clear that the totality of his poetic production is eerily in harmony with the concerns of contemporary poets and critics alike, with its overt metatextual focus, and unremitting fascination with the limits of language and artistic representation. His use of ekphrasis both as a representational strategy and as a metaphor of the (im)possibility of representation itself reflects this poet's skepticism toward, yet celebration of, the process of creating and communicating signification, whether verbal or visual. By simultaneously surrendering to yet having sovereignty over the visual arts within his poetic texts, he frames the question of representation in a way that foregrounds not only the verbal/visual medium, but also the medium itself as message. Moreover, his questioning stance toward representation itself firmly align the poetry of Machado with other modernists such as Gertrude Stein, William Carlos Williams, and Ezra Pound.[12] This similarity suggests the need for a reconsideration of his poetic production, as well as that of his contemporaries, in order to explore the possibility of further affinities with the broader European modernist tradition.[13]

3

The Writerly/Painterly Text: Rafael Alberti and Pablo Picasso

Rafael Alberti's first vocation as a painter has already been well-documented. As a young boy, his initial aspiration was to dedicate himself to the visual arts, and it was only after a few expositions of his work in Madrid that he finally decided to turn over his attention and considerable creative energy primarily to verbal rather than visual expression.[1] But as many critics, as well as Alberti himself, have noted, this generation of '27 poet's work demonstrates a decided propensity toward the visual, whether it be his metaphors of vision, light, and color, his "pictorial memory" (Jiménez Fajardo, *Multiple Spaces*), his use of ekphrasis as a form of (auto) biography (González Martín 1972), his experimentation with various graphic art forms as supplements to his written texts, or his continual and lifelong fascination with the pictorial arts as a thematic source for his own poetic texts.[2] While the poet seemingly accepts the poetry/painting dialectic, his attempts to transpose or translate (or is it traduce???) the tradition (or is it treason???) of the visual arts within a verbal medium continually work to call into question, undermine, and subvert not only that very distinction, but also the sign systems and the different contexts of the two different media. As C. Christopher Soufas comments, "To seek to overturn a predominant set of artistic values while remaining absolutely dependent upon them to accomplish its purposes is the central contradiction that informs all of Modernist art" (Soufas 1985–86, 24). It is not surprising, then, that Rafael Alberti returns again and again in his work to that of Pablo Picasso, a contemporary whose creativity was a catalyst for Alberti's own. But more importantly, Picasso, from a variety of perspectives, is the emblem for the process of creation, undertaken by the two artists within a specific historical and cultural milieu. The person "Picasso," the word "Picasso," the artwork signed "Picasso" become the poet's coun-

terpoint in the paradigm of Self and Other. Alberti's verbal creations utilize the multivalent sign of Picasso to represent the
interdependence of the verbal and the visual. The sign Picasso
codifies that that simultaneously can and cannot be subsumed
by the process of writing, the process of artistic creation, the
carnival of signification that is the signature of the Modernist
period.[3] Alberti and Picasso, in their two distinct yet related
modes of creation, enter into intertextual dialogue, as the sign(s)
for Self and Other define yet subvert each artist's creative
process.

Picasso describes his own artistic process of presence and absence in the following manner: "It is as though I have never been
able to build up a painting myself. I begin with an idea and then
it becomes something else. After all, what is a painter? He is a
collector who gets what he likes in others by painting them himself" (Livermore 1988, 154). This process of "becoming something else" may well also be applied to Alberti's poetry, and
clearly identifies the modernist undertaking reflected in both
artists' work. As Wendy Steiner explains, "Unlike such moments
in scientific history where one paradigm directly supplants another, the avant-garde model was instead superimposed upon
the Renaissance norm, and carried with it not only its own meaning and power but the marker of newness and success" (Steiner
1988, 121).

In his "Ecrivains et écrivants" (1960) Roland Barthes proposes
a telling distinction between "priestly" authors and "clerical"
writers opting to privilege the task of the former, who produce
what he terms the "writerly Text." (Barthes, 145) This productive
and open-ended relationship between writer and Text illuminates the function of both Picasso and Alberti in their individual
artistic quest. John Sturrock comments that the "écrivain" produces a Text, which "is a sort of verbal carnival, in which language is manifestly out on parole from its humdrum daily tasks.
The writer's language-work results in a linguistic spectacle for
its own sake rather than to look through language to the world.
A Text comes, in fact, from consorting with the signifiers and
letting the signifieds take care of themselves" (Sturrock 1981,
69). But what is fascinating to note is that while Alberti, on and
through "parole," attempts to envision not the objective world
but rather the visual and visionary world of Picasso's art, that
which inevitably and inexorably comes into focus is the medium
of language—how it sounds and how it looks—and the techniques that the poet has at his disposal within that medium to

make his own sign system (dis)appear in the ebb and flow, the waxing and waning of the subversive presence/absence of the sign "Picasso" within his texts. Picasso's sign is the Other who can never be fully possessed but who defines, frames, reflects, and refracts the Self, and the Self's process of signification. Alberti both succeeds in and fails to transpose Picasso's creativity in the discourse of the visual arts. As will be shown, by turns the visual simultaneously cedes to yet overpowers the poet's verbal medium, just as Picasso's artistic presence surrenders to yet maintains sovereignty over Alberti's own creation.

Alberti's artistic and symbiotic relationship with Picasso is that of endless reflection (in both senses of the word), reelaboration, and concatenation, an image in and of itself of the Modernist perspective. In *A la pintura (To Painting)* (1948) the poem entitled "Picasso" appears at the very end of the collection, which could be construed as Alberti's view of Picasso and his work as the culmination of artistic evolution in the Western world. This collection contains poetic compositions that focus on the masters of Western art, beginning with Giotto, and continuing with such renowned artists as Leonardo da Vinci, Michelangelo, Titian, Velázquez, Goya, and Renoir.[4] The speaker utilizes a purely chronological order to present all the painters; this organization in and of itself is reminiscent of the Renaissance view of reality, in that the reader of *A la pintura* is encouraged to perceive this presentation based on a diachronic view of Western art as having a fixed beginning and ending.[5] This same composition then reappears as a newly inserted fragment in *Los 8 nombres de Picasso y no digo más que lo que no digo (The 8 Names of Picasso and I Do Not Say More Than I Do Not Say)*, first published in 1970, but now carrying the title of "De azul se arrancó el toro" ("The Bull Was Torn Out of the Blue") thus clearly exemplifying the process of "becoming something else" identified by Picasso. In this manner, as has been suggested by Steiner, Alberti adopts the avant-garde stance by superimposing the Modernist model upon the Renaissance one, just as Picasso did in his own work. And poem 71, the second *last* of *Los 8 nombres* and that is entitled "No digo más que lo que no digo" ("I Do Not Say More Than I Do Not Say"), originally appeared as Alberti's prologue to Picasso's own study and interpretation of *El entierro del Conde de Orgaz (The Burial of the Count of Orgaz)* (1969), the painting by El Greco still housed in a Toledo chapel.[6] In a subsequent edition of *Los 8 nombres* entitled *Lo que canté y dije de Picasso (What I Sang and Said About Pi-*

casso) (1981) Alberti includes not only his collection of poetry dedicated to his prolific artistic contemporary, but also three prose works, the first of which is entitled "Visitas a Picasso" ("Visits to Picasso"), which he explains are "recuerdos para *La arboleda perdida* (1968–1972)" "memoirs for *The Lost Grove* (1968–72)," Alberti's own previously published autobiography.[7] The revealing vignettes and illuminating snippets of conversation contained in *Lo que canté (What I Sang)* shed light not only upon Picasso's art, but also upon Alberti's prismlike modernist introspective view—personal, emotional, aesthetic, philosophical—of Picasso the man, the friend, the artist, the institution, and how the poet has gone about formulating and framing his own artistic creation, his Text, that he has entitled "Picasso."

The second and third prose sections of *Lo que canté y dije de Picasso* also had been published previously, and are Alberti's introductions to two separate publications of Picasso's work, *Picasso en Aviñón (Picasso in Avignon)* (1970) and *Picasso, le rayon ininterrompu/Picasso, o el rayo que no cesa (Picasso, the Ray that Does Not Cease)* (1972). The latter title is taken from the verse line by the Spanish poet, Miguel Hernández. It is difficult to categorize these works, since in their fragmentary, essayistic orientation they are alternately narrative, dramatic, and lyric, all within a prosaic frame; they depend for their vibrance upon the fragmentary and intertextual nature of their composition. For example, the text speaker of *Picasso en Aviñón* opens with a decidedly journalistic yet ironic, slyly ludic account of Picasso's arrival at Avignon, which in the blink of an eye/I transforms itself into a dramatic presentation of Picasso's cast of characters:

NOTICIAS DE ULTIMO MOMENTO

1 de mayo de 1970. *(Urgente.)*

Pablo Picasso invade el Castillo de los Papas de Aviñón al frente de una columna de más de 100 hombres, acompañados de más de 30 mujeres, dos enanos, dos arlequines y un pierrot, varios niños, algunos ramos de flores y unas frutas. En su mayoría son gentes de grandes dimensiones, surgiendo de los trajes y los fondos más diversos, de las más violentas disonancias, los arabescos más inusitados, las rotas explosiones más armoniosamente desarmónicas. Han tomado las más grandes y solemnes estancias de los Papas—la inmensa capilla de Clemente VI, la cámara del Camarero y la de los Notarios—, y en una misteriosa y muda algarabía se han colgado de

las paredes, los muros del palacio inexpugnable. Luego, han comenzado a hablar:

Hemos llegado aquí recién nacidos. Tenemos poco más de un año.
Hemos visto la luz allá en la altura de Mougins, en Notre-Dame de
Vie, desde enero de 1969 al 2 febrero de 1970. (Alberti 1970, 173)

(THE LATEST NEWS

1 May 1970. (Urgent.)

Pablo Picasso invaded the Papal Castle at Avignon at the head of
a column of more than 100 men, accompanied by more than 30
women, 2 dwarfs, 2 harlequins, and 1 Pierrot, various children, some
bouquets of flowers, and some fruit. Most of them are people of large
dimensions, flowing out of their costumes and out of the most diverse backgrounds, from the most violent dissonances, the most un-
usual arabesques, the cloven, most harmoniously disharmonic
explosions. They have taken the largest and most solemn papal
rooms—the immense chapel of Clement VI, the chamber of the
Chamberlain, and that of the Notaries—, and in a mysterious and
silent jabbering they have hung themselves from the walls, the ram-
parts of the impregnable palace. Then, they began to speak:

We have arrived here recently born. We are little more than a year
old. We first saw the light at the top of Mougins, at Notre-Dame de
Vie, from January 1969 to 2 February 1970.)

In the classical ekphrastic tradition, Alberti has given voice to
the mute art object, and allowed Picasso's works to "speak for
themselves" in an oratory and vernacular sense, but has placed
this classical tradition within the contemporary context of a
press release upon the occasion of a gala opening night. At first
the reader might be predisposed to imagine the opening of an
art gallery, since, after all, Alberti has chosen to focus on Picasso,
the visual artist. But the reader's expectations receive a jolt, since
the "opening night" is that of a dramatic performance, where
Picasso's characters come to life, and play out their roles in ani-
mated and quite verbal fashion. At another moment, the speaker
inserts the purportedly verbatim account of the "Diálogo al ama-
necer" ("Dialogue at Dawn") between Pablo and Pedro. Within
the dialogue it is revealed that Pablo is Picasso and Pedro is none
other than "Pedro de Luna. Benedicto XIII. El último papa de
Aviñón" ("Pedro de Luna. Benedict XIII. The last Pope of Avignon") (Ibid., 213). The text speaker intervenes to present yet another text, "una carta condenatoria, firmada por el mismo
Lucifer—Epistola Luciferi—" ("a condemnatory letter, signed by

Lucifer himself—*Epistola Luciferi*—") and also acts as text editor, declaring "He aquí algunas de sus estrofas, entre burlonas y mordaces, escritas en versos de cuaderna via ("Here you will find some of his strophes, between mocking and biting, written in medieval rhymed quatrains"):

> El fuego del infierno corre por Aviñón.
> Papas y cardenales le dan su bendición.
> Ya ni San Pedro puede pedir su excomunión,
> dicen que de Mougins llegó tal perdición.

> (Ibid., 176)

(The fire of hell runs through Avignon. / Popes and cardinals give it their blessing. / Now not even Saint Peter can ask for his excommunication, / they say that from Mougins such eternal damnation arrived.)

And in *Le rayon ininterrompu* the text speaker continues with the process of intertextual weaving of fragments, revealing not only Alberti's debt to Picasso, but Picasso's debt to Alberti as well as to other writers and creative artists and their creations, whose traces are eternally discernible in both Picasso and Alberti's work:

> Aquí nada está muerto, nada se ha acabado. Aquí se alzan, otra vez, espectadores y héroes a un mismo tiempo de esta última y dramática fiesta, sus 201 cuadros, esta enorme multitud de ojos que iguales casi siempre a los del propio Picasso contemplan al pintor que se halla en multiplicada presencia y ahora erguido para siempre en la capilla clementina. (Alberti 1972, 231)

(Here nothing is dead; nothing is finished. Here spectators and heroes hoist themselves up at the same time from this last and dramatic celebration, their 201 portraits, this enormous multitude of eyes, which, equal to those of Picasso himself, contemplate the painter who is to be found in multiplied presence and now erect in the Clementine chapel.)

Thus, the process of "becoming something else" signaled by Picasso in his own work and that of painters in general, extends as well to the verbal domain and also more specifically to diverse literary genres in Alberti's text(s) on Picasso. The poet creates a collage of texts taken from different media and genres, puts a frame around them, and allows each fragment to speak for itself as well as to speak of the interpersonal and interartistic dialogic process of creation. The relationship between Alberti and Picasso is given form by the dialogue between poet and painter, poetry and painting, poetry and prose, text and intertext, frame and text, text and Text. The Text, as proposed by Barthes in his article "From Work to Text" (1979), is the verbal and visual carnival made manifest by both Alberti and Picasso.

In Alberti's account of his affiliation (*affiliare*, "to adopt as a son" [Who has adopted whom???]) with Picasso, the poet brings to the forefront and utilizes a media mix of visual and verbal strategies, and in this manner there is established a complex intertextual, interartistic, temporal, and spatial relationship not only between Alberti's own works of verse, but also between the poet and the painter, between Picasso and other painters and artistic traditions, and between visual and verbal art forms. According to Murray Krieger, *ekphrasis* is "the imitation in literature of a work of plastic art. The object of imitation, as spatial work, becomes the metaphor for the temporal work that seeks to capture it in that temporality. The spatial work freezes the temporal work even as the latter seeks to free it from space" (Krieger 1967, 107). But as always artful representation is never as simple as it seems at first glance. Alberti's analysis of, and meditation on, the work of Picasso places the visual artist's plastic object in a new dimension, one that is touched by time, just as Picasso's experimentation with multiple visual perspectives opened up to question the strictly three-dimensional view of reality, an inheritance of the Renaissance tradition. Alberti, for his part, in his work on Picasso pays homage to both traditions of temporal representation, that of the Renaissance and the avant-garde. In *A la pintura* Alberti expresses his esteem for and debt to Picasso within a Renaissance framework, demonstrating how Picasso's genius may be viewed from that perspective as a most obvious successor and artistic result of the Western aesthetic tradition. The poetic homage to Picasso appears at the end, with the collection's overall structure based on the temporal chronology of the painters whom Alberti chose to include. And in *Los 8 nombres*, Alberti places Picasso's artistic genius within a different framework, that of the avant-garde, using this second perspective to demonstrate how Picasso's work is simultaneously a result of previous artistic tradition as well as a basis for a new and original way of viewing the world. The sign Picasso takes on the characteristics of the cubist collage, namely, "the transfer of materials from one context to another, even as the original context cannot be erased" (Perloff 1986, 47). And as we shall see later, this subversive contiguity of planes and perspectives, temporal and otherwise, irrevocably leads to metatextual considerations. Marjorie Perloff cogently comments that "each element in the collage has a dual function: it refers to an external reality even as its compositional thrust is to undercut the very referentiality it seems to assert" (Ibid., 49). By utilizing both styles of temporal representation, the fixed-point narrative style of the Renaissance tradition and the multiperspectivalism of the avant-garde, Alberti's Text on Picasso is metatextual and metacubist. Because of its overall chronological style of organization, the poet pays homage to fixed-point representation in *A la pintura* and in individual works of this same collection as well as in subsequent works that subvert it in the (re)elaboration of each version of Picasso, in a slightly different context.[8] In his *Los 8 nombres* and *Lo que canté* the art of Picasso serves as the (pre-)Text for Alberti's own meditations on the process of artistic creation and the (im)possibility of the discrete work of art. Yet, ironically, the poet both succeeds and fails in that the reader of his text(s) is still and forever trapped in the temporal flow of literature, and in the reality of temporal perception of the literary work.

The complex intertextual and interartistic relationship of *Los 8 nombres* is further strengthened by the presence of many Picasso sketches and other memorabilia interspersed among Alberti's poetic texts.[9] Many of the drawings are of Alberti himself, dedicated to him or to Maria Teresa de León, the poet's wife. For example, on the back cover of the 1978 Kairós edition, there is a profile sketch of the poet's head, which faces toward the left, with its easily recognizable and distinctive long, flowing hair. The likeness is accompanied by a scrawled phrase, presumably in Picasso's own hand, that reads

> para Rafael Alberti
> Su amigo
> *Picasso*
> el 10.7.70

(Alberti 1978)

(for Rafael Alberti / His friend *Picasso* / 10 July 1970)

In a powerfully stunning inversion effected by the use of two distinct sign systems, Picasso creates two juxtaposed versions of Alberti, communicating his perception of the poet by way of one that is visual as well as another that is verbal. But this verbal version is visual as well, since it is a handwritten message of

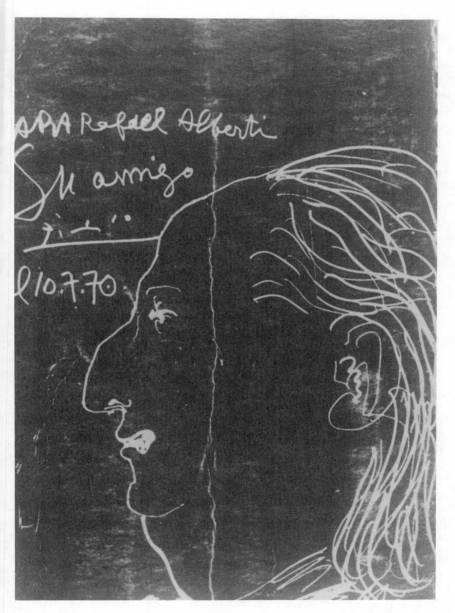

Sketch of Rafael Alberti, by Pablo Picasso. © 1995 Artists Rights Society (ARS), New York / SPADEM, Paris.

curves, lines, and dots that the reader interprets as Picasso's own
dedicatory and personal signature. Just as Alberti's words create
"another" Picasso in a different medium, so Picasso's dedicatory
words and drawings in turn create "another" Alberti, one ex-
trapolating the other in an artistic process of creativity and simultaneity. Of course, the question must arise: who is the creator,
and who is the created? The answer is to be found in the creative
dialogue between Alberti and Picasso within the mixed media
that is this text, between art and the context that produced it.

The other interpolated seemingly extraneous fragments contribute in various ways to the elaboration of Alberti's forever
incomplete sign for Picasso. For example, there are several pages
upon which appear the colophons of previously published works
in France, presumably of Picasso's artistic production. The following is one of several that are included by Alberti in his
collection:

ACHEVé D'IMPRIMER
EN MARS 1964 PAR
EMMANUEL GREVIN et FILS
A LAGNY-SUR-MARNE
Dépôt légal: 1945
N° d'éd. 10214.-n° d'Imp. 7598.
Imprimé en France.

(Alberti 1978, 49)

Picasso has added a scrawled dedication and signature that
gracefully surrounds and encloses the officially printed notice,
that states "Para Rafael Alberti su amigo Picasso el 11.12.68"
("For Rafael Alberti his friend Picasso 11 December '68"). The
simultaneous and juxtaposed planes of these two distinctly
coded verbal messages function on several different levels at
once. The poet points to the official context of art as well as
the interpersonal relationship, business versus pleasure. There
is also the contrast of the differing language codes, French versus
Spanish, as well as the differing forms of their presentation, cursive script versus printing. Moreover, the two distinct messages
communicate an aspect of Picasso's human and personal history,
namely, his personal, cultural, and psychological roots in Spain
versus his public artistic development and success in France.
Through this juxtaposition of two distinctly coded planes, one
may also observe how the poet depends upon the fixed-point
temporal perspective only to subvert it in the process of creation.
By enclosing this supposedly extraneous page from an unidenti-

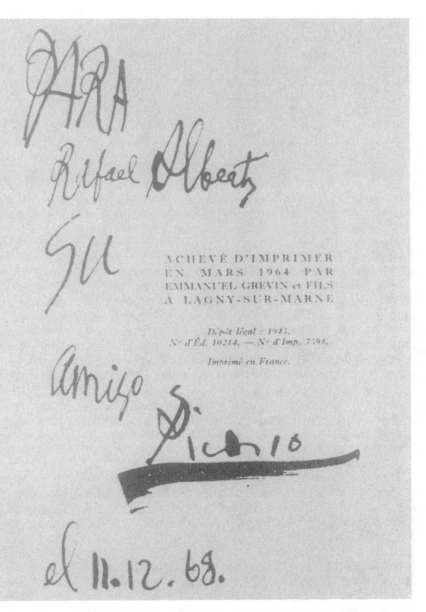

ACHEVÉ D'IMPRIMER
EN MARS 1964 PAR
EMMANUEL GREVIN et FILS
A LAGNY-SUR-MARNE

Dépôt légal : 1945.
N° d'Éd. 10214. — N° d'Imp. 7598.

Imprimé en France.

Picasso: colophon signature, by Pablo Picasso. © 1995 Artists Rights Society
(ARS), New York / SPADEM, Paris.

fied published text, Alberti makes reference to Picasso's existence as a cultural icon in the chronology of Western art. The
trace of Picasso's sign is the circumstantial evidence proffered
by the colophon. There is underlying this odd page of poetic/
legal text a trace of the chronological story of Picasso's life. Alberti acknowledges those links to the outside world, yet simultaneously undercuts that very narration and referentiality that he
seems to affirm, by including this page as one more facet of
his own cubist collage. Picasso counterbalances the official and
impersonal printed typeface with a cursive dedicatory in his
own hand. The question that arises for the reader is in regard to
a work that bears Picasso's signature. By signing this work, has
Picasso metamorphosed a simple colophon into a work—*his*
work—of art? And what of Alberti's complicity in the frame-
up? How does the poet contribute to the artistic process, the
jouissance produced by this odd text, by including this multivalent page within a work of his own creation?

Alberti contravenes referentiality in yet another way. In the
tradition of collage, the poet subverts the original context, in that
the colophon would not necessarily be viewed as a lyric element
in and of itself. But because the poet includes this graphic representation in his poetic collection, he calls into question a purely
monosemic reading of a seemingly marginal element of a book's
overall composition. And finally, by including this extraneous
page from yet another text on Picasso, Alberti makes reference
once again to the concepts of the fragment, the frame, and the
eye of the beholder. By including the colophon of an unnamed
text on Picasso, the poet acknowledges the unfinished nature of
any attempt to (en)close Picasso's representation. Alberti celebrates yet calls into question both the diachronic and the syn-
chronic view of Picasso as sign.

Pieter Wesseling in his *Revolution and Tradition: The Poetry
of Rafael Alberti* sees a similar attitude of playfulness in the
work of both Alberti and Picasso, an attitude that will appear as
the "pursuit of the essence of each moment" (Wesseling 1981,
117). One has only to recall Picasso's series of etchings on the
bull, in which the artist presents a satyrlike alter ego in taurine
form, to come face-to-face with this playfulness. The dedicatory
poem of introduction to *Los 8 nombres* repeats that playfulness
in verbal rather than visual form, and suggests Barthes's concept
of the verbal carnival that was mentioned earlier.

> Dios creó el mundo—dicen—
> y en el sétimo día, cuando estaba tranquilo
> descansando,

se sobresaltó y dijo:
He olvidado una cosa:
los ojos y la mano de Picasso.

(Alberti 1978)

(God created the world—they say—/ and on the seventh day, when he was tranquil resting, / he jumped up with a start and said: / I have forgotten one thing: / the eyes and the hand of Picasso.)

With this ludic opening composition Alberti's speaker points to such issues of artistic import as the relationship of life to creativity, tradition, art, poetry and painting, poet and painter, sound and sight, inner and outer reality, reality and illusion, visual and verbal art, Self and Other, and artful representation as truth versus history turned into art. But just as was the case with Alberti's subversion of the two distinct modes of temporal representation, fixed-point versus multiperspectival, here in this opening composition there is established a series of oppositions which ultimately serve to undermine a monosemic reading of the collection in its totality. The poet surrenders to the authority of Picasso's visual art, but on (and in. . . .) his own terms. Ultimately, Alberti's power and the concomitant pleasure of the reader derive from his simultaneous success and failure in making visible Picasso's art in and through the medium of language. Alberti attempts to make language be "seen" in a new way, while permitting its oral/aural aspects to (dis)appear in "a new light."[10] "Picasso" and Picasso's visual art are and are not present in the play of Alberti's Text. His desire to (re)create and communicate "Picasso," celebrating the painter's visual art, succeeds in foregrounding the difficulties of language in referring to something other than itself. Paradoxically, by heralding the visual discourse(s) of Picasso, Alberti also profiles verbal language's transparent power and self-referentiality.

The title of this collection is a case in point. Alberti signals the number *eight* as that which identifies the names of Picasso. In the first poem of the collection the speaker begins with the query "¿Qué hubiera sido de ti, Pablo, / si de entre los ocho nombres / con que fuiste bautizado / hubieras preferido al de Pablo Picasso" ("What would have become of you, Pablo, / if from among the eight names / with which you were baptized / you would have preferred one [other than] Pablo Picasso") (Alberti 1978, 11) and then goes on to specify other combinations of names by which the artist could have been named. Of course this brings to mind the line of verse which states "A rose is a rose is a rose," that is, a rose by any other name is still a rose. This poem ends with "Sólo PABLO PICASSO" ("Only PABLO PICASSO"), as if to signify that the simplicity of the painter's name cannot diminish his greatness. The artist's work is his finest signature on culture, one that is recognizable in many forms, and one that does not have to depend on mere linguistic tags in order to be recognizable. Yet another manifestation of Picasso's work is to be found in this collection by Alberti. Picasso's essence and style have passed through the lamina of a parallel artistic medium, and have been metamorphosed into verbal form.

The collection itself is divided into seven (rather than eight) unequal sections, perhaps indicating that the eighth is to be provided by the reader, who must create a vision of Picasso just as Alberti has done. In addition, the second half of the title folds back upon itself: one would expect it to state "yo no digo más que lo que digo" ("I do not say more than I say"), but in point of fact an intrusive supplementary negative appears, "lo que *no* digo" (that which I do *not* say"). The effect is to subvert that that has come before. Thus, it would seem that Alberti wishes to communicate that his meditation upon Picasso is a mere approximation of the artist's essence and worth, one that is necessarily incomplete. Just as Picasso's vision of the world refuses closure, so too that of the poet, and of the reader. In the silence that surrounds the poet's rendition of the visual artist, in the lack that he acknowledges in his "no digo" ("I do not say"), in the space between what Alberti has said and not said, lies the true message and the true encapsulation of Picasso's sign. The simultaneous surrender and sovereignty signaled by Robert Scholes resides for Alberti in the (im)possibility of bridging the gap between poetry and painting, between "decir" ("to say") and "no decir" ("not to say"), between "ver" ("to see") and "oír" ("to hear"). His best approximation is to make language be seen, to defamiliarize it sufficiently so that it will be seen as it has never been seen before, from the perspective of a visual artist who uses it not only for its possibilities as a transparent communicative system, but also for its inherent beauty as a set of graceful lines, curves, dots, pauses, and spaces. As Alberti's speaker comments in section 6, "No digo más que lo que no digo,"

Es el idioma en vértigo.
Es la pintura en vértigo.
Metamorfosis siempre de todos los colores.

Felipe IV, Diego de Velázquez. © Museo del Prado, Madrid.

El infante don Carlos, by Diego de Velázquez. © Museo del Prado, Madrid. All rights reserved.

Les Demoiselles d'Avignon, by Pablo Picasso. Oil on canvas, 8′ by 7′8″. Courtesy of the Museum of Modern Art, New York. Acquired through the Lillie P. Bliss Bequest. Photograph © The Museum of Modern Art, New York.

Hotel Room, by Edward Hopper. Courtesy of the Fundación Colección Thyssen-Bornemisza. © VEGAP, Madrid, 1996.

Escenas entrevistas surgidas sin aviso y desaparecidas al mo-
mento.
La tierra y la subtierra de la mano que va escribiendo.
Y el ojo inquisidor de este pintor tan poeta como pintor.
Que es una sola cosa y no dos, pues no es posible en él un poeta
    de quítate tú para ponerme yo.

(Ibid., 143)

(It is language in dizziness. / It is painting in dizziness. / Metamorphosis always of all colors. / Vaguely conjured scenes sprung up
without warning and vanished in-/ stantly. / The earth and the under-
ground of the hand that goes on writing. / And the inquisitive eye of
this painter as much a poet as a painter. / Verily it is one thing and
not two, since it is not possible for him to be a / poet only in terms
of divesting yourself of this in order to put on that.)

In his analysis of Alberti's poem "Un pintor de domingo" ("A
Sunday Painter") of *Poemas escénicos (Scenic Poems)* Wesseling
comments that Alberti offers "an engaging presentation of the
artistic experience of inspiration and creation. . . . At a given
moment the painter feels that he is inspired and has at least
caught the truth of the scene he tries to paint. . . . However, immediately afterwards he begins to doubt that in fact he has captured the right qualities. . . . The joy that accompanies the
moment of insight is not long-lived but his insight into the im-
pression has acquired a life of its own" (Wesseling 1965, 119–
20). This, I believe, is also the thrust of Alberti's meditation upon
the work of Picasso in his *Los 8 nombres*. In his poetry he attempts to approximate the spark of creativity, individuality, and
innovation of the visual artist; but at the same time he goes beyond a simple description of the painter's discourse to present
to the reader a kaleidoscope of color, line, movement, personal
anecdote, interior monologue, and historical context. And the
poet's task is complicated by the paradox of conflicting artistic
media: color, line, texture, shape, and the combinatory power of
visual collage for Picasso; word, form, printing style, and typographical distribution for Alberti. As Murray Krieger comments,
"every poem's problem has its own aesthetician, and every
critic's problem after it, is essentially the problem of Keats with
his Grecian urn: how to make it hold still when the poem must
move" (Krieger 1967, 124).
    Alberti's verbal collage imitates the visual artist's experimen-
tation on the one hand, but on the other, because of language's
essentially temporal orientation, imposes a kinetic element upon

Picasso's medium. But there is a further complication: Alberti does not seek to achieve a complete vision of Picasso in just one poem, or for that matter, in the entire collection. The verbal collage created by Alberti around the polyvalent sign of "Picasso" that is *Los 8 hombres* typifies beautifully the issue convincingly argued by Joseph Frank, the "internal conflict between the time-logic of language and the space-logic implicit in the modern conception of the nature of poetry" (Frank 1945, 229). Frank further suggests that "modern poetry asks its readers to suspend the process of individual reference temporarily until the entire pattern of internal references can be apprehended as a unity" (Ibid., 230). Alberti approaches Picasso's work from various perspectives, juxtaposing these facets, in order to allow the reader the opportunity to create a unique configuration of the elements, and concomitantly, to come to an individual conclusion about Picasso and his work, and by extension, about the appropriateness of attempting to translate Picasso's artistic genius into verbal form. This method repeats in linguistic form Picasso's experimentation with collage and with the multiple perspective of his cubist period. Just as modernist art depends upon the Renaissance perspective, the reader of *Los 8 nombres* must keep in mind Alberti's previous context for the sign that he names Picasso, namely, his book *A la pintura*. In *A la pintura*, Picasso appears as the latest of a long list of visual artists, while in *Los 8 nombres* the poet examines the various facets of Picasso's work from a variety of perspectives. But because Picasso's creativity and originality depends in a certain sense upon the work of his predecessors, the reader must continually frame his work so as to see it as new, while at the same time view it as dependent upon the artistic traditions from which it resolutely sets itself free. Therefore the Renaissance-modernist dialectic in a certain sense reflects and sustains the time-space problematic of the ekphrastic work. In each duality both elements serve to define as well as subvert the other in an unending course of combined affirmation and negation. I will now consider some of the specific techniques that Alberti utilizes to communicate the "still movement" of his verbal compositions in the encapsulation of Picasso's visual art.

In her article on visual art in literature, Diane Chaffee comments that "By arresting time in space through composite description of plastic art or by employing the techniques of juxtaposition and simultaneity, writers produce visual art. The verbally illustrated story with its digressions and spatial progressions contribute to the graphic quality of language" (Chaffee 1984, 318). Alberti's ekphrastic poetry depends on a "visual" approach, in that he uses imagery that appeals most directly to the sense of sight, but the poet also allows other sensory perceptions to influence and be influenced by sight. Thus, his "seeing images" may be seen, perceived, and experienced in a new way.[11] His fascination for painting and painters and the ever-present painter's I/eye in his poetry manifest themselves in his use of color, in his manipulation of line and movement, as well as in his chronicling in poetic form the historical epochs and major historical figures of visual art. Moreover he has demonstrated an affinity toward communicating ideas through objects.[12] What attracts the reader to *Los 8 nombres* is the manner in which Alberti transmutes into verbal form the juxtaposition, simultaneity, and multiperspectivalism of Picasso's cubist style, but achieves his particular effect through the medium of language, whether in its aural, oral, or visual manifestation. This simultaneity has been variously named as "geometrización, perspectiva múltiple, descontinuidad, dislocación" ("geometrization, multiple perspective, discontinuity, dislocation") (Caparrós Esperante 1981, 13). For example, in "De azul se arrancó el toro" ("The Bull Torn Out of the Blue") (Alberti 1948, 14–18), which is the text entitled "Picasso" in *A la pintura*, the speaker describes Spain using fleeting and subconsciously connected images of various tones and textures:

> España:
> fina tela de araña,
> guadaña y musaraña,
> braña, entraña, cucaña,
> saña, pipirigaña
> y todo lo que suena y que consuena
> contigo, España, España.
>
> (Ibid., 14)

(Spain: / fine spiderweb, / scythe and shrew, / summer pasture, gut, greased pole, / fury, pinching game / and all that sounds and that rhymes / with you, Spain, Spain.)

But ironically, the poet emphasizes Picasso's Spanish roots by choosing words in the original Spanish that contain the relatively infrequent "ñ," a graphic and graphemic visual sign that appears solely in the Spanish alphabet. This sound may be transcribed in other ways, such as by "gn," "n," "ni," or "ny," but its

written representation as "ñ" identifies it as pertaining to a certain well-defined, culturally bound set of graphemic characters.
Thus, while suggesting in Picassian fashion jarring and disparate
visual images by way of the semantic content of the words themselves, the speaker in addition forces the reader to be aware of
not only their phonological impact, but also in a broader sense,
their place within the uniquely Spanish graphemic system.
Moreover, on another level, he asserts Picasso's provenance in
the general Spanish cultural system. The character "ñ" as well
as the character "Picasso" reside within, pertain to, and identify
the systems to which they belong, and this relationship is based
upon the faculty of vision, whether neurological or epistemological. The sound that is produced for the character "ñ" may be
represented using other symbols, but the allograph "ñ" is unique,
existing only within the Spanish context.[13] Concomitantly, Picasso's art has been copied by many, but he too is a unique
"monstruo de la naturaleza" ("monster of nature"), a dear and
clearly recognizable icon of Spanish origin.[14]

From this same text the speaker paints Picasso's verbal portrait
in a similar fashion:

Picasso:

Maternidad azul, arlequín rosa.
Es la alegría pura una niña preñada;
la gracia, el ángel, una cabra dichosa,
rosadamente rosa,
tras otra niña sonrosada.
Y la tristeza más tristeza,
una mujer que plancha, doblada la cabeza,
azulada.

(Alberti 1948, 15)

(Picasso: / Blue motherhood, rose harlequin. / A pregnant girl is pure
joy; / grace, the angel, a lucky goat, / rosily rose, / behind another
blushing girl. / And sadness more sadness, / a woman who irons,
with bent head, / blue.)

This poetic text may be read from both a diachronic and syn-
chronic perspective, since on the one hand it offers a collage of
Picasso's various artistic styles and favored hues, and on the
other, relates the "story" of a woman's life. The visual leitmotivs
of color (referring to Picasso's own blue and rose periods) appear
within several contexts, woven together by a tenuous thread de-

tailing the various stages of existence, for Picasso the man and for Everywoman. The two biographical planes conflate into one: there is the story of woman's birth, development, sexual awakening, and disillusionment, from innocent, rosy girl-child to a marginalized, defeated, and sad woman weighed down by daily, monotonous toil; her story is told in and through Picasso's development as an artist, and through the stages through which he himself passed in his aesthetic evolution. Now, his / her / their story is simultaneously told once again, in and through the prism of Alberti's biographical version of the sign named Picasso.

Another form of juxtaposition employed by Alberti plays upon a single word, placing it in succeeding, anaphoric lines of verse in different contexts. In the following text taken from "Tres retahílas para Picasso" ("Three Series for Picasso"), the speaker creates a concatenating, metonymic effect with the verb "salió" ("he came out" of):

> ¿De qué plata y de qué oro
> era a fin de cuentas el toro
> que le salió al pintor
> que salió de una flor
> que salió de una hoja
> que salió de un pincel
> que salió de un palito
> que halló Pablo Picasso en el Perchel?
> Puedes preguntárselo a él.
>
> (Alberti, 21)

(Of what silver and of what gold / was after all the bull / that came from the painter / that came out of a flower / that came out of a leaf [sheet] / that came out of a paintbrush / that came out of a little stick / that Pablo Picasso found in el Perchel? / You can ask him about it.)

The reader must take into account the totality of this particular composition, which is comprised of three separate sections. All of them begin with "Pablo Picasso nació en Málaga" ("Pablo Picasso was born in Málaga"), and end with a variation of one message: "Puedes preguntárselo a él" ("You can ask him about it"), "Sólo a él se lo puedes preguntar" ("Only him can you ask about it"), and finally "Sólo Pablo Picasso te puede contestar" ("Only Pablo Picasso can answer you"). The metonymic effect of the aforementioned verb "salió" ("it/he came out of") is tem-

pered by the metaphoric concatenation of the text's overall structure. In addition, two verses by the Golden Age author Luis de
Góngora appear as an epigram at the poem's opening, "Mátanme
los ojos / de aquel andaluz" ("The eyes of that Andalusian /
slay me"). In the closing section of Alberti's poem, the speaker
intercalates Góngora's words, and with paradoxical anachro-
nism, they effectively subvert the underlying, parallel chronological structure and order that were suggested by each stanza's
opening and closing, and the repetition of the verb "salió":

> Y gritó rabiosa la luz
> al sentirse morir de tanta luz:
> *Mátanme los ojos*
> *de aquel andaluz.*
> ¿Quién este andaluz
> que al sentirse morir la luz de tanta luz
> . . . halló todo lo que quiso encontrar?
> Sólo Pablo Picasso te puede contestar.
>
> (Ibid., 22)

(And the light shouted furiously / upon feeling itself die from so
much light: / *The eyes of that Andalusian / slay me.* / Who [was] that
Andalusian / who upon feeling the light die from so much light /
. . . / discovered all he wanted to find? / Only Pablo Picasso can
answer you.)

The reader is thus encouraged to look upon the phrase "aquel
andaluz" ("that Andalusian") from a new perspective, with a
new sense of vision, one that will allow Picasso's creativity to
enter into that of Góngora, and Góngora's into Picasso's as well
as into Alberti's. The three Andalusians—Góngora, Picasso, and
Alberti—all are suffused with the light of their native land, and
Alberti gives witness to their interwoven/intertextual geographic,
social, cultural, literary, and visual heritage in this text, through
the medium of language. The multivalent sign "luz" ("light")
pays homage to their commingled history, origin, shared motif,
and artistic testament as well as achievement.

Yet another form of simultaneity to be found in *Los 8 nombres*
is the juxtaposing of one artistic era with another, one artistic
creation with another; this technique is similar to the strategy
employed by Alberti to graft Góngora's words to his homage of
Picasso.[15] In section 3 Alberti offers a series of poetic meditations
in classical sonnet form. These poetic texts focus on several classic painters, and create a dialogue between painter and painter,

painter and poet, artist and viewer/reader. Upon reading the title of "De Rafael a Picasso" ("From Raphael to Picasso") and the first few lines of verse, for example, the reader is uncertain whether the name "Rafael" ("Raphael") refers to the renowned Renaissance artist, or to the twentieth-century Spanish poet, or to both. The vocative emanates not from the present to the past, but from the past to the present, the exact opposite of what occurred in *A la pintura*:

> Maestro, no soñaba yo que un día
> me dibujaras tan divinamente
> el gallo erguido de la cresta ardiente
> dentro del horno que jamás se enfría.
>
> (Alberti, 74)

(Master, I did not dream that one day / you would draw for me so divinely / the erect rooster with the fiery crest / within the oven that never cools down.)

And in the same fashion Michelangelo addresses the twentieth-century painter, as if to defend himself and his own unique style, faced with the prolific, larger-than-life creator who is his successor:

> Peligroso maestro respetado,
> que sin respeto por mis compañones
> me haces mirar entre los cortinones
> lo que en mi alcoba ver quisiera alzado.
>
> (Ibid., 75)

(Dangerous respected master, / who without respect for my buddies / you make me look at between the large curtains / that which in my bedroom I would like to see hidden.)

Interestingly enough, in *Los 8 nombres* Alberti for the most part does not pause to meditate upon many specifically named paintings by Picasso, in contrast to what we saw in Manuel Machado's work, for example.[16] "Balada de les Demoiselles d'Avignon" ("Ballad of les Demoiselles d'Avignon") is an obvious exception. In this poetic text, the poet communicates Picasso's transgression of many artistic norms by a similar style of transgression in his own work. Just as Picasso had experimented with multiperspectivalism in his visual work, Alberti here emulates the visual artist's innovation in verbal form. (See color plates.)

The poet approximates in linguistic form Picasso's use of "primitive art as a battering ram against the classical conception of beauty" (Janson 1962, 521). Alberti gives echo to Picasso's cubist undertaking by constructing a verbal text of exquisitely crafted verbal shards, collagelike scraps of language that at once recall classical models of composition and beauty as well as signal that the stylishness of these art forms has long since passed:

> Venus podrida. La sublime
> belleza eterna al panteón.
> Un salvaje asesino surge.
> Les demoiselles d'Avignon.
>
> Pasmo. Al burdel nuevos clientes.
> El siglo entero en conmoción.
> Irrumpen ángulos en furia.
> Les demoiselles d'Avignon.
>
> Hieren a pico nalgas, codos,
> narices, ímproba agresión.
> Castigo en formas que se aplastan.
> Les demoiselles d'Avignon.
>
> Grito el espacio sin espacio.
> Libertad. Descomposición.
> Rayan las tripas, no soportan.
> Les demoiselles d'Avignon.
>
> Cementerio de lo agradable.
> El buen gusto, la picazón
> de fornicar con lo pintado.
> Les demoiselles d'Avignon.
>
> Día y noche el portón abierto.
> Hoy visitas sin restricción.
> Cuidado. Muerden todavía.
> Les demoiselles d'Avignon.

(Alberti, 31–32)

(Putrefied Venus. Sublime / eternal beauty to the pantheon. / A savage assassin appears. The young ladies of Avignon. // Wonder. To the brothel new clients. / The entire century in commotion. / Angles erupt in fury. / The young ladies of Avignon. // They wound with beak bites buttocks, elbows, / noses, dishonest aggression. / Punishment in forms that crush. / The young ladies of Avignon. // I shout the space without space. / Liberty. Decomposition. / The belly underscores, does not endure. / The young ladies of Avignon. // Cemetery of what is charming. / Good taste, the itch / of fornicating with what is painted. / The young ladies of Avignon. // Day and night the open door. / Today visits without restriction. / Careful. They bite still. / The young ladies of Avignon.)

Alberti chose for this text the nine-syllable line of verse, no doubt influenced by the acoustic effect of the painting's title. But it is revealing to note that this lyric meter manifests in and of itself the transgression that characterizes the painting as well as the entire poetic composition. In his well-known *Manual de versificación española (Manual of Spanish Versification)* Rudolf Baehr states: "Es difícil dar un resumen histórico del eneasílabo. La cuestión de su procedencia en las distintas épocas, y en parte en lo que se refiere a los diferentes tipos, ha sido explicada de manera diversa, a pesar de que se está de acuerdo en que, por vía directa o indirecta, remonta al octasílabo provenzal-francés. . . . El desarrollo histórico del eneasílabo acontece en dos planos: uno estrictamente popular, y otro artístico" ("It is difficult to give an historical summary of the nine-syllable verse line. The question of its origin in various epochs, and in part in reference to the different types, has been explained in various ways, in spite of everyone being in agreement that, directly or indirectly, it goes back to the French Provençal eight-syllable verse line. . . . The historical development of the nine-syllable line occurs on two planes: one strictly popular, and another artistic") (Baehr 1981, 121). The bilateral manifestation "en dos planos: uno estrictamente popular, y otro artístico" ("on two planes: one strictly popular, and another artistic") refers as well to the painting's and the poem's artistic originality. H. W. Janson describes Picasso's achievement in the following manner:

Not only the proportions, but the organic integrity and continuity of the human body are denied here, so that the canvas (in the apt description of one critic) "resembles a field of broken glass." Picasso, then, has destroyed a great deal; what has he gained in the process? Once we recover from the initial shock, we begin to see that the destruction is quite methodical: everything—the figures as well as their setting—is broken up into angular wedges or facets; these, we will note, are not flat, but shaded in a way that gives them a certain three-dimensionality. We cannot always be sure whether they are concave or convex; some look like chunks of solidified space, others like fragments of translucent bodies. They constitute a unique kind

of matter, which imposes a new integrity and continuity on the entire
canvas. (Janson, 521–22)

The common strumpets of Avignon Street in Barcelona have
been transformed by Picasso's creativity. As Janson reminds us,
the painting "can no longer be read as an image of the external
world; its world is its own, analogous to nature but constructed
along different principles" (Ibid., 522). Similarly, Alberti's text
may also be read on two distinct planes, one popular and another
artistic. Through his verse form and the provocative erotic imagery, he recalls the popular origins of his verse as well as the
classical tradition of medieval, Renaissance, and baroque love
poetry, from the "canciones de amigo" ("medieval lovers" bal-
ladry") to the ribald and bawdy verse of Lope and Quevedo. Also,
the cyclic repetition of the painting as well as the poem's title
as the final verse of each strophe contributes to the cubist message of the poetic text. The repetition of "Les demoiselles d'Avignon" ("The young ladies of Avignon"), much as a refrain in
traditional verse, frames each stanza as a separate entity, as well
as miters them all together into a cohesive totality. With this
bipolar function of separating and joining simultaneously, the
line evokes a self-conscious reading from both a visual and linguistic perspective, and elicits a new plane of awareness, in fine
cubist fashion, for the discerning reader.[17]
   Alberti's text contains yet a further extrapolation of the world
created by Picasso. The opening line of verse refers obliquely to
the classical representation of Venus, as in Botticelli's famous
work, but Alberti's Venus is by contrast "podrida" ("putrified").
As in the Picasso version/vision, where a world is "constructed
along different principles," this putrifaction takes on a positive
value, "La sublime belleza eterna al panteón" ("Sublime eternal
beauty to the pantheon"). The second stanza adopts another perspective and may be viewed from at least two angles. It may be
interpreted as a reading from within the painting itself, where
new clients become patrons of the willing women. Or from another perspective, the "nuevos clientes" ("new clients") may be
read as those who open their eyes to the modernist perspective,
whether as patrons of the arts or museum-goers in general, or
as commercial patrons and supporters of specific artists. The
"ángulos" ("angles") to which the speaker refers in the second
quartet could be in reference to either Picasso's visual style or
to the commercial success that followed the cubist explosion.
The poet transposes Picasso's visual angles in yet another way,

in that he utilizes end-line stop, which lends to his work a broken and staccato cadence, thus offering to the poetic text's reader a collagelike assemblage of verbal scraps and pieces. Like the cubist elements in the Picasso visual text, each fragment speaks for itself, simultaneously against *and* with the others with which it shares space in the framework of the text as a whole.

In the center two stanzas the speaker attempts to re-create the breaking up "into angular wedges or facets" noted by Janson, such as in the "nalgas y codos" ("buttocks and elbows") that "hieren a pico" ("wound with beak bites"), the "castigo en formas que se aplastan" ("punishment in forms that crush"), and the "Libertad. Descomposición" ("Liberty. Decomposition"). The final two quartets adopts yet another angle or perspective. Here, the speaker retreats from a direct observation of the painting itself to comment upon and offer an opinion of Picasso's treatment of the past, as well as the painter's artistic achievement, but he expresses it in common erotic terms, "la picazón / de fornicar con lo pintado" ("The itch of fornicating with what is painted"), which reminds the reader of Picasso's own combination of the plebeian and the artistic, his prostitutes metamorphosed onto the canvas according to the cubist principle. Likewise, the speaker invites the current reader of his own text, the poetic composition, to form an individual opinion, and with tongue-in-cheek seriousness issues a warning as to the danger of such an undertaking, in spite of the passage of time. The door remains open and "Hoy visitas sin restricción" ("Today visits without restriction") are an oblique reference to the bordello in the painting and in Alberti's opening stanzas. But on another level, the speaker through these lines of verse challenges the reader to experience individually and contemplate freely upon the cutting edge creativity of Picasso, in his *Les demoiselles d'Avignon*. Picasso has opened the door to a new way of organizing reality, one that cannot be denied because of its impact on all Western art that followed in Picasso's wake.

There are many other poetic compositions in Alberti's *Los 8 nombres* where the poet does not name directly a certain Picasso painting but rather alludes to a specific theme or visual strategy.[18] For example in the synesthetic "Oyes, ¿Qué música?" ("You hear, What music?") (Alberti 1978, 36) the speaker suggests Picasso's studies of the musical medium and various musical instruments, such as "Still Life with Violin and Fruit" (1913), "Three Musicians" (1921), or the Blue Period "Old Guitarist" (1903). The speaker, in directing himself to the painter in apostrophic fashion, marvels at Picasso's ability to capture in visual form lyric compositions perceived by the auditory faculty. The speaker ends this particular poetic composition with the simple statement "Tú has sentido la música que miras" ("You have felt [heard] the music that you look at"), where he plays on the multivalent "sentir," both as "to feel" and "to hear." The speaker suggests that Picasso does both with his artistic achievements: he hears, feels, and creates the visual music and harmony that humanity longs for. The will to sustain the artistic tradition is a sign of that very humanity and a guarantee of immortality, a proud and Promethean challenge to divinity. But the marvel of sensorial delight is also communicated to Alberti's reader on another level. One must be aware that Alberti in turn has transmuted yet again Picasso's transposition of sound to vision, to yet another form of artistic creativity. As Luis Caparrós Esperante suggests, the poet has captured in linguistic terms the fleetingness of sound as it passed into a visual medium (Caparrós Esperante 1981, 13). Or in "Escultura" ("Sculpture") the poetic speaker assures us of Picasso's magic, "Cuando él construye una guitarra es otra" ("When he constructs a guitar it is another"). If perchance someone would object to Picasso's creative power, the speaker has a ready answer:

> Ah, pero si se te ocurre ir a su taller,
> en el acto Picasso te construye otras manos
> capaces de tocarla
> y otras nuevas orejas
> perfectas para oír sus hondos aires de hojalata pintada.
> (Alberti 1978, 41)

(Ah, but if it occurs to you to go to his studio / instantly Picasso fashions for you other hands / capable of playing it [the guitar] / and other new ears / perfect for hearing its deep plaints of painted tinplate.)

Picasso's hands are godlike in their creative capacity, in their power to create flesh that comes to life through his art. In "Consejos picassianos" ("Picassian Advice") Alberti effects a significant inversion: whereas in previous texts, the poet usurps the visual discourse of Picasso, in this poetic composition, the poet creates a speaker named Picasso who usurps the verbal discourse of his creator. Picasso as a first-person speaker forms neologisms of all types, transposing nouns into verbs, to create a highly suggestive and surreal text, where reference is deferred yet present:

Almejo todo, escobo, aljofifo, limono
sin ensartar lo que nunca naranjo.
Encubo, escoplo cuanto desatornillo,
descoso, descalabro, deslibero,
membreto bien, salitro,
pajareo lo que atrapo.
Es mi virtud.
No olvides.
Siempre descalandrájate.

(Ibid., 39)

(I mussel everything, I broom, I floor cloth, I lemon / without thread-
ing what I never orange. / I vat, I chisel as much as I unscrew, / I
unsew, I harm, I unliberate, / I letterhead well, I saltpeter, / I bird flock
what I trap. / It is my virtue. / Don't forget. / Always untatter yourself.)

This poetic text reminded this reader of Picasso's sculpture
entitled *Bull's Head* (1943), a work of art that had been constructed of a discarded handlebars and bicycle seat. The two
elements were pirated from their original context, a mechanical
means of transportation, and combined in a playful fashion so
as to suggest the skeletal remains of a bovine head; yet they also
refer in a novel way to one facet of Picasso's cultural heritage,
the Spanish bullfight, and the lasting trophy via the art of the
taxidermist of a mythical contest between man and beast, played
out in a sunbaked and dusty bullring, in some half-forgotten
corner of Spain. In parallel fashion, Alberti allows Picasso's
voice to playfully draw existing morphological segments from
the Spanish system to create new words, and to endow them
with new meaning, as for example, the verb "limono" ("I lemon")
from "limonar" ("lemon grove" or as a verb "to lemon") or "almejo" ("I mussel") from "almejar" ("mussel bed" or as a verb "to
mussel"). Both "limonar" and "almejar" are conventional nouns
in Spanish, but look as if they could be verbs, because of the
telltale (or is it tell-tail??) infinitival morphological marker, "-
ar." The speaker of this text is the Picasso created by Alberti, and
he creates from old linguistic segments some new and resonant
combinations, just as he did in the visual medium. In his own
voice he forcefully speaks out from a first-person viewpoint his
process of creation, utilizing this strange yet recognizable vocabulary. The verbal artistic objects "speak for themselves" in
their own (de)familiarizing way.

In addition to "Consejos picassianos", there are several other
texts of *Los 8 nombres* where Alberti gives voice to the mute art

object in the classical sense of ekphrasis, and allows that art object to speak for itself. For example, in "Escena picassiana" ("Picassian Scene") the speaker of the poetic text is the male figure of a Picasso portrait, obviously from the artist's blue period, who tells his own story:

> Soy un mendigo azul.
> El año tres del siglo
> me senté en este azul junto a mi nieto.
> Pido limosnas. Fueran
> azules las limosnas.
> Mas como no lo son. . . .
> Nadie me escucha. Pido.

(Ibid., 30)

(I am a blue beggar. / The year three of the century / I sat down on this blue next to my grandson. / I beg for alms. Would that the alms were blue. / But as they are not. . . . / No one listens to me. I beg.)

The speaker has identified the year, 1903, and so the reader may surmise that the portrait is from that year, and could be identified as *The Old Jew*. It is interesting to note that at the end of the poetic text, the speaker makes reference not to how the figure looks, cast in overriding shades of blue, but rather to what he says and his lament that "Nadie me escucha. Pido" ("No one listens to me. I beg"), which brings into focus not the visual but the verbal aspect of his relationship to the world. But ironically, the reader of Alberti's text is aware of his plight, what he hears and what he says, through the sense of sight, since reading is a visual rather than aural act of reception. Thus from a different perspective Alberti encourages the reader to see verbal language in a new way. The poet allows Picasso's vision of the world to be seen and heard, and for that which is heard to be seen, as letters on the printed page.

And in "Sucedido" ("Happening") the poetic speaker relates an odd but charming and captivating ekphrastic experience. He is seated at a sunny outdoor café and is accompanied by a very delicate female companion, who is temporarily set free from the frame of a Picasso painting. Picasso is present in the text not only by way of reference to the name of one of his paintings but also because the text-speaker directs the text to him in apostrophic form:

Hay una silla libre.
En ella siento a tu
"Mujer sentada con sombrero lila".
Llega el mozo:—Señora. . . .
—Un helado de fresa—le responde,
correctamente hablando por un ojo.

(Ibid., 79)

(There is a free chair. / In it I seat your / *Seated Woman with Lilac Hat*. / The waiter arrives:—Madam. . . . / —A strawberry ice cream— she tells him, / correctly talking through an eye.)

The speaker effects a conflation of the visual and the verbal by both celebrating and subverting the frame of the artistic text, whether visual or verbal. The combined celebration and subversion of framing is underscored in the intercalation of several surrealist details, such as that his companion eats her strawberry ice cream through her "inmensa nariz, / a grandes picotazos como haría un pelícano" ("immense nose, / with great beak gobbles as a pelican would do"). The surrealist portrait, whether in its visual or verbal composition, is so normal, that at the end, "un caballero / se acerca cortésmente y le propone: / —Señora, / ¿aceptaría ir conmigo a cenar / y luego al baile?" ("a gentleman / approaches courteously and suggests to her: / —Madam, would you accept going to dine with me / and then to the dance?") Picasso's portrait of the seated woman wearing a lilac hat comes to life, the central figure speaks for herself, and elicits the amorous attention of a gallant gentleman. The speaker-witness calls attention to the portrait's title, and frames that name visually for the reader of the poetic text. But that same speaker-witness deliberately subverts the act of framing by allowing the framed figure to speak for herself, to decide her own boundaries and choices, rather than those imposed upon her by the painter, the poet, the speaker, or the amorous suitor, all of whom are male. The text ends with a question, so that the frame is forever open from a variety of perspectives. The questioning stance allows the reader to answer—or decide *not* to answer—the many questions posited by this, or any, text's eternal closure and aperture, most especially from an ekphrastic perspective.

Similarly, in "Suceden cosas" ("Things Happen") the poetic speaker anthropomorphizes the very substances, the artistic materials, with which Picasso's hands come in contact. By defamiliarizing them in such a way, he privileges them with voice, volition, and feeling:

Suceden cosas, pasan
cosas en cuanto tocas con tu mano.
Suceden y se escuchan. Así hoy:
Grita el cobre mordido por el ácido,
tatuada piel estremecida
de arañazos, zarpazos, gañafones
. . . Así el metal contigo está orgulloso
de existir, se te ofrece a cada instante
complacido, dispuesto
a resistir tranquilo las puntas, los mordientes,
los bisturíes que desgarran
su pecho rutilante,

(Ibid., 69)

(Things happen, they occur / these things as soon as you touch with
your hand. / They happen and they are heard. Thus today: / The
copper gnawed away by the acid, / tatooed skin shocked / by claw
scrapes, / paw blows, farmhand manhandling / . . . / Thus, the metal
with you is proud / of existing, it offers itself to you at each instant /
content, disposed / to resist tranquilly the tines, the acids, the scal-
pels that rend / its shining breast,)

In her brilliant chapter on James Joyce and Pablo Picasso,
Steiner asserts that Picasso's oeuvre represents a sustained visual
inquiry into the connection between narrativity and the modernist revolution (Steiner 1988, 131), between the fixed-point and
multiperspectival view of reality. She points out that "Cubism
neglected the romance possibilities of pictorial perception, and
Picasso later dramatized this fact in his *Vollard Suite*" (Ibid.), a
series of drawings that meditates upon the "connection between
love, sexuality, art, and vision" (Ibid., 133). She comments that
"Sometimes there is a perfect circuit of communication among
sculptor, model, and work, with eyes interconnected and eros
and aesthesis bound" (Ibid.) Moreover, "the act of beholding is
by implication a discovery of the self in the work, as it is for the
model, and a creation and act of love, as it is for the sculptor.
Viewer and work are intimately connected—encircled by the
same garland—so that the etching, through its connection to the
work within it, establishes a special kind of intertextuality: that
between itself and us, whom it has made into a text for the occasion" (Ibid., 134). In his meditation on the work of Picasso, Alberti plays upon the various definitions of vision that connect
the two artists, whether in the philosophical sense of worldview
and aesthetic commitment, in the capacity of divine revelation

and inspiration, or in the more corporal, neurological acceptance of the word, from a purely sensory perspective.

It is not surprising then that Alberti utilizes as one of his principal images in *Los 8 nombres* that of the eye, both of Picasso and of the beholder, be it of his own text-speaker, one of Picasso's subjects, the museum-goer, or the reader of his own poetic text.[19] It is an interesting play, too, on the painter seen from outside, as a person, and his eyes as organs of sight. As viewers, we see through the eyes of the painter and poet, as well as conjure up a picture of what the painter and the poet are like as people. Thus, Self and Other simultaneously become one, frame one another, yet separate under our gaze as readers of the various texts that come into (our) sight. In "Los ojos de Picasso" ("The Eyes of Picasso") the poet captures with mesmerizing verbal effect Picasso's predilection for large eyes, which are able to see the world in all of its complexity and splendor, as well as to represent the painter's unique vision of that world. This poem in particular repeats in linguistic form the painter's study of a particular subject from various perspectives. Thus, it is significant that the poet has chosen *eyes* as his central image to communicate Picasso's inventiveness in breaking down the traditional boundaries of height, width, and depth, in order to add another which is simultaneity. Alberti's "vision" of Picasso is complicated still further by the fact that "Los ojos de Picasso" is inspired by some poetic lines by Vicente Huidobro, which Alberti cites/sights at his own poem's beginning:

> El ojo humano, el ojo luz,
> el ojo caos, el ojo universo,
> el ojo eternidad. . . .
> VICENTE HUIDOBRO
>
> (Alberti 1978, 23)

(The human eye / the eye light, / the eye chaos, the eye universe, / the eye eternity. . . . / VICENTE HUIDOBRO)

Alberti in this fashion once again brings to the forefront the intertextual nature of this collection as well as the essentially simultaneously derivative yet altogether original nature of Picasso's art. Alberti's vision of Picasso—and Picasso's vision of the world—is tempered by artistic context as well as by the individual creative genius. As Alberti states,

El ojo en vela
centinela,
espuela,
candela,
el que se rebela y revela.

(Ibid., 24)

(The eye awatch [set sail/ablaze]/sentry,/spur,/candle, / the one that
rebels and reveals itself.)

The "vela" ("vigil" or "sail" or "candle") of "El ojo en vela" (The
eye awatch [set sail/aglow]") just cited, could be read as an
oblique intertextual reference to Federico García Lorca's "con-
flicto de luz y viento" ("conflict of light and wind") from his
Poeta en Nueva York (Poet in New York) (1940), since "vela"
has three radically different translations, either "vigil" or "ship's
sail" or "candle." The evocative Albertian image of Picasso's "eye
at vigil," with traces of "eye ablaze" and/or "eye at full sail"
expressively conflates with synesthetic economy the painter (and
the poet's) breathtaking originality. The final homonymic "se
rebela y revela" acknowledges the painter's simultaneous break
from, and debt to, his predecessors, and mimics the constant
flickering of a taper and/or billowing of a sail from slack to full-
ness in the wind. This poetic text ends with the line of verse
"La eternidad para esos ojos" ("Eternity for those eyes"), which
returns the reader to the beginning of the poem, and to the words
of Vicente Huidobro. But the Latin American poet's words have
been refracted through the prism of Alberti's vision of Picasso.
Once again, the verbal artist has foregrounded in linguistic form
the intertextual nature of art, regardless of the medium.[20] The
verbal strategy of ekphrasis powerfully emblemizes language's
(in)ability to represent an object exterior to itself. The ebb and
flow of presence/absence of one text within another, of Text(u-
ality) as an epistemological undertaking, of Alberti's/Picasso's/
Huidobro's vision, underscore and problematize art's questionable object of representation of anything exterior to itself.

In many poems of *Los 8 nombres* the poet captures a vision
of himself viewing Picasso's work, as in "Escribo lejos" ("I Write
Far") (104–5) or in "Este museo de mi barrio" ("This Museum
of My Barrio") (109–10).[21] These poetic texts in effect bring to
the forefront from yet a different perspective the relationship
between the art object and its viewer, and thus create a distinct
type of frame, wherein the person viewing a framed artwork is
framed and memorialized by the new text, which itself is en-

closed by a frame. (The example of Velázquez's *Las Meninas* is an excellent visual example of this type of painting.) These poems tacitly acknowledge the concept of the frame while at the same time they encourage the reader to both acknowledge *and* subvert the frame, by entering into the text. This verbal strategy is reminiscent of that of Picasso in his *Vollard Suite*, in a "perfect circuit of communication among sculptor, model, and work" (Steiner 1988, 133), but here it is the circuit of painter, poet, Text, and viewer/reader. Alberti furthers the chain by including himself as the poet, the poetic speaker he has created, and the viewer/reader of both painting and the poetic text. This textual receptor breaks the frame of not only the visual work of art, but also the verbal one. For example, in "Mañana boca arriba" ("Morning Face Up") the poet's first-person speaker pays homage to the inter-and metatextual nature of the Alberti-Picasso dialectic by acknowledging the *differénce/differánce* of the sight/sound dichotomy:

> Todo se ve, se escucha.
> Picasso—sso—Picasso
> y hasta un gato feroz
> se lo come el agua.
> Leo cerca de una fuente.
>
> (Albert, 111)

(Everything is seen, is heard. / Picasso—sso—Picasso / and the water drinks up even a ferocious cat. / I read close to a fountain.)

These enigmatic lines of verse confess to Picasso's all-consuming talent ("se lo come el agua") ("the water drinks it up"), and in the sibilant, suggestive "—sso—" of his surname may well allude to the "secret" ("¿sigiloso?") (ssecretive?) power of creation at his disposal, the water that paradoxically drinks in the powerful cat as a mysterious life force. The poetic speaker gives pause for thought, not only in the evocative and multivalent images of cat and water, but in the typographical spacing on the printed page. The speaker's text is doubly framed, separate from, yet inextricably bound to, his verbal portrait of Picasso and his art. The reader of Alberti's text also reads "cerca de una fuente" ("close to a fountain"); the wellspring could be interpreted as the entire cultural corpus upon which the intertextual relationship is based. Or in "No digo más que lo que no digo" (141–45) the speaker inserts an apostrophic and seemingly parenthetical comment to the reader of his "derived" text, which he offers as a commentary on Picasso's comments upon El Greco's visual text of *The Burial of Count Orgaz:* "(No intente poner comas ni otros signos el que esta obra leyere. Léala sin aliento, pues puede sucederle si se para ser sepulto en la onda y arrastrado y tundido, sin socorro posible. Será siempre mejor que comience de nuevo)" ("Do not try to put commas or other signs, the one who may read this work. Read it without taking a breath since it could happen to you if you stop that you will be buried under the waves and dragged and thrashed about, with no aid possible. It will always be better that you begin anew") (Ibid., 142).[22] This advice to begin anew is relative at best, since the reading of a text/Text does not begin or end with the individual text at hand. Rather, the speaker signals that the reading process is a continual and continuous act of creating, that knows no beginning or end. All creative works are born from and cede to others, one giving way to another in a constant interchange unmarked by artificial frames, temporal restrictions, or points of punctuation. Just as Alberti's text/Text frames and is framed by Picasso and *his* text/Text, so too the latter's obligation to El Greco. Alberti defers to this limitless textual concatenation by closing this text with "Leemos El entierro del Conde de Orgaz. / Todos buscamos como locos el Conde. / Era el único que no se hallaba en el relato y no le fue posible escuchar la lectura" ("We read The Burial of the Count of Orgaz. / We all search madly for the Count. / He was the only one who was not to be found in the story and it was not possible for him to listen to the reading") (Ibid., 146).

In and through Alberti's Text on Picasso, the poet succeeds in producing a study of the multiple facets of this visual artist's work, an artist who broke the limits of the artistic endeavor as they had been previously defined. But more importantly, in his rapprochement with the contemporary painter's work through the medium of language, the poet's own text is foregrounded, and with it the modernist undertaking and how it relates to the fixed-point view of reality that is both its basis and its antithesis. Alberti's multifaceted and multiperspectival Text on Picasso succeeds in bringing to the forefront not only the creativity and originality of the visual artist and his work, but also the relationship between the Renaissance heritage and the modernist undertaking in both the visual and the verbal format, and the metatextual problematic of verbal representation. Moreover, in the poet's attempts to approximate the painter's creativity with line, color, simultaneity, and juxtaposition, there is both success and failure. The poet simultaneously succeeds and fails, in that the sign for Picasso is both present and absent, forever deferred by the subversion of the visual/verbal dialectic. In Alberti's writerly/painterly Text on Picasso, the poet offers a metatext concerning his own work, and from a much wider perspective, one on the interartistic relationship and the artistic creative process, whatever the medium. As Krieger has commented, "literature retains its essential nature as a time-art even as its words, by reaching the stillness by way of pattern, seek to appropriate sculpture's plasticity as well. There is after all, then, a sense in which literature, as a time-art, does have special time-space powers. Through patterns, through context, it has the unique power to celebrate time's movement as well as to arrest it, to arrest it in the very act of celebrating it" (Krieger 1967, 125). Alberti's meditation upon Picasso, his life, his art, and his creativity, has succeeded in moving beyond a static representation of the visual artist, to achieve a timelessness and synergistic dynamism that pays tribute as well as responds to Picasso's own artistry. Through the techniques of simultaneity and juxtaposition—of artistic eras and personalities, of visual and verbal texts, of sound, vision, and silence—Alberti has been able to communicate in spite of the difficulties and failures of discourse(s) of that still movement described earlier, which is the (un)bridgeable chasm between literature and plastic art. By presenting to his reader an opportunity to perceive the sign Picasso in an original way through the prism of language, Alberti also allows the reader to perceive language anew and to see how language in and of itself is a verbal as well as a visual art form, and to appreciate the reader's relationship to language, art, and language as art. The portrait of Picasso and the entire modernist undertaking that emerges is not a static representation, but rather an approximation to the artist in verbal collage, an artist who was both the product and creator of his historical context. As Alberti states:

> Un día,
> cuando después de cientos de miles de años,
> si es que al hombre aún le exalta el pasado remoto,
> se dirá al hallar tantos residuos de cerámicas,
> ojos alucinados, buhos, caballos, toros,
> senos, palomas, arabescos raros:
> Una vez en tierra existió una edad maravillosa
> a la que llamaremos picassiana.
>
> (Alberti 1978, 125)

(One day, when after hundreds of thousands of years, / if it is that man still exalts the remote past, / it will be said upon discovering remnants of ceramics, / dazzled eyes, owls, horses, bulls, / bosoms, doves, strange arabesques: / One time on earth there existed a marvelous age / which we will call Picassian.)

4

Shot Out of the Can(n)on: Gloria Fuertes, Carmen Martín Gaite, and the Problem of Liminality

In his *Literature and Liminality: Festive Readings in the Hispanic Tradition*, Gustavo Pérez Firmat notes that certain texts tempt (and [at]tempt to go beyond) the limits of conventional discourse within their genre. This type of text is "one that in a given situation takes up a position of eccentricity, one that occupies the periphery in relation to a contextually determined center" (Pérez Firmat 1986, xiv). Paradoxically, the central focus in these texts is the very issue of their marginality. As Pérez Firmat states, this type of text is "constituted by a productive tension between restraint and mobility, order and disorder, tradition and treason" (Ibid., xviii). The ekphrastic text fits well within this definition, since there is a rupture in a poetic text's boundaries by the problematic presence/absence of a visual art work. The poet attempts to (re-)create this art object through the medium of language and must necessarily celebrate yet suspend and defer the art object's original discourse, be it of painting, architecture, or cinematography, for example, in order to effect a transmutation of that visually and spatially defined object into linguistic form, which manifests a decidedly temporal cast.[1] Thus, there is a continual play of presence and absence of the visual art object, in that its presence/absence is (dis)covered through verbal discourse. Its visual discourse must (dis)appear within the context and the frame of the linguistic one. In and through the verbal medium on the printed page, the poet encourages the reader to simultaneously forget and remember the visual dimensions of the desired object: the reader remembers/desires the visual object, but continually defers possession of the visual object because of the barrier of linguistic mediation. Thus, a poem or a collection of poems that utilizes ekphrasis as a central discursive

89

strategy dances on the border, and in that act, realigns the focus from centrality to marginality, where marginality comes to occupy a not very firmly grounded center.

The reading of an ekphrastic text must take into account the issue of liminality. And this concept is inextricably bound to the question of gender. As noted in the introductory chapter of this study, the vast majority of visual art objects are created and/or viewed from the vantage point of the male gaze. But when the visual artist, poet, or reader is female, or when a male wishes to consider the ramifications of change from the male to the female point of view, sensory as well as philosophical, then the patriarchal frame becomes a part of the focus; the marginal comes to occupy a central position. As Dale M. Bauer suggests in her *Feminist Dialogics: A Theory of Failed Community* where there is a tension between the marginal and the central, so also one will find an equal tension between the eccentric (read here, the feminine or gynocentric), and the phallocentric (Bauer 1988; xiii). Traditionally, art forms have been defined and classified by the norms of patriarchal culture. Art forms that utilize the female I/eye as their locus bring into question not only the structures and norms closed to them by definition because of female Otherness, but also the position of eccentricity* [*ec, "out of," + kentron, "center; deviation from the norm"] formulated by the patriarchal order.[2] Thus it is inevitable that not only the subject/object relationship must come under scrutiny, but also the borders and the gatekeepers.

Bauer has developed a fruitful line of inquiry in order to dismantle the tradition of the male gaze. Her point of departure is especially germane to a discussion of the ekphrastic text, since this particular type of literary work depends on a visual art object as one of its points of reference. She suggests that "the feminist voice (rather than the male gaze) can construct and dismantle the exclusive community and patriarchal critical discourse" (Bauer, 2). Her thesis is predicated upon an extrapolation of the dialogism proposed by Mikhail Bakhtin, where the disruptive feminine voice places itself in opposition to the patriarchal surveillant gaze. This Other voice goes against the commonly held axiom that women, like children, should be seen and not heard. Bauer's critical stance outside the border of patriarchy permits and encourages a reading where the text is able to speak "out," to speak for itself, from a position of Otherness. And as we saw in chapter 1, this ability to speak out, is indeed one of the definitions of ekphrasis in general, to give voice to an otherwise mute art object. But for a female artist, the art object traditionally has been mute twice over: first, because art has been the exclusive domain of men, and second, because the object itself most often reflects the masculine concept of female beauty, namely, to be silent, passive, malleable, virgin, and submissive to possession. Thus, for Bauer there is a basic tension between seeing and saying, which reflects that of centrality and marginality, Self and Other, phallocentric and gynocentric.

The two poets whose work I have chosen for consideration here are Gloria Fuertes and Carmen Martín Gaite. The former is the author of *Obras incompletas* (*Incomplete Works*) (1978) and the more recent *Historia de Gloria: amor, humor y desamor* (*History of Gloria [Glory]: Love, Humor and Indifference*) (1981).[3] And the latter, in addition to her many novels, stories, and essays, has published only one collection of verse, entitled *A rachas* (*With a Gust of Wind*) (1976), which was written over a span of many years and encompasses early poems from her student days in Salamanca as well as her more recent efforts at poetic expression.[4] In a sense, both Fuertes and Martín Gaite perfectly exemplify the concept of liminality as poets. Both of them began their writing careers and achieved fame as well as status before publishing works of poetry intended for an adult audience. Fuertes was first known as a children's writer, who later gained renown as a poet of legitimate verse. It is well-known that Fuertes's lyrics has received only grudging and/or marginal acceptance by the established and canonized community; this is perhaps because her poetry wholeheartedly embraces liminality as one of its central characteristics. For her part, Carmen Martín Gaite is a very wellknown and highly acclaimed contemporary novelist and essayist, who only recently was persuaded to publish her sole collection of poetry.

In looking at how these two female poets approach the issue of ekphrasis, the reader must also confront how each in her own way brings into question discursive practices and methods of representation of the (patriarchal) literary and artistic canon. In the case of Fuertes and that of Martín Gaite, and the younger female poets whose work will be considered in chapter 6, it is evident that female writers must utilize the codes and conventions of discourse that in and of themselves often objectify or totally exclude women. By speaking of and through these codes and conventions, the female writer reveals an entirely new level of communication, one that repeats and even parodies the patriarchal mode, but that simultaneously allows the female gaze and voice to make themselves known. This female presence responds to and goes beyond the imposed limitations that are in place because of the patriarchal point of view, and sets them into a new framework, one that acknowledges and celebrates the female voice and gaze. And in the process of this recontextualization of codes and conventions, that which is foregrounded is not only the work of art in and of itself, but also the canon, its limits, and the role of women, either closed in as object, or closed out as a freely speaking subject. This absent yet present female gaze and voice may manifest itself, for example, in the manner in which a female writer offers a tongue-in-cheek version of a cultural artifact revered by the patriarchy. The female rendering of the desired object permits a space for the reader to consider not only the object itself, but the conventions by which that object has come to represent certain patriarchal values, which often contribute to the subjugation of women.

By way of example, let us begin with Fuertes's representation of the Virgin Mary. According to the traditional manifestation of the ekphrastic principal, a painting or other work of art is described in a written text in order to elicit a specific reaction—be it of nostalgia, of religious devotion, or of singular appreciation of beauty—on the part of the receiver. But Fuertes views this issue of representation from an entirely different perspective. In her text entitled "Virgen de plástico" ("Virgin of Plastic" (Fuertes 1978, 283–84), she implicitly compares the traditional, canonized religious image of Mary put forward and held up as exemplary by the prevailing cultural standard—the patriarchal one, to be sure—with another more blatantly materialistic format that has become so prevalent in the second half of the twentieth century.[5] In reading Fuertes's text, one is reminded perhaps of Manuel Machado's "Las Concepciones de Murillo" ("The Conceptions of Murillo") already mentioned in chapter 2, where the generation of '98 poet evokes the ethereal representation of the Virgin Mary by the Golden Age painter. Thus, Machado's text is a possible intertext that is, as we shall see shortly, in a certain respect in ideological and aesthetic counterpoint to that of Fuertes.

The contemporary Virgin Mary evoked by Fuertes has "su manto de nylon / y la corona eléctrica, / con pilas en el pecho / y una sonrisa triste." ("Her cloak of nylon / and the electric crown, / with batteries in her breast / and a sad smile.") Fuertes makes specific mention of Mary's breast, an outstanding female attribute that could be construed as either maternal or sexual, or perhaps as an undecidable reference to both, which defies the patriarchal classification of woman as either mother or sexual object. The undecidable nature of Fuertes's reference to Mary's battery-laden breast attests to the patriarchal frame that is both present and absent in the representation of the Virgin. This is definitely *not* the traditional "Virgen" ("Virgin") of the heavenly spheres, but rather one who is "un cruce de Virgen entre Fátima y Lourdes, / un leve vaciado con troquel "made in USA'" ("a cross of Virgin between Fatima and Lourdes, / a light casting marked with a die "made in USA'"). Thus, the poet brings Mary figuratively and literally off her pedestal, and subverts the image of her as pure, untouchable, and out of touch with modern culture and society. The speaker makes reference to the Virgin as being removed from the context normally ascribed to her. Here, she is found not on a pedestal in a sacred environment but in "las vitrinas de todos los comercios / y en los sucios hogares de los pobres católicos" ("the display windows of all the shops / and in the dirty homes of the poor Catholics"), thus making oblique mention of the church's preferred and zealously guarded affinity with members of the more moneyed class. Similarly, the speaker indicates that the Virgin has found refuge among another group of outcasts who venerate her image in the most unlikely of places, if one judges according to the standard conventions of religion and its "acceptable" context: "En Nueva York los negros / tienen su virgen blanca / presidiendo el lavabo / junto a la cabecera . . ." ("In New York the Blacks / have their white Virgin / presiding over the washbasin / next to the headboard. . . ."). Fuertes underscores the Otherness that is Mary: she is female, and thus outside the frame of patriarchal power, but her image is controlled by the patriarchy's dominion. Her Otherness is further emphasized by grouping her with the marginalized outcasts, "los pobres católicos" ("the poor Catholics") as well as "los negros" ("the Blacks").[6] Thus, the speaker of the text places Mary in a realm that is physical, presiding over a bathroom sink, rather than spiritual, as in a chapel or church. Wayne C. Booth, in commenting upon Bakhtin's study of carnival, comments: "When the natural forces of joyful celebration of the lower body reached their peak, in time of carnival, mankind was healed with a laughter that was lost, when, in later centuries, the body, and especially the lower body, came to be viewed as entirely negative and shameful" (Booth 1983, 162). Mary's placement on a sink rim, presumably in a bathroom, and beside a bed with its unmistakable trace of sexual activity, puts her clearly in this carnivalesque tradition. And Booth, citing Bakhtin, further comments that the "popular comic tradition . . . viewed women as representing the material bodily lower stratum; she is the incarnation of this stratum that degrades and regenerates simultaneously. She is ambivalent. She debases, brings down to earth, lends a bodily substance to things, and destroys; but, first of all, she is the principle that gives birth. She is the womb. Such is woman's image in the popular comic tradition" (Ibid., 162). Thus, the Virgin described by Fuertes's speaker is more corporal than spiritual, much more akin to an Earth Mother than to an intercessor between the earthly and celestial realms. Fuertes has given back to her an element of affirmative and healthy earthiness that all but disappeared in the sanitized image projected by the official, patriarchal church.

The speaker lobbies for the acceptance of this Virgin, pointing out, as a used-car salesperson would, the advantages of this representation over another: "es lavable y si cae no se descascarilla. Las hay de tres colores, / blancas, azules, rosas / —las hay de tres tamaños—/ —aún la grande es pequeña—" ("She is washable and if she falls the paint doesn't peel off. She comes in three colors, / white, blue, and pink / —she comes in three sizes—/ — even the big one is small—"), all characteristics that would seem to be of great import to the female, rather than to the male perspective. The image is unbreakable, the colors are attractive, and there is a size to suit everyone's need.[7] Fuertes very skillfully manipulates the discourse of marketing and consumerism, which are yet other patriarchal strongholds. But this discourse is transparent, since it reflects (upon) not only its own value within a certain cultural framework but also upon how simultaneously it devalues and displaces more eternal ideals. The application of the commercial discourse to the Virgin's attributes as a spiritual model effectively defamiliarizes the role of discourse per se in the process of reception and interpretation. It is no wonder that at the end of the text the speaker ruefully comments, "Virgen de resultado, / me diste tanta pena, / Virgen pura de plástico, / se me quitó la gana de pedirte un milagro" ("Virgin of consequence, / you gave me so much pain,/ Virgin pure[ly] of plastic / that I no longer feel like asking you for a miracle"). The beautifully ambiguous placement of the adjective "pura" causes the reader to wonder whether the Virgin is pure because she was conceived without sin (the canonical view. . . .), or because she is made purely/totally of plastic (the "extra-canonical" view. . . .). The speaker allows the reader to decide, or decide *not* to decide.

There are several concerns that are brought to the forefront in this text, one of which is liminality. The speaker playfully jousts with the entire tradition of religious representation and implicitly questions why one should or should not be inspired by a representation in oil versus one in plastic with electric light bulbs. After all, illumination is the bottom line, regardless of the source. Secondly, the iconic representation becomes symbolic, in that the tawdry image of the Virgin with batteries in her breasts comes to be a loaded image. This image speaks out against the conceptualization of Mary, the Mother of God, as the ideal woman, one who is silent, passive, receptive, and virgin. Mary's image in this text "speaks for itself" by implicitly or explicitly contradicting (*contra* "against" + *dicere*, "to speak") the role assigned to her by the patriarchy. On the one hand, it also speaks out against the crass commercialization of religion with its too simplistic formulas for religious intervention. "Prop a Virgin up on the sink, and you'll get a miracle, one-two-three." And on the other hand, this iconic representation also becomes symbolic of a discourse seeking to grasp within its boundaries Reality or *a* reality, Truth or just simply a truth, and Beauty, or,— more realistically—an individual perspective on beauty. Also, by choosing to represent this particular image of the Virgin, Fuertes establishes as a point of reference the questions of artistic, social, and religious value, from both a phallocentric and gynocentric perspective. Implicitly she stresses that value is conferred only by codes and conventions. Thus, Fuertes's image, the so-called traditional one, or the mass produced representation of the Virgin—in oil, words, or plastic—is worthy (or not worthy) of being considered good, valuable, and valid only by social contract. By implication, this text questions several canons at once—religious, artistic, and literary—and also the gatekeepers who guard entry to their hallowed confines. In the final analysis, this text speaks of not only the product of the artistic process, but of the process itself, and questions how poetic discourse, indeed artistic discourse in general, defines (and defies. . . .) the limits and conventions of "acceptable" representation, whether poetic or religious. Similarly, it challenges the reader to question not only the limits imposed by the canon, but also the ramifications of those limits. By distancing and defamiliarizing the image of the Virgin Mary, by creatively applying the coded language of vulgar consumerism to her sacredness, Fuertes utilizes the creative

masque of carnival in order to invert and subvert the presuppositions concerning the role of women, the sacred, and the lyric
within patriarchal society.

Similar in impact but different in composition and style is the
cryptic Fuertes text entitled "Arquitectura—Elche" ("Architecture—Elche"). In this poem, the poet evokes not a painting but
rather an architectural construct. It consists of only one and a
half lines of verse, and like "Virgen de plástico" ("Virgin of
Plastic"), suggests to the reader the simultaneous, dialectical
maintenance and rupture of limits, whether those concerning
discourse, or those having to do with the tensive voices of gender.
The text reads:

> La primera columna fue de madera,
> fue una palmera.
>
> (Fuertes 1981, 374)

(The first column was of wood, / it was a palm tree.)

In Bakhtinian terms, the speaker allows several voices to emerge
in the text, voices that attempt to disrupt the superficial serenity
of the surveillant gaze. Among them, there is that of the official
exaltation of art, which makes reference in oblique fashion to
the grand, classical (and patriarchal) Greco-Roman tradition of
architecture and to its central position in the creation and dominance of Western civilization. But this declaration is made
tongue-in-cheek, with a tone that is imbued with humor, folk
wisdom, and basic simplicity, since the speaker points out that
this classical tradition of architectonic perfection is based upon
Mother Nature's "grand" design of the palm tree.[8] There is another that requests recognition of the historical process and evolution of artistic forms, whatever their nature; this voice
acknowledges that human history may look back upon its accom-
plishments with both pride and humility. Third, there is the
voice that refers to the Derridean traces of origins, at once forgotten and remembered, both present and absent in modern manifestations.[9] The open-endedness of this text, in both form and
content, suggests to the reader that the process is not quite finished yet, that there is more to come, literally and metaphorically,
from both a microcosmic *and* a macrocosmic perspective. The
column's metamorphosis from a natural form to a humanly constructed one is bound to continue, just as the text's reception
and interpretation repeats the same process. The silence of the

text speaks, ironically, to the issue of the dialogue that is art, between past and present, old and new, tradition and treason, centrality and liminality. Thus, in spite of its truncated form, there is a definite metapoetic and self-referential dimension to this cryptic text.

And one also has to take into account the second word of the title, the proper noun "Elche." With it, the speaker conjures up for the reader images of "La dama de Elche," the bust of the enigmatic priestess, discovered on Iberian soil. The voices that push to the limit and beyond the representative nature of this poetic text make reference to Spain as well as to the Greco-Roman cultural context; the richness of artistic heritage; the undeniable presence of the past in the here and now, the traces, in the deconstructive sense, that one can perceive in any sign. Furthermore, the Elche reference brings with it an image of the feminine. In this text there is a convergence of woman as (art) object ("La dama") ["The Lady"] and subject / creator (Fuertes) of art. Just as the feminine as art's object may once have resided outside the canon, namely, may have been marginalized, and then been accepted only gradually, so too, the idea of woman as the creator of acceptable art has now begun to pass to within the limits of respectability and tradition. There has been resistance, but the process has begun. The image of woman has begun to metamorphose from that of passive muse to active creator. Just as the patriarchal Greco-Roman tradition has been the dominant one and has flourished, there has been a parallel though an anonymous tradition of female art, one whose sources can be traced to nature itself, the realm of the feminine.[10] Through this text, Fuertes proposes Mother Nature as the ur-Creator of Western art. The Greco-Roman world is present from yet another feminine perspective as well, since the name of the goddess Hera appears in shadowy phonological echo in the final syllables of "primera" ("first), "palmera" ("palm tree"), and "madera" ("wood").[11] Hera, queen and wife to the Olympian god Zeus, is the protectress of all women and symbolizes the feminine aspects of nature. It is fitting that the sign of Hera, her name, be both absent and present, as is the gynocentric tradition. The absence / presence of Hera's name echoes and reflects that of the feminine inscription upon Greco-Roman architecture, in the curved rectitude of the first column, the graceful, natural palm tree.[12] In this particular text Fuertes makes reference to the issue of liminality, and of the tension between the phallocentric and the gynocentric, which is a salient feature of her work. For this twentieth-century poet, the poetic text comes to be an uncanny self-reflective meditation on the process of artistic representation, one that is based on the questioning of limits and the issues of pragmatism versus beauty, phallocentric versus gynocentric, tradition versus treason, acceptable versus unacceptable, canon versus its contravention, centrality versus liminality. The matter-of-fact tone, with its lack of editorializing on the part of the speaker, draws the reader into a participatory role, thus allowing that reader to mull over and come to private conclusions about the issues hinted at only glancingly on the superficial level of the text. The reader must first fill in the blanks in the creative jump between the palm tree and the stately column, and then continue the process of evolution, taking into account the gynocentric tradition.

Keeping in mind Fuertes's questioning stance in regard to the issues of discourse, representation, and their limits, it is much easier to view the corpus of her work as a whole, and see it as one that is simultaneously inside and outside the bounds of acceptability. As Pérez Firmat comments, "the liminal entity, whatever its nature, is one that in a given situation takes up a position of eccentricity, one that occupies the periphery in relation to a contextually determined center" (Pérez Firmat, xiv). But in affirming this position of liminality, the poet also affirms tradition, for the two are inextricably bound. Pérez Firmat further comments: "To traduce tradition is to affirm tradition: nothing is more traditional, in one sense of the word, than the break or discontinuity achieved by an act of treason" (Ibid., xvii). Thus a most obvious treasonous yet traditional aspect of Fuertes's oeuvre is the inspiration that she gleans from a variety of sources, which are most clearly outside the canon of accepted lyric topoi: to treason tradition *is* her tradition. One only has to refer to other titles such as "Guía comercial" ("Commercial Guide"), "Galerías Preciadas" ("Valued Galeries" [a pun on the Madrid department store chain of "Galerías Preciados"]), "Telegrama" ("Telegram"), and "Menú de guerra" ("War Menu"), to see the dialectic of liminality and tradition that prevails, and that we saw so well in "Virgen de plástico" ("Virgin of Plastic") and "Arquitectura" ("Architecture"). In all of these texts, she represents twentieth-century society, utilizing disarming yet uncanny images borrowed from other modes of discourse that call attention to themselves as artistic artifacts of the current age as well as to the rules and conventions of artistic discourse, whether canonized or not.

The second set of examples that I wish to consider here are two poetic texts by Martín Gaite, entitled "Espiga sin granar"

("Unripe Wheat Spike") (1976, 35–36) and "Todo es un cuento roto en Nueva York" ("All Is a Fractured Story in New York") (Ibid., 86–90), from her collection, *A rachas*. Like the texts by Fuertes, these also boldly confront the doubling and double issue of gynocentric representation and discourse, but in a different fashion. Bauer has demonstrated that all too often "the silencing of the female voice takes place under the discipline of the gaze" (Bauer, xiii), where the gaze is generically masculine. But in the two poetic texts by Martín Gaite, the speaker successfully subverts the stereotypical image of woman's silence as a negative, in order to imbue that silence with power. And it is not the male gaze that effects this radical change, but rather woman's own. In the hauntingly beautiful "Espiga sin granar" ("Unripe Wheat Spike"), the speaker confronts her future self, when her youthful visage silently gazes into a mirror, and subverts the silence of the gaze by describing through the poetic text what she sees. In this manner, the visual portrait evoked is a self-portrait framed not only by the mirror's edge but also by the temporal flow of present into future and back again, as well as the presence/absence of voice/silence and gaze. The youthful Self attempts to catch a glimpse of the future adult Self that is and is not Other, and that is and is not present. Jenijoy la Belle comments that

> an understanding of the mirror scenes in literature will tell us much about feminine consciousness in its relation to body and to world. Through the mirror, we can gain insight into the reciprocal interchanges between interiority and exteriority as these create what a woman is to herself and to her culture. The reflection in the glass is at once both the self and radical otherness, an image privileged with a truth beyond the subjective and at the same time taken to be the very essence of that subjectivity (La Belle 1988, 9).

Whereas men utilize the mirror as a practical tool, women use it in an act of ego formation (Ibid., 22). And furthermore, "in European culture for at least the last two centuries a female self as a social, psychological, and literary phenomenon is defined, to a considerable degree, as a visual image and structured, in part, by continued acts of mirroring" (Ibid., 9). In Martín Gaite's text, ironically, in the silence of that mirrored image is captured the power of essence and presence, combined with female potentiality and creativity:

Nunca me acerco tanto a ser mujer
como cuando abandono mis palabras,
repliego el abanico
tras el que ensayo risas de gioconda,
desciendo del tinglado de mis gestos
por peldaños estrechos y gastados
y me quito en silencio, a oscuras,
los adornos.
Alguien está conmigo a quien no veo,
que me recoge el alma como un traje arrugado
y me la va subiendo de los pies a los hombros:
la mujer que seré.

(Martín Gaite 1976, 35)

(Never do I get so close to being a woman / as when I abandon my words, / I fold my fan / behind which I rehearse Mona Lisa giggles, / I descend from the ruse of my gestures / by narrow and worn steps / and I take off in silence, in the dark, / my adornments. // Someone is with me whom I do not see, / who gathers up my soul as a wrinkled gown / and goes about raising it from my feet to my shoulders: / the woman that I will become.)

The play of images puts into dialectic oscillation those that are feminine versus those that are masculine. The speaker plays upon the opposition and synthesis of the phallocentric and gynocentric in the poem's title, "Espiga sin granar." The formation of the wheat spike is decidedly masculine, whereas the expression "sin granar" ("unripe") lends a feminine cast, through its reference to the grains' incipience and roundness. This contrast is further emphasized through the juxtaposition of the traditional feminine images of the first strophe, such as "el abanico" ("the fan"), "gioconda" ("Gioconda"), "los adornos" ("the [my] adornments"), and "un traje arrugado" ("a wrinkled gown"), with the scene's outward structure based on the male gaze. A woman adorns herself in order to make herself more attractive to men. As Bauer suggests, the source of the gaze is generally masculine, whereby a male viewer observes the mute object of beauty, usually represented by the female body.[13] But here, the gaze emanates from a female point of departure. Even though the female object partakes of conventional female activity—gazing into a mirror, recognizing that the viewer is mentally disrobing her for the voyeuristic pleasure of that viewer, letting escape innocent giggles and mysterious little smiles—the erotic scene does not lead to seduction in the (hetero)sexual sense, but rather in that of the creative and artistic. The female viewer/

speaker gazing upon herself leads her to give herself over to the creative forces within herself. She is seduced by herself, by her power, and gives voice to herself, acting as her own muse. Moreover, the source of those creative impulses is female. Svetlana Alpers posits "a "female" way of experiencing the world, through alternative modes of perception, such as fragmentary perception, a nonpossessive relation between artist/observer and female subject, and the pictorial presentation of monumental female figures, who in their exclusive attention to their own affairs are supremely "self-possessed" (Broude and Garrard 1982, 8). I believe that Martín Gaite effectively communicates this attitude of self-possession in the verbal/visual self-portrait of this ekphrastic text, in that the framed gaze of herself empowers her to become the speaking subject of her text, rather than the mute object. Her sexuality gives way to textuality; she writes her own body in the body of her text.[14] The inversion and subversion of the traditional female role and of the conventional silencing of woman's voice is marked by the positive value given to silence by the speaker, wherein the woman she is to become in the future, but paradoxically has *already* become in the text, finds herself in the enriching void that is beyond words.[15] The reader must take note of how the text is framed: the poem opens with a reference to silence, "como cuando abandono mis palabras" ("as when I abandon my words"), where the speaker in an act of will embraces silence. And the poem ends in a similar fashion, when the speaker makes reference to the pause, once again willed into existence, that precedes plenitude. But this pause or silence itself is given voice, in that the speaker names it by allowing the wind to speak the word "espera" ("wait") thrice over:

> "Espera—espera—espera",
> canta el viento azotando mi guarida
> y apagando la llama
> del último candil.
> Y la palabra espera es un camino
> serpenteando incógnito
> entre rachas de bruma.
>
> (Martín Gaite 1976, 36)

("Wait—wait—wait", / sings the wind thrashing my lair / and extinguishing the flame / of the last oil lamp. / And the word wait is a path / snaking incognito / among gusts of mist.)

The unfolding of the speaker's image, visual as well as verbal, is further witnessed by the youthful Self who describes the "mujer secreta" ("secret woman") who awaits a future meeting, and who will ultimately take possession of physical characteristics which now seem so alien, the "ojos de sibila" ("eyes of [a] sybil") and receives the "mensajes como éste que ahora escribo" ("messages such as the one that I am now writing"). Paradoxically, this alien Other's presence is marked by absence, silence, mystery, and shadowy incertitude. The present speaker continually plays with the presence/absence of the "Other" she imagines what "she" will be like, comments upon her own presuppositions about that future self, and looks back upon herself as an adolescent from that future vantage point, thus neatly inverting the point of view with which the text began. Ultimately the speaker must ask the Other, her distanced Self, "Dime dónde estaremos cuando lo leamos, / qué habrá sido de mí dentro de ti" ("Tell me where we will be when we read it, / what will have become of me within you"). Thus, in this last instance, we see the manipulation effected by the (auto)biographical "I" of the text, who apparently manifests herself as present.[16] And this I does it in such a way as to evince solidarity with the Other of the future, by asking "dónde estaremos" ("where we will be"), slyly utilizing the inclusive "nosotras" ("we" [fem.]) pronoun form. At this juncture the reader becomes aware that this I is not the I of physical presence, but only another fictional creation, one who (dis)appears in the text at the beck and call of the Martín Gaite who is not in the frame of the textual portrait, either visual or verbal. (This reminds me of the text by Borges entitled "Borges y yo." or Unamuno's *Niebla*.) And in truth, this text does end "entre rachas de bruma" ("among gusts of mist"), where woman's silence, rather than being imposed by the male gaze, is more akin to the reticence of the enigmatic sphinx or to the mysterious stillness of the Gioconda. But whereas those two are male objectifications of woman, Martín Gaite's framed self-portrait offers a woman's own self-possessed view of her Self as potential Other, free of the ruled impositions of patriarchy. Her silence is her own, through which she expresses her potential, her power, and her wholeness.[17]

The second poem, "Todo es un cuento roto en Nueva York" ("All Is a Fractured Story in New York") (Martín Gaite, 86–90) is too long to cite here in its entirely, but I will refer to its various modes of discourse as a focal point for my discussion. First, one should note its title, with its direct reference to narrative rather than to poetic discourse. Thus, the speaker immediately puts up for close inspection a text whose discourse will be the main event. Secondly, the reader will take note of the dedicatory within parentheses *(En memoria de William Carlos Williams)* where the speaker in a sense undermines and subverts that which has come before, by dedicating the text (poem or narrative?) to William Carlos Williams, an American poet of considerable stature.[18] Here the reader is at once encouraged to approach the text, that is, to attempt to resolve these apparent superficial anomalies, and also to step back, to ponder their significance at a higher level of interpretation.[19]

Those familiar with twentieth-century Spanish poetry cannot help but note the similarity between the opening lines of this text and another by Rafael Alberti, "Los ángeles muertos" ("The Dead Angels"), which begins with "Buscad, buscadlos: / en el insomnio de las cañerías olvidadas, por el silencio / en los cauces interrumpidos de la basura" ("Search, search for them: / in the insomnia of the forgotten pipe-lines, through the silence / in the interrupted garbage ditches"). The Martín Gaite text makes use of the same "vosotros" ("you" [fam. pl.]) command to draw the explicitly named multiple readers into the text: "Buscadla por Manhattan, / entre las escombreras de chatarra, / los coches de bomberos, / los anuncios, los locos, los cubos de basura" ("Search for her throughout Manhattan, / among the rubble heaps of scrap iron, / the fire trucks, / the advertisements, the crazy people, the garbage cans" (Alberti, 86). Like Alberti's, Martín Gaite's speaker evokes an urban wasteland similar to that of T. S. Eliot (*The Waste Land, Collected Poems, 1919–1962*) that silently screams its wretched message of despair. These readers are pulled into a vortex of texts wherein the speaker pursues a mysterious figure through the streets, scenes, experiences, and incoherence of New York City, but at the same time she pulls the reader with her through a succession of frames and discourses. The cityscape of alienation and discarded waste sets the tone for both the Alberti and Martín Gaite text. Thus, immediately the female poet sets up an intertextual dialectic of source(s) and echo(es) among the various texts to which her speaker makes reference. As in the case of Fuertes, paradoxically, the liminality of the Martín Gaite text is defined by uncanny and unsettling centrality. The search for something absent and currently "real" only in the speaker's imagination—her allusion to other texts, the elusive protagonist, the desire for coherence and/or determinacy—is the core of the text itself.

Martín Gaite also uses another technique in this poem which makes reference to other modes of artistic discourse in twentieth-century society. But let us return for a moment to the opening lines of verse of her text, where the speaker states "Buscadla por Manhattan" ("Search for her throughout Manhattan"). As the poem progresses, it is evident that the speaker walks in the wake of an illusionary figure, and bids her readers to join her in her chimerical quest: "Se habrá desvanecido la ilusión de su imagen / y no quedará rastro / de la silueta vaga, fugaz, y discutible / que llevabais soñada en la retina / porque acaso la visteis en un film" ("The illusion of her image will have vanished / and no trace will remain / of the vague, fleeting and debatable silhouette / that you [fam. pl.] carried dreamily on your retina / because perhaps you saw her in a film") (Martín Gaite, 86–87). As in the case of the Alberti text, where that poet's speaker creates a poetic presence through silence, Martín Gaite's is defined by the dialectic of presence and absence, or, presence defined only by the delineation of absence. Over and over again, the speaker makes reference to a lack which is the illusionary figure; the reader must create an image of that figure through a description of her disappearance. The speaker has recourse to such expressions as "no la encontraréis" ("you [fam. pl.] will not find her"), "manchas movedizas" ("movable smudges"), "jugando al escóndite" ("playing hide-and-seek"), "camuflada" ("camouflaged"), "habéis creído atisbarla" ("you [pl. fam.] probably believed that you observed her"), "no quedará rastro" ("no trace will remain"), "la silueta vaga, fugaz y discutible" ("the vague, fleeing and debatable silhouette"), as well as many more. We follow the speaker, who in turn follows the shadowy female being whose world is punctuated by the flash of a walk-don't walk sign, or who looks into the "vacío en el subway" ("the void in the subway") or who "finge embeberse en los sucesos / de crímenes y guerras y desfalcos / que vienen relatados en el Times, / tras el cual se amuralla" ("feigns absorbing herself in the events / of crimes and wars and embezzlements / that come to be reported in the Times, / behind which she walls herself") (Ibid., 87). The indeterminacy of the speaker's focus may suggest to the reader the "film noir" atmosphere of the Hitchcock style of cinema or of a popular detective novel. The reader is constantly placed in a position of wondering whether the pursued figure is indeed "real" or a figment of the speaker-pursuer's imagination.

Robert Pring-Mill views this mode of discourse as *documentary poetry*, in which the poet "sets out to "document" reality, selecting, shaping, and imposing interpretive patterns on the world with liberal use of such filmic "editing" techniques as crosscutting, accelerated montage, or flash frame" (Pring-Mill, ix). Martín Gaite extends the definition of ekphrasis to include a decidedly twentieth-century visual art form, that of the cinema.[20] And in point of fact we see the shadowy protagonist of the poetic text pursued by the speaker in a variety of circumstances, frozen with cinematic exactness on the screen/page before us: "Bus-cadla entre la gente que hace cola en el cine, / o al borde de la acera a la caza de un taxi / o en algún "ladies room" donde pudo meterse / entre un tarantuleo de cucarachas rubias / a limpiar sus lentillas" ("Search [you fam. pl.] for her among the people who line up at the moviehouse, / or at the edge of the sidewalk in hunt of a taxi / or in some "ladies room" where she was able to slip in / among a fandango of blond cockroaches / to clean her contact lenses") (Martín Gaite, 88). This illusionary figure takes on a variety of guises as the speaker pursues her throughout the city, and throughout the text. First, as in an enticing snippet of a detective film, the speaker points out that "Tal vez habéis creído atisbarla un instante / en la calle catorce con la quinta avenida" ("Perhaps you [fam. pl.] probably believed that you observed her for an instant / at Fourteenth Street and Fifth Avenue") (Ibid., 86). Or, "Tal vez, se ha disfrazado / de esa vieja señora con la gorra calada" ("Perhaps she has disguised herself / as that old woman wearing the hemstitched cap") (Ibid., 87). Or, after all

> Puede haberse mudado en esa chica
> de caderas potentes y paso un poco raro,
> a quien de pronto un guardia ha cogido del brazo,
> se la lleva a tirones y ella se le recuesta
> con los ojos nublados por la droga
> y dice que no ha sido,
> que ella no sabe nada de ese bolso que buscan.
>
> (Ibid., 89)

(She could have changed into that girl / with powerful hips and a rather strange gait, / whom a cop hastily grabs by the arm, / carries her off with a few good jerks and she goes limp on him / and states that she was not the one, / that she knows nothing about that handbag that they are looking for.)

The speaker encourages the reader to overstep the bounds of poetic discourse by two different means. First, she encourages the reader to "see" the scene of the narration within this poetic text in a very cinematic sense, in such phrases as "diréis "allí la veo'" ("you [fam. pl] will say "I see her over there'"), "si alguna vez la visteis" ("if some time you [fam. pl.] saw her"), or "tal vez la visteis en un film" ("perhaps you [fam. pl.] saw her in a film"). In fact the speaker mentions at several moments in the text this cinematic "reality" of the artistic experience.[21] It is interesting to note that the gaze, rather than the voice, defines itself as a characteristic of emergent female discourse. Since patriarchal structures have consistently denied to the female author the right and privilege of voice, female authors in their texts often have recourse to a description of visual experience, having been previously and resoundingly excluded from the verbal sphere. This seems to be the case in this poetic text. While in the previous text, Martín Gaite utilizes silence in a productive fashion, here the verbal description of gaze is a subversion and contravention of the taboo against female voice. Thus, Martín Gaite with this ploy brings into question not only the issues of representation and discourse, but also those of gender and genre.

The reader is also drawn outside the bounds of poetic discourse by the stance of the speaker, who removes herself for the moment from her pursuit of the protagonist, to make a comment upon the course of events as they have developed in the text. In this commentary, the speaker refers to the text's ultimately undecidable nature:

> Todo es un cuento roto en Nueva York
> donde ninguna trama se ha de tener por cierta,
> recitado de forma intermitente
> entre guiños de flash
> en el gran escenario giratorio
> al que afluyen en mezcla simultánea
> la basura y el oro,
> gente que tira y gente que recoge.
>
> (Martín Gaite, 89)

(All is a fractured story in New York / where no plot is a given, recited in intermittent form / among winks of flash / on the great revolving stage / to which they flow in simultaneous mixture / garbage and gold, / people who throw out and people who pick up.)

At the end of this poetic text, Martín Gaite subtly but forcefully brings the reader face-to-face with the ephemeral and ultimately questionable nature of literary discourse and of all artistic representation, whether verbal or visual. The speaker returns once

again to her pursuit of the mysterious woman whom she has so
assiduously sought throughout the length of the poem, and invites her readers to consider a possible solution to the text's
enigma: "yo puedo revelaros una pista" ("I can reveal to you a
hot trail to follow").[22] But once again certainty is defined by
indeterminacy, for the speaker voices her invitation in undecidable terms, "una pista" ("a track to follow"), followed by a question, "¿Por qué no entrar un rato en el Museo Whitney?" ("Why
not go into the Whitney Museum awhile?") (Martín Gaite, 90).
The speaker then describes the silent, chimerical figure whom
she has been pursuing through the streets of Manhattan and
through her text. The concept of movement is key to Martín
Gaite's version of ekphrasis, and finds form in the obvious pursuit of the protagonist by the speaker. (See color plates.) This
protagonist escapes not only *from* a work of art, but also *into*
one. The speaker finally catches up with the shadowy figure,
who has found refuge in a painting by Edward Hopper located
in that very museum. Thus, the breaking of the frame and the
text's ultimate undecidability represents also the breaching of
representational and textual limits. Martín Gaite very evidently
is playing with the problem of artistic representation and of the
boundaries that are crossed, recrossed, and double-crossed in
her text(s). And as Marcia L. Welles so cogently demonstrates,
for Martín Gaite, "truth in discourse, true communication as dis-
tinguished from its alienating versions, is posited in terms of a
search for the perfect interlocutor" (Servodidio and Welles 1983,
201). It is significant that the search ends in silence as the
speaker gazes in hushed awe in front of a mute painting, whose
frame catches in suspended animation the protagonist who remained so elusive to the poem's speaker. The pursuit of the shadowy figure may well be symbolic of the author's pursuit of
Oneness, that she achieves only partially and imperfectly in each
of her texts. The speaker's representation of a painting within
her own text, a deferred image that frames, distances, (dis)covers,
and captures the poet's enigmatic and silent quarry, becomes
symbolic of the Text, and ultimately, the sign: mutable, deferred,
present, absent, and indeterminate:

> Cansada de rodar,
> de soñar apariencias,
> de debatirse en vano
> ensayando posturas de defensa o de ataque,
> de convertirse en otra,

esa mujer perdida por Manhattan
se ha escondido en un cuadro de Edward Hopper,
se ha sentado en la cama de una pensión anónima
y ya no espera nada.

Sin abrir tan siquiera la maleta,
acaba de quitarse los zapatos
porque los pies le duelen,
y se ha quedado sola entre cuatro paredes,
condenada a aguantar a palo seco
esa luz de la tarde ya en declive
que se filtra en la estancia
veteada de brillos engañosos,
con los brazos caídos y la mirada estática,
clavada eternamente de cara a una ventana
que de tan bien pintada parece de verdad.

(Martín Gaite, 90)

(Tired of shooting [cinem.], / of dreaming appearances, / of fighting
herself in vain / rehearsing postures of defense or of attack, / of turn-
ing herself into another, / that woman lost in Manhattan / has hidden
herself in an Edward Hopper painting, / she has seated herself on the
bed in an anonymous boardinghouse / and no long awaits anything. //
Without having even opened her suitcase, she has just removed her
shoes / because her feet hurt her, / and she has ended up alone
between four walls, / condemned to endure without ceremony / that
afternoon light already sloping downward / that filters into the room /
mottled with misleading glitters, / with disheartened arms and her
gaze static, / nailed eternally facing a window / that [is] so well
painted that it seems real.)

The woman who is in Manhattan in the story (remember the
title?), is the one in the poem, who is in the film, who is in the
painting. Or is she? The window painted so well on the wall
seems to be the truth. Or does it? The reality/realities described
here (where?) seem(s) so real. Or do they? The speaker asks us,
the readers, to participate in the willing suspension of disbelief,
to enter into the reality of the text. Which reality and which text?
Is the "pista" ("hot trail") proposed by the speaker at the end
really a solution or yet another blind alley?[23] The poem seems
to describe the painting and/or the film and/or the story. Or does
it? What is the story here???

There is an overriding aura of indeterminacy that extends
throughout this particular text, encompassing not only the context that it suggests from an artistic, historical, and geographic

perspective, but also from that of the dialectic of reality and illusion upon which it plays. And this indeterminacy extends to both the sender and the receiver of the text as well. The author creates a discourse, a speaker, and a protagonist, all of whom go beyond the frames and limits of convention. For their part, the readers also go beyond the limits of convention, since we are called upon to give up our conventional and very comfortable passive role of being the final judge and arbiter of what goes on in the text. Our pursuit is parallel to that of the speaker, who pursues the shadowy, silent protagonist. The discourse of this poem is dialogic, a dialogue of other forms of representational discourse, such as narrative, film, and painting. The speaker of the text supposedly speaks the truth, yet continually crosses boundaries and in the process double-crosses the limits of artistic representation. It is significant that the illusionary figure who is pursued by the speaker and who weaves her way through the text(s)—poem, story, film, and painting—and passes imperceptibly through the boundaries of those various forms of representation is a woman. She could represent the breaking of limits that gynocentric discourse represents. The feminine gaze puts into question preestablished boundaries, limits that previously had not had to take into account her presence. Thus it is that the female protagonist can pass imperceptibly into another medium, and "disappear" into its confines, while still remaining clearly in view.

In her collection of verse *A rachas* Martín Gaite incorporates into her poems textual desire, the wish for oneness, and wholeness, just as she did in her novel entitled *El cuarto de atrás* (*The Back Room*).[24] But as Welles suggests, "The absolute wholeness or 'Oneness' of a self reunited with its image can be recaptured only in death, as was the fate of Narcissus. Although its fulfillment is unobtainable, the desire cannot be stopped. . . ." (Servodidio and Welles, 205). In this collection there is a stubborn refusal to closure, where the poet questions the limits of text, genre, memory, telling, writing, and experience, and wills the Self to continue the search for identity. Like Fuertes, Martín Gaite rejects the traditional limits of ekphrastic representation, and brings marginality to a central position. But she accomplishes this feat in a manner quite different than Fuertes. Her speaker purposefully lulls the reader into believing that the poem will utilize the realistic mode of literary discourse; but then she abruptly juxtaposes the discourses of both film and painting, and consequently introduces implicit questions about the viability of *any* mode of discourse and of its questionable success in representation, as well as the reader's ability to define the text and how it is that one decides what exactly is inside and outside its frame. (Remember that the poem ends with "que de tan bien pintada *parece* de verdad." ("that [is] so well painted that it *seems* real.") [Italics mine.] Thus, the reader is left to ponder a variety of tantalizing issues that present themselves for consideration. Martín Gaite very evidently is playing with the problem of artistic representation and the boundaries that are crossed, recrossed, and double-crossed in her text(s). Where does one text begin and the other end? Where does one representation begin and the other end? How does the reader "read" the modes of discourse—of narrative, film, journalism, poetry, and painting—that collide in this text? What are we to make of the dialectic of reality and illusion that is so craftily presented and subverted here? How does the female "gaze" enter into the question of voice and poetic discourse and indeed all artistic representation? Needless to say, as in the case of the Fuertes text "Virgen de plástico" ("Virgin of Plastic"), this poem by Martín Gaite converts the iconic into the symbolic: it points out that what is "there" is only an illusion. The reader is then left to ponder whether what the poet says is there in linguistic terms may be an illusion as well. Thus, this poem subtly indicates to the reader that there is more than meets—or doesn't meet—the eye.

Just out of curiosity, I myself went to the Whitney Museum, to see if I could possibly find the painting to which Martín Gaite makes reference in her poetic text. And in so doing I further blurred the distinction between reality and illusion, fact and fiction, allusion and representation, text and intertext, creator and created, author and reader. I became in fact the one who wends her way through the labyrinth of New York City, as well as the one who pursues the illusionary figure of the text, I myself having become part of Martín Gaite's "text" as it metamorphosed into yet another form of representation. Was I then the speaker of the text? The reader? Perhaps the shadowy figure in the text? Or possibly the author of a new form of the text? Or was I indeed all of these? By taking on the role of the author, speaker, reader, and protagonist, I entered into Martín Gaite's work of art by playing out its blurring of reality and art within my own context, just as the shadowy figure entered that of Edward Hopper.[25]

At the museum I did indeed find a painting entitled *Hotel Room 1931* by Hopper (1882–1967), in a catalog of the painter's complete works, but the painting itself is currently housed in the Thyssen-Bornemisza collection in Madrid. Ironically enough, this detail removed me one step further from the "reality" of the illusion of representation: I viewed not the painting itself, but a photographic representation of that Hopper portrait.[26] This painting contains all the elements of the final scene described by Martín Gaite's speaker, except for one absolutely tantalizing detail. In the Hopper portrait, the mysterious woman whose face is swathed in shadows, is staring blankly at an open book. It is significant to note that the poet in her poem does *not* make reference to the "text" as poetic product—as a printed object on a page in a book—but only to the product in its visual and filmic form. We as readers of the poetic form must create this text out of the silences and absences that Martín Gaite has provided. And the silence of Martín Gaite's text in regard to this telling detail perhaps in and of itself is a paradoxical metatextual reference, a pointer to the text's signs of presence and absence as well as presence in absence, limits, and liminality, and also to the reader's role in the creation of a version of the text. That text exists only in the act of reception, and must be continually created anew with each reader and reading. But in another sense, Martín Gaite is true to the visual intertext to which she alludes in her poem. Just as Hopper in his work of art refers to another art form—the written word—but does not evince his own medium, so too Martín Gaite attempts to capture an artistic medium of a visual nature, but remains "silent" as to the verbal creation in her own poetic text. The absence of the text so visible in the painting may be implied as a fragment of the "cuento roto" ("fractured story") of the poem's title. This poem may also offer to the reader for consideration a commentary on how the artist must attempt the impossible, which is to capture reality with a preestablished set of codes, be they verbal or visual.

These poetic texts by Gloria Fuertes and Carmen Martín Gaite, each in their own way address the issues of artistic representation, the female gaze and female writing, ekphrasis, liminality, carnival, and poetic discourse in the closing years of the twentieth century. Fuertes, for her part, in underlining the liminality of her poetic texts, ironically pays homage to the classical ekphrastic tradition that serves as a substructure to the iconoclasm in her verse. Through her poetry, and because of its stance

at the margins of the literary canon, Fuertes brings to the forefront the setting of limits and the place of discordant voice(s) in
relation to those preestablished limits. Martín Gaite begins by
borrowing the rules of discourse from other media, in order to
return to the ekphrastic tradition of the portrait poem, but not
in the traditional sense. As we saw earlier, the portrait that
emerges at the end of her text, and in(to) which her protagonist
ultimately and ironically "(dis)appears," is used not as a representation but rather as a subterfuge of reality. In so doing, she
also calls into question the accepted limits that separate one
mode of discourse from another, one text from another, one reality from another. Her representation, at the end, is only an illusion, one that has been borrowed, and is not really "real" after
all. The central question that she posits, of course, is whether
representation in any medium, or across media, is possible at all.

The common thread that we can find between Fuertes and
Carmen Martín Gaite is that poetry can and should be enriched
with elements that are decidedly "liminal" for whatever reason,
or rather, "liminal" according to the standards that have long
outlived their usefulness. The ekphrastic techniques espoused
by these two poets may cause fireworks, but it is ultimately the
two poets themselves who have shot themselves out of the (literary) can(n)on, with such creative results. The carnival mood and
mode is quite different for Fuertes and Martín Gaite. Fuertes
openly encourages bawdy laughter, surrounded by common folk,
glaring lights, and raucous noise, and invites her reader to leave
inhibitions and preconceived notions behind. Martín Gaite's text
produces an effect in the reader that emulates the eerie silence
of the fun house after closing time. The rules of the society that
surrounds the carnival are still supposedly in place; but the very
existence of the carnival fun house, with its subversion of socie-
tal laws and limits gives witness to the uneasy, ever-changing
amity/enmity between centrality and marginality. The reader has
been encouraged to use those limits as a handy point of reference, but then those boundaries are inexplicably and abruptly
taken away. By questioning in radically different forms, both explicitly and implicitly, the limits of conventional poetic discourse as well as the traditional expectations of the reader as
well as the presuppositions based on gender, these poets not
only put into effect a new definition of poetry, but they also
cleverly bring to the forefront various issues of primary concern
to author and reader alike. By means of ekphrasis, the poems
considered here point to the fascinating yet troubling problems

of discourse, voice(s) and silence, liminality, framing, representation and its many manifestations, Self and Other, gender and genre, the gaze, and the artist and reader's complicity in the artistic process of the Text's production, reception, and changing signification.

5

(Self-)Portraits, (Dis)Guises, and Frames: The (Dis)Figuring Gaze of Jaime Gil de Biedma and José Angel Valente

THE unsettling relationship between verbal text and visual imagery presents for the reader of the verbal text a variety of theoretical problems to be faced but not necessarily resolved. In the case of ekphrastic literature, the writer, in his role as the reader of yet another text from another medium, has to confront the naming and breaking of artistic limits of various genres, literary as well as visual. As we saw in chapter 1, Mary Ann Caws refers to these interartistic "translations" as "stressed readings." The seductive play of the various definitions of stress inserts into the ekphrastic text the ambivalence to which W. J. T. Mitchell refers (Mitchell 1994, 156), and leads to the reader's sense of (im)possibility in regard to the simultaneous presence/absence of the alien text, the alien other that is the visual art work.*

According to the ideas that were developed in the introductory chapter, I define a poetic text as ekphrastic when it makes reference to a visual work of art, whether real or imagined, canonized or uncanonized, and thus allows that art object, in truth, the object of (artistic) desire, to "speak for itself" within the problematically ruptured framework of the poetic text. This art object's ability to speak for itself is dependent upon the intertextual, stressed status of its problematic presence in the verbal text as well as the status of the reader who attempts to participate in the economy of power and pleasure as well as in the surrender and sovereignty of the reading process.[1]

---

*Because of copyright restrictions, no English translations will appear for the poetry of Jaime Gil de Biedma. Verses cited from the original Spanish are reprinted by permission of the estate of Jaime Gil de Biedma. © Jaime Gil de Biedma, 1982 y Herederos de Jaime Gil de Biedma.

In the case of Jaime Gil de Biedma, the recently deceased Catalan writer, his ekphrastic poetry both problematizes and celebrates the stressful, elusive, magnetic, and ultimately
undecidable relationship between verbal and visual art, as well
as art and life. The first poetic text that will be considered is
entitled "Trompe l'oeil" (Gil de Biedman 1966, 95–96), and is
taken from his *Moralidades, 1959–1964* first published in Mexico in 1966.[2] As defined by *Webster's New World Dictionary* this
French term (literally translated as "it tricks the eye") refers to
"a painting, etc. that creates such a strong illusion of reality that
the viewer on first sight is in doubt as to whether the thing depicted is real or a representation" (1524). The *Langenscheidt
Standard Dictionary of the French and English Languages* defines it as a "still-life deception; illusion. Tromper: to deceive,
cheat, mislead or delude" (499). This definition of a visual work
of art, of course, suggests to the reader a myriad of possibilities
in regard to the dialectic of inside/outside, Self/Other, reality/
illusion, presence/absence, word/silence, and ultimately art/life.
It is interesting to note that Gil de Biedma in a certain sense
from the outset performs what his title purports to "borrow"
from the painting that is the focus of the poetic text. The more
common expression is "trompe d'oeil." The sly and slight change
in the title deceives the reader; we *think* we see something that
is not really there, namely, the commonly held version that is
"trompe d'oeil." (Or is it?) This process of verbal suggestion mimics the feigned presence of objective reality in the type of painting which is suggested in the title.

Dionisio Cañas, in a recent article concerning the poetry of
Gil de Biedma, views the trajectory of the poet's work as "del
idealismo romántico al nihilismo posmoderno" ("from romantic
idealism to postmodern nihilism") (Cañas 1990, 1010), which in
effect is the subtitle of his perceptive piece on Gil de Biedma's
journey through the ruins. But in taking a closer look at a few
of the ekphrastic texts of this gifted writer, it seems to me that
rather than an evolution from the romantic to the postmodern
positionality of the subject, there is a subtle deconstructive subversion of the idealism/nihilism binary opposition. Instead of
(re)presenting reality, Gil de Biedma's portraits in words (dis)-
figure what they purport to convey, portraying not the world,
other art forms, or even himself, but the way in which the poetic
speaker filters objective reality through the lens of the speaker's
own perspective, under the (dis)guise of doubled artistic discourse. Thus, the romantic ideal of perfect correspondence be-

tween an object and its artistic representation bespeaks its own failure in the very act of its own communication, in true "trompe l'oeil/trompe d'oeil" fashion.

The poem with this same title begins with a commentary by the speaker/viewer in which he admits to the simultaneous reality and illusion of the "world" before him: "Indiscutiblemente no es un mundo para vivir en él".[3] The clarity and assertiveness of the opening adverb loses its direction with the subversive "no" that immediately follows it. Negation, by its very nature communicates inherent and systematic ambiguity, which decenters any one intepretive path for the reader.[4] The opening word, "Indiscutiblemente", belies the speaker's own questioning stance, faced with (ir)reality of the work of art, be it visual, verbal, or experiential. "No," as suggested previously, imposes unavoidable ambiguity, since its focus could be logically applied to negate the value of the following noun ("mundo"), or the verbal phrase that states "para vivir en él." In a similar vein, the "mundo" of this opening verse may be read as referring (un)decidedly to that which is both inside and outside the frame of this visual art object, as well as to the poetic text in which the speaker's comments appear. This undecidability leads to metapoetic considerations, a perspective that enriches the reading of this text from beginning to end. The unsettling no of this same opening line of verse causes the reader to ask the question "Why?," which receives a possible answer from the poetic speaker in the second stanza.

He comments that this world is "una experiencia literal/mejor organizada que la nuestra." But the "literal experience" to which he refers leads subtly but inexorably to a dead end, since its "literal" character may refer to the literal/literary text that we as readers must confront (in contrast to the reality outside the frame of any artistic experience), or also may refer to the delicious but duplicitous "reality" of the "trompe d'oeil" painting that is being evoked in the poetic text. The speaker in this stanza deliberately merges several levels of meaning and reference, and the effect is similar to what occurs when the viewer takes in a painting of the type evoked by the poem's title. For example, he refers to specific details, such as "esas antenas" or "lo mismo esos barcos como cisternas madres/amamantando a los remolcadores", as if to draw the viewer into the reality of the visual text. But simultaneously he emphasizes that these details have been created and appear "sobre el papel" and thus points out to the reader/viewer that those realistic details also contribute to the work's artifice and nature as an object created to seem what it is not, that is, reality as illusion and/or illusion as reality. Similarly, he resorts to "flowery" (excuse the pun. . . .) metaphoric rather than unadorned language when he states "son la flora y fauna de un reino manual." With the copulative "ser" he creates an equation of and between the realistic details and the artistic illusion to which they contribute. The speaker's words and his use of those same words function on the mimetic, semiotic, and metapoetic levels simultaneously. Through and with them he paints a reality that seems real, but in and through those very same words he signals that the reality so represented points to its own nature as artifice.

In the third stanza the seemingly realiable speaker continues his commentary concerning his "reading" of the duplicitous painting, but once again the reader of the poetic text must be simultaneously both inside and outside this speaker's artistic experience. The speaker slyly invites the reader's complicity in the act of reading by stating that

> Aunque la vaguedad quede en el fondo
> —la dulce vaguedad del sentimiento,
> que decía Espronceda—, suavizando
> nuestra visión del tándem y la azada
> de todos cuanto útiles importa conocer.
> (Gil de Biedma 1966, 95)

The expression "nuestra visión" demands the reader's presence and participation in the speaker's artistic experience of reading another text, but also signals quite firmly the frame that is both present and absent in the conflation of visual image and verbal strategy. In addition, the "vagueness that remains as a backdrop" craftily ("craft" in the sense of deceit as well as artistry) seems to point to the vagueness of an artistic work's background (verbal or visual), but in the silent void between the first and second verse of this strophe, the speaker enriches this vagueness to include feeling, a feeling that is a part of "our" experience of the world of art, whether verbal or visual, the world that is outside both of these frames of reference. Or is it the frame of representation and reception? By purposefully bestowing the polysemic value on the concept of vagueness, the speaker also by association equally bestows polysemy on that of vision: "nuestra visión" may refer to our purely physical and neurological capability as well as to our ability to see beyond the merely physical.

The speaker's reference to Espronceda, a romantic poet par excellence, allows the reader of the poetic text an intertextual digression, but also points to the poetic text as the object of artistic desire. That that fades momentarily to the "vagueness that remains in the background" is the painting that is supposedly the focal point and reference of the verbal text. The poem and painting rupture each other's frames and (dis)appear at the critical artistic vanishing point.[5] The allusion to Espronceda establishes a "frame of reference," but problematizes this very frame, since Espronceda and his poetic work are both inside and outside the frame; they are both present and absent, framing and framed by the text(s) evoked by the poetic speaker. The presence of Espronceda suggests another level, since he is both inside and outside the frame of reference of the present text, that is, a poem of the twentieth century that evokes the presence of one or several works of visual art. In addition, Espronceda's chimerical presence in Gil de Biedma's text makes possible the play of presence and absence on yet another level: the nineteenth-century poet appears in the Catalan poet's text in an aside, which is in itself a manifestation of romantic irony, which "is equated with the deliberate intrusion of the author who interrupts the fictitious action in order to destroy artistic illusion and thus prove the absolute power of the artist" (Bretz 1982, 258). The speaker of Gil de Biedma's text uses the literary strategy that characterizes the poet's work in order to enrich yet problematize the literary, artistic illusion of his own. In other words, the use of romantic irony by Gil de Biedma's speaker simultaneously supports and subverts the artistic illusion of his poetic text, in that it underscores the nature of poetic language, but also because of its function, it brings to the forefront the contrived artifice of that same language, and the poet's control over it. This duplicity mimics the status and effect of the "trompe d'oeil" type of painting, as well as points to a metapoetic reading of the text as a whole.

This vision to which the speaker refers from a multiplicity of perspectives applies to the following strophe as well, but the reader of the poetic text is caught in a "trompe d'oeil" reality/illusion dialectic and labyrinth. The speaker places the focal point of his commentary in this strophe upon a type of artwork within the frame of parentheses, miming in linguistic and typographical form the separation that obtains between what is inside and outside the limits of artistic representation:

(Como aquellos paisajes, en la Geografía
Elemental de Efetedé,
con ríos y montañas abriéndose hacia el mar,
mientras el tren, en primer término,
enfila el viaducto junto a la carretera,
por donde rueda solitariamente
un automóvil Ford, Modelo T.)

(Gilde Biedma 1966, 95)

But ironically, his commentary refers not to the original painting evoked by the poem's title, but rather to yet another visual text "(Como aquellos paisajes, en la Geografía / Elemental de Efetedé. . . .)". In this manner, the speaker points not to some original landscape but rather to their representation that appear in yet another text, "la Geografía Elemental de Efetedé" a simple textbook directed at Spanish primary schoolchildren. These landscapes are simultaneously and subversively both inside and outside the frame of representation. They are securely inside, since the speaker is comparing them with the "trompe d'oeil" painting of the poem's title; but they are ouside, since the landscapes are separate works of art. Moreover, their presence is deferred twice over, since Gil de Biedma's text makes subversive reference not to them directly but rather to their reproduction in yet another text, as a part of a store of images to which the reader/viewer may or may not make reference.

The speaker's comments about these landscapes are set off by parentheses, which serve visually and typographically as a frame of both inclusion and exclusion in the poetic text. The parentheses underscore the inclusion or framing of the speaker's personal comments concerning the painting(s), in addition to his meditation on the work(s) of art; in a sense, the parentheses emblemize the presence of the viewer of a work of art. The parentheses also serve to exclude, since they attempt to separate or frame off those very comments from the main focus, which is the "trompe d'oeil" visual work of art. In this latter case, they serve to keep the visual work of art from being sullied by the alien other, the viewer, who is permitted to ponder but not to touch. The parentheses are the frame of the visual work of art, and also the museum guards. The former's function is to keep in, the latter to keep out. And finally, the parentheses also serve a metapoetic function, since they remind the reader of the poem's existence as a linguistically and typographically visual artifact. They are two discrete, vertical curves on the page, which by convention, represent the (un)necessary supplement. The strophe in parentheses draws the reader's attention to the inside/outside dialectic of the framing device, whether visual or verbal, and also points out that textuality, whatever the discourse, is based upon convention.

It is interesting to note that the speaker makes reference to that which appears in the foreground, "en primer *término*" ("term, place, boundary"), rather than in "primer *plano*" ("plane, distance"). The word "término" may be used to signify "word" or "term," and thus brings with it a suggestion of metapoetic implications. In this poetic text there is a constant fluctuation among the mimetic, semiotic, and metapoetic readings, which is similar to the consistent inconstancy of the reality/illusion dialectic in the "trompe d'oeil" type of painting. Once again, by making reference to seemingly realistic details, in that very act of reference, the speaker undercuts and brings into question art's ability to refer to and represent the "objective" world.

The poem ends with yet another type of commentary offered by the speaker of the poetic text, and may be read from a variety of perspectives:

> Que la satisfacción de la nostalgia
> por el reino ordenado, grande y misterioso
> de la tercera realidad
> no sólo está en el vino y en las categorías:
> también hacen soñar estas imágenes
> con un mundo mejor.
>
> (Ibid., 95–96)

His commentary may be in reference to the "reino ordenado" ("ordered world") of the visual "trompe d'oeil," which catches in suspended animation a given artistic but ultimately deceptive representation of the world. Secondly, his reading may as well refer to the idealized and R/romantic "mundo mejor" that is the poetic text. At this point the reader of the text may elect to remember the opening lines of the poem, "Indiscutiblemente no es un mundo / para vivir en él." This "mundo," "mejor" or not, has attempted to capture the speaker's vision in its undecidable trajectory into linguistic form. Or third, the speaker's final commentary may refer to the poetic speaker's metapoetic insights in regard to the reading process as a whole, and the difficulty of transposing one discourse, that of visual imagery, into another, that of verbal representation. This strategy is made all the more complicated, since we as readers of the poetic text inexorably are pulled into the vortex of the sign's undecidability. As readers, we are witnesses as well as participants in the speaker's reading of yet another text. The process continues in us, since our own methods of reading will reveal what aesthetic ideals we have chosen, favored and valued, just as those of the poetic speaker's are revealed in *his* reading of the visual text(s) to which he makes reference. And lastly, the speaker's satisfaction and nostalgia may be inspired by his sense of this "mundo mejor," or only his longing tempered by an alcohol induced vision. His comment that "no sólo está en el vino" may well be a reference to the Latin expression "in vino veritas," which implies that many "eternal truths" find their way out of an uncorked bottle of wine.[6]

Gil de Biedma's speaker closes the poem with the following lines of verse:

> Las lecciones de cosas siempre han sido románticas
> —posiblemente porque interpretamos
> los detalles al pie de la letra
> y el conjunto en sentido figurado.
>
> (Ibid., 96)

The "sentido figurado" of the speaker's final commentary once again suggests to the reader of the text (verbal or visual) a meta-poetic perspective, since the term "figurado" carries with it several denotative possibilities: (1) in reference to language style; (2) to depict, represent, draw, and outline; (3) to feign; and (4) to imagine or to fancy. The speaker includes "us," observers and receivers of any kind, in the interpretive process ("interpretamos"), and allows us to choose the focus (I use this visual image with a purpose. . . .) on "los detalles" and "el conjunto." So the "trompe l'oeil" of the title may be in reference to our reading of a specific painting, to the specific poetic text being read, or to the poetic speaker's summation of our own paltry attempts to read the so-called reality (or is it illusion???) that surrounds us all. The poem ultimately leads toward its own sub-version, since it too may be read in "trompe d'oeil" fashion: its realistic details and linguistic specificity simultaneously attempt to capture objective reality, but also in the very act signal language's failure to refer to anything except itself.

Another aspect of ekphrasis in Gil de Biedma's poetry is to be found in his verbal self-portraits, specifically in the texts entitled "Contra Jaime Gil de Biedma," and "Después de la muerte de Jaime Gil de Biedma," both of which are from his *Poemas póst-*

umos, first published in 1968. Both of these poems address the problematic of (self-) portraiture and representation, and complicate the issues of verbal and visual imagery as well as the dialectic of surrender and sovereignty that were mentioned earlier. This latter issue of surrender and sovereignty is made manifest in the breaking of the frame, since the representation posited in the verbal text is that of Self and Other, Self by Other, Self inside and outside Other. Both of these texts offer to the reader seductive possibilities of reading, and suggest many images, visual as well as verbal, that ultimately lend a metapoetic dimension to both texts.

The unfolding of the Self is exemplified most clearly by the lengthy poem of some fifty-five lines entitled "Contra Jaime Gil de Biedma" (Gil de Biedma 1968, 145–146), in which the author of flesh and blood creates a "tú" who also bears the name of Gil de Biedma. Because of the unfolding of Self as critic into Other, who is criticized in the poem could be viewed as an interesting play on essayistic convention where the essay's narrator attempts an ill-fated objectivity to convince the reader of the narrator's own viewpoint. The title of this piece embodies in and of itself the verbal artifice that obtains in the work as a whole. The preposition "contra" in Spanish has two distinct meanings: it may be understood in the sense of "against, in opposition to, in conflict with," as in the Spanish sentence "Lucharon contra la opresión" ("They fought against oppression"). Or secondly, it may be understood as "facing, toward, finding support," as exemplified in the Spanish "Apretó con fuerza al niño contra su pecho" ("He/she/you [fam. sing.] held the little boy tightly against his/her/your breast"). The reader is already aware of the fact that the flesh-and-blood author is himself a man named Jaime Gil de Biedma, and so is faced with the problem of the author who creates a speaker of the same name, who in turn creates an Other in opposition to the Self, and who begins by providing a title based on an inherent semantic indeterminacy as well as a focal ambiguity. As will be shown in the analysis of the text, the author plays upon the dual meaning of the Spanish word "contra" by both maligning and eliciting support for the poetic persona of the Jaime Gil de Biedma portrayed in the text.

The speaker begins with what appears to be a statement of concession and exasperation,—"De qué sirve, quisiera saber yo" and continues with a string of infinitives, "cambiar de piso," "dejar atrás," and "poner visillos blancos," whose subject is not as yet disclosed. It is only when the speaker tries to disassociate himself from the Other in line 7, "si vienes luego tú, pelmazo" that the reader becomes aware that the preceding verbs do indeed refer to the Self's attempts at autonomy from the Other. The speaker states that he wishes to "dejar atrás un sótano más ne- gro / que mi reputación" in lines two to three, but perhaps this statement contains a Freudian hypallage for the true state of af- fairs, namely, "dejar atrás una reputación más negra que mi só- tano."[7] In other words, the speaker refers to the place, "el sótano" instead of the more revealing personal characteristics, which, according to the speaker, describes not the Self, but the Other. And this reference to "sótano" relates directly to the expression "cambiar de piso" seen earlier: the speaker may indeed be exhib- iting yet another (un?)conscious Freudian projection, in that it is much easier to name a move to the nether regions of a house- hold than to those of one's own character. The Self is and is not the Other; inner is and is not outer; subject is and is not object; reality is and is not illusion. The Other in this case is a distanced and not so neatly framed image of the Self, "framed" in the sense of being held within a border as well as being incriminated in questionable behavior. The Other is one given to dissolute living, a bohemian lack of concern for practicality and, presumably, in- considerate behavior, in contrast with the more staid characteris- tics of the straitlaced speaker. The speaker depicts the alien Other:

> embarazo huesped, memo vestido con mis trajes,
> zángano de colmena, inútil, cacaseno
> con tus manos lavadas,
> a comer en mi plato y a ensuciar la casa?
> (Gil de Biedma 1968, 2. 8–11, 145)

The situation described by the speaker is that of the host, albeit a reluctant one, and guest. But as J. Hillis Miller points out, this relationship is none too clear. The concept of host contains within it "the double antithetical relation of host and guest, guest in the bifold sense of friendly presence and alien invader. The words "host" and "guest" go back in fact to the same etymologi- cal root: *ghos-ti*, stranger; guest, host, properly "someone with whom one has reciprocal duties of hospitality" (Bloom et al. 1979, 220–21).

In viewing the relationship of Self to Other in Gil de Biedma's text, one could say that it is parasitic, where the guest takes advantage of the host. But once again, the speaker encourages the reader to become aware of how language betrays itself. Miller points out that "the 'para' of parasite is a double antithetical prefix signifying at once proximity and distance, similarity and difference, interiority and exteriority, something inside a domestic economy, and at the same time outside it, something simultaneously this side of the boundary line, threshold, or margin and also beyond it" (Ibid., 219). In the case of the poetic text "Contra Jaime Gil de Biedma," is it this very linguistic indeterminacy of words such as host, guest, and parasite that is reflected by chance in the two protagonists, who are both simultaneously inside and outside the frame of the text, or is it something entirely different? Is it that the poet wants the two protagonists to embody the linguistic indeterminacy by which the poet attempts to describe them? The complementarity of opposition is paramount: Self is and is not Other; the observer is and is not the observed; the word is and is not silence; the poet is and is not the poem.

In the second stanza the Self amplifies upon the peccadilloes of the Other—his socializing habits, his unconventional friends, and the odd hours that he keeps. But in the selective reading of the portrait of the Other that he presents to the reader, the speaker also presents a faceted portrait of himself: for just as the Other must look in a mirror and see the Self, so the Self, upon viewing the Other also sees his own image. It is a hall of mirrors that continues in its dizzying process of reflection, in both senses of the word. The Self attempts to chide the Other, who in return effortlessly breaks the fragile frame established by the Self, in order to maintain an unsustainable distance: the Other reminds the Self of their unbreakable bond in the passage of time: "me recuerdas el pasado / y dices que envejezco" of lines 21 and 22. Now the tables have been turned. Instead of the Self viewing the distanced Other as a separate entity, the reader is faced with the Self viewing the Other who in turn is viewing the Self. Instead of the Self framing the Other, the Other paradoxically frames the Self.

Beginning in stanza 3 with line 23 the speaker distances himself once again from the Other, but this time in a different fashion: he enters into a soliloquy while taking on yet another persona, that of a disapproving father with a recalcitrant and impetuous son:

> Podría recordarte que ya no tienes gracia.
> Que tu estilo casual y que tu desenfado
> resultan truculentos

cuando se tiene más de treinta años,
y que tu encantadora
sonrisa de muchacho soñoliento
seguro de gustar—es un resto penoso,
un intento patético.

                    (Gil de Biedma 1968, 2.23–30, 145–46)

The Self recounts, presumably for the benefit of the reader, the details of what he could say to the son, but of course does not. Ironically, what he says by not saying it becomes a part of the portrait that we have of the Other. The words that he uses to describe his distance and absence from the Other contribute to the Other's presence. Thus, the double meaning of the word "contra" manifests itself in the waxing and waning of the Self's words and of the Other's presence/absence, and suggests the function of the frame, namely, to include as well as exclude.

The portrait of the Other in turn allows the reader metapoetic considerations, in that by portraying the Self as Other the poet in turn gives up for consideration, as Françoise Meltzer comments, "literature's views on itself, on representation, and on the power of writing" (Meltzer 1987, 1). The Other is the object of artistic desire, forever present, forever absent to the writer. The reader is left to conjecture why the Self cannot bring himself to face directly the Other and to express his distress. Perhaps it is because the Self does not want to alienate the Other and in essence fears his loss, which in turn would be a loss of a part of the Self. Once again Gil de Biedma, the flesh-and-blood author, underscores the tenuous yet mutually begetting relationship of Self and Other. With the foregrounding of the Self, the Other is destroyed and vice versa. The Guest becomes the Host, and the Host the Guest. Or the Host as welcomer becomes the Host as destroyer. In turn, the guest as friendly invited presence becomes the alien invader.

Stanza 4 culminates in the as yet undecided tug-of-war between Self and Other, father and son, host and guest, observer and observed. In the first line of the strophe (Gil de Biedma 1968, 1.34), the Self once again derides the Other—"si no fueses tan puta!"—while in the second (Ibid., 1.35) he recognizes his own failings, but also his own power and knowledge—"Y si yo no supiese, hace ya tiempo." It is then that the Self faces up to the fact that even though he detests having to admit it, he is inextricably bound to the Other, who, in a certain sense, is the prime mover, the Father, the Host, the observer of the Self: "que tú eres fuerte cuando yo soy débil / y que eres débil cuando me

enfurezco. . . ." Even though he abhors the social infractions of
the Other, he cannot hide his desperation over the mere thought
of the Other's abandoning him. The exchange of power and pleasure that enters into the contract of reception and representation
frames and informs this duplicitous relationship and portrayal
of Self and Other. Thus, the Self longs for total and unconditional
intimacy with the Other but fears the overwhelming feelings of
powerlessness accompanying such an emotional commitment.
In lines 38 to 44, the speaker utilizes exclusively negative terms
to describe the feelings of revulsion: "impresión confusa/pánico/
 pena/descontento/desesperanza/impaciencia/resentimiento/vol-
ver a sufrir/humillación imperdonable."

The denouement of the Self's confrontation with the portrait
of the Other is laden with sexual and erotic overtones, and reflects in human terms the (pro)creative aspect of (verbal) [self]-
portraiture: using a metaphor of carnal and metaphysical proportions, the Self and Other go off to bed together.[8] "A duras penas
te llevaré a la cama, / como quien va al infierno / para dormir
contigo" (Gil de Biedma 1968 2.45–47, 146). This highly symbolic action pays homage to the closest physical proximity between two human beings, yet the Self recognizes the
impossibility of perfect union and harmony, in spite of the attempt at intimacy: "Muriendo a cada paso de impotencia, / tro-
pezando con muebles / a tientas, cruzaremos el piso / torpemente
abrazados, vacilando / de alcohol y de sollozos reprimidos"
(Ibid., 2.48–52, 146). The ultimate act of life, intimate sexual
union, with its possibility of creation, only leads to destruction
and death. The Self recognizes his fate, yet must give himself
over to this experience, over and over again. Self and Other surrender to one another, knowing full well that their attempt at
union will only lead to despair and defeat. The poet, by creating
himself anew in the verbal portrait of Self and Other loses a facet
of the Self, surrenders to the Other, one that is now free of the
Self's control and domination by the very fact of alterity in the
text's verbal portrait. The Self surrenders sovereignty to the
Other, in the act of representation. But in so doing, the Self
claims for himself (in the name/word[s] of the Other) the power
of this representation, and the pleasure that this process of representation renders. The reader enters into the verbal and visual
economy of this (ex)change by carrying it one step further: the
reader is both Self and Other by virtue of identification with
the I/eye of the text, simultaneously inside/outside the frame of
the portrait(s).

The poem ends with a depersonalized vocative. It is a disembodied voice, perhaps of both Self and the Other. . . . or of neither. In spite of the difficulties inherent in reception, (self-)expression, and subsequent (self-)representation, Self, Other, Poet, speaker, and reader must continue on the path of simultaneous deconstruction and creation, ignorance and knowledge, intimacy and alienation, enmity and amity. The closing lines of this poetic text lament "Oh innoble servidumbre de amar seres humanos, / y la más innoble / que es amarse a sí mismo!" (Ibid., 2.53–55, 146). The speaker here hands over his thoughts as embodied in a verbal (self-)portrait now not to the Other, but to the reader/viewer, whose task it is to continue the process of in(tro)spection, (pro)creation, and (self-)knowledge. This vocative is stated not in the "tú" ([fam. sing.]) form that was employed previously, but in the impersonal "se" ("one"). The portrait that emerges at the end is both of both Self and Other, where each is mutually and reciprocally "framed," consumed, subsumed, constituted, and subverted by the disruptive alien presence. The questionable behavior of the Other that was mentioned earlier may now be viewed as a metaphor for writing and for all forms of representation. The very act of writing, portraying, and representing brings into question the value and truth of that very process.

Through this particular poetic text Gil de Biedma also profiles the relationship of poet and poem, (self-)portrait and artist, text(s) and reader, word and image (both verbal and visual), the frame and its contents, word and silence, art and life. From a metapoetic perspective, it offers a record of the poet's failed yet successful attempt to finally get it right, to overcome the barrier of language. The battle of Self and Other could be interpreted as a metaphor for the artist's struggle with Otherness, that which is forever beyond the artist's grasp. One should note the use of vocabulary in lines 38 to 44, just cited above. These same words—confusion, panic, pain, discontent, despair, impatience, resentment—could as well be used to describe the agony of the artist, verbal or visual, in the act of creation. Otherness is and is not a part of the creative spirit. The artist can and cannot control it, yet wishes to represent and control the alien Other in order to become one with the alien object of desire: otherness is forever exterior to the Self: the Self always must fail to express and possess that very object of desire. In this narcissistic act of self-begetting, Gil de Biedma's speaker has been defeated in a certain sense, but has also gained an important victory. On the surface level of the text, the Self does not finally possess or control the image of the Other, but at least recognizes and allows the reader to recognize the mutual dependence of the relationship. Concomitantly, the poet has not broken through the barrier of artistic expression to possess the desired object, but rather has produced another in the form of the verbal (self-)portrait of the poetic text, one that simultaneously pays homage to and yet undermines the concept of the frame. The text is magical, in that it captures and encapsulates, if only momentarily, the multivalent sign we know as "Jaime Gil de Biedma": persona, poet, protagonist, portrait, poem. It is the author himself who is and is not in the picture, in a literal as well as metaphoric sense, part of and yet separate from the Self and the Other.

In a similar poem of this same collection, "Después de la muerte de Jaime Gil de Biema" (Ibid., 155–57), the poet pays homage to this simultaneous presence and absence of Self and Other, but once again cannot resist the temptation to have the poetic text open and then fold back upon itself. The poet/speaker describes the process of textual creation, from the vantage point of the present looking toward the past. And as in the previously considered text, there is a disassociation from and depersonalization of the poetic I/eye. He offers a portrait of the "tú" ([fam. sing.]), who is objectified by means of the speaker's gaze:

> Yo me salvé escribiendo
> después de la muerte de Jaime Gil de Biedma.
> De los dos, eras tú quien mejor escribía.
> Ahora sé hasta qué punto tuyos eran
> el deseo de ensueño y la ironía,
> la sordina romántica que late en los poemas
> míos que yo prefiero, por ejemplo en Pandémica. . . .
> A veces me pregunto
> cómo será sin ti mi poesía.
>
> (Ibid., 2.59–67, 157)

The first two lines of verse just cited can be read in two ways: they may either refer to the poet's self-help methods upon the death of his self-begotten and self-begetting portrait, or they may also refer metapoetically to the creation of the text being read by the reader, namely, the poetic text entitled "Después de la muerte de Jaime Gil de Biedma." In either case, once again the poet draws the reader's attention to not only the theme at hand, but also to discourse, the creative process, framing, and the rupture of that frame. The Other portrayed in the text is both the mirror and the mask of the Self who appears therein.[9] Thus, the reader is encouraged to be inside and outside the frame of the (self)-portrait simultaneously, in order to accept the perspectives of both the Self and the Other. And the speaker graciously accepts the knowledge and finesse with which the Other provided him, attributing to that Other what he considers the best characteristics of his written work, the beguiling touches of "ensueño y la ironía, / la sordina romántica que late en los poemas / míos que yo prefiero." The text folds back upon itself, the Self, and the Other, in yet another manner, since the "Pandémica" referred to in this text is an intertextual reference to a Gil de Biedma poem from *Moralidades* entitled "Pandémica y celeste."

The (dis)figuring gaze of Gil de Biedma in his ekphrastic texts brings into focus not only the unsettling relationship between verbal text and visual imagery, but also the process of reading and seeing double for both poet and the reader. In allowing the object of artistic desire to speak for itself within the ruptured framework of the poetic text, the poet enters actively into the problematic economy of power and pleasure as well as surrender and sovereignty of the reading process. Thus, for Gil de Biedma, the "trompe d'oeil" technique of the visual work of art (dis)covers itself in the poetic text as well, since we as readers along with the poetic speaker are drawn into the duplicitous reality of the poetic representation. In like manner, Gil de Biedma's (self)-portraits (re)present the artist's success and failure in capturing objective realty. The Self/Other dialectic is a metaphor of a metaphor: it (re)presents in diligent "trompe d'oeil" fashion the artist's particular quandary in attempting to simultaneously grasp and set free the unattainable object of artistic desire. Here, a poet named Jaime Gil de Biedma creates in a clearly unamunesque move an alter ego who carries the same name, who in turn bifurcates into a Self-Other. One reading of the artistic representation of the Self could well point to a metamorphosing of the Self into a sign for artistic (pro)creation; and the further doubling into the Self-Other dialectic could well refer to the exposed and precarious nature of that sign, since the Self does and does not control the Other. The Other, by the very position of alterity, is not a part of the Self, but is ultimately dependent upon the Self for representation. As Meltzer cogently comments, "the portrait in a literary text is at once a pleonasm (representation representing itself) and a point of danger: the moment when the text risks annihilation by the power of representation itself, of which the

text is but one facet" (Meltzer, 215). Self and Other coincide in
the false reality of illusory truth that is all art.

In a similar fashion José Angel Valente also participates in
the economy of power and pleasure as well as surrender and
sovereignty in his renditions of literary (self-)portraiture.[10] But
the (self-) portraits that emerge in his case effect a doubling between Self and Other, a distancing between the two poles of the
dialectic, that utilize differing strategies in order to bring about
the act of framing and its simultaneous rupture that was seen
previously in the case of Gil de Biedma's poetry. For example,
in "El espejo" ("The Mirror") of *A modo de esperanza* (*In the
Same Way as Hope*) (Valente 1955, 15–16), Valente's first published book of verse, the poetic speaker makes reference to the
means by which the self-portrait's image is to be perceived by
the Self as well as by the observer (spectator and reader), that is,
through the double lens of the duplicitous mirror and the
speaker's eye. The question that arises for the observer is "Which
of the two lenses will be most (un)faithful to that which is being
framed?" namely, the distanced view of the Self as Other. In
utilizing the image of the mirror the poet invites the reader to
access such diverse intertextual echoes as the fairy tale of Snow
White ("Mirror, mirror on the wall, who is the fairest of them
all?"),[11] Alice in Wonderland taken from Lewis Carroll's classic
Alice Through the Looking Glass, the myth of Narcissus, or the
so-called mirror stage according to one branch of current psychological theory.[12] As Joan E. Cirlot suggests, the mirror is the symbol par exellence of the imagination and consciousness, yet
is ambivalent in regard to representation. In Valente's text, the
Self views the Other as distanced and marked by the effects of
time's passage:

> Hoy he visto mi rostro tan ajeno,
> tan caído y sin par
> en este espejo.
> Está duro y tan otro con sus años,
> su palidez, sus pómulos agudos,
> su nariz afilada entre los dientes,
> sus cristales domésticos cansados,
> su costumbre sin fe, sólo costumbre.
>
> (Valente 1955, 2.1–8, 15)

(Today I have seen my face so belonging to another, / so fallen and
without equal / in this mirror. // It is hard and so other with its

years, / its pallor, its sharp cheekbones, / its fine-drawn nose amid
[the] teeth, / its tired domestic glasses, / its habit without faith,
only habit.)

Memory serves to contrast the present Other with another (and
an Other) who has been lost in the course of time. "También fue
niño / este rostro, otra vez, con madre al fondo" ("It also was
boyish / this face, again with [a] mother in the background")
(Ibid., 2.11–12, 15), thus insuring the repetition of the act of
doubling. This last image, of mother and child, offers yet another
example of multiple framing, and brings to mind several examples of earlier portraiture, such as those executed by Renaissance
artists of the Madonna and Child, later ones by Velázquez or
Goya of the Spanish nobility, or the more recent ones by Picasso
of the working class in his blue and rose periods, or in his later
Vollard Suite, where satyrs and women are reflected in, and reflect upon, their own and each other's mirrored gazes.[13] The poetic speaker further distances the Self from the image in the
mirror by making reference to childhood activities and objects
such as "frágiles juguetes" ("fragile toys"), "el parque infantil"
("the children's park"), or the "niño municipal con aro y árboles"
("municipal boy with hoop and trees").

In the final stanza the speaker returns temporally as well as
imagistically to the visage of the not-so-distanced yet unknown
Other who is framed by the concrete aspect of the mirror itself,
framed by time's passage, framed by the speaker's physical and
psychological perspective, and also framed by the act of poetic
creation. He states:

> Pero ahora me mira—mudo asombro,
> glacial asombro en este espejo solo—
> y ¿dónde estoy—me digo—
> y quién me mira
> desde este rostro, máscara de nadie?
> (Valente 1955, 2.18–22, 16)

(But now it looks at me—mute fright, / glacial fright in this lone
mirror—/ and "where am I?"—I say to myself—/ and "who looks at
me" / from that face, mask of no one?)

But now it is the Other who gazes at the Self—"Pero ahora me
mira—mudo asombro, / glacial asombro en este espejo solo—"
("But now it looks at me—mute fright, / glacial fright in this lone
mirror—")—and causes the Self to question his own frame of

reference (pun intended. . . .), from a temporal, spatial, and existential perspective as well. These final verses are enigmatic, in that the reader must ponder the reference point of "asombro" in the sense of the negative "fright" or the more affirmative "amazement," or both, as well as "este rostro, máscara de nadie" ("this face, mask of no one"). This final expression may refer to the face of the Self looking at the Other, or that of the Other looking at the Self. In either case, the Self reflects an Other (or the Other reflects a Self) who is eternally present, yet eternally absent under the watchful, full frontal gaze of a fully visible and present yet totally enigmatic mask. In the (dis)guise of the known, the Self/Other (Narcissus, Alice, the fairest, the subconscious) looks straight into the face of the mystery of identity, textuality, and representation. From a metapoetic perspective, this attitude of self-contemplation is continued, if one considers that the poetic speaker contemplates the unknowable Other that is the sign in the very act of writing. As in the case of Jaime Gil de Biedma's poetic self-portraits, the mutual confrontation of Self and Other here in Valente's text may be interpreted as a metaphor of writerly creativity. There is a continual and ultimately undecided and undecidable play of surrender and sovereignty, presence and absence, framing and rupture, in the process of self-reflection that is the poetic text itself.

Two other texts where Valente presents self-portraits commemorate his thirtieth birthday and fortieth year respectively, and thus are also marked by the sign of time's passage, just as in the case of the previously considered "El espejo" ("The Mirror"). In "El autor en su treinta aniversario" ("The Author on his Thirtieth Birthday") (Valente 1966, 159–62) of *La memoria y los signos* (*[The] Memory and [the] Signs*) the poetic speaker immediately establishes a frame for his readers, and invites those readers to consider a possible world, "as if" it were real:

> Como si estuviera desnudo
> o al borde de nacer o de morir,
> en la terrible red del aire detenido,
> en el trigésimo año de mi juventud.
>
> (Valente 1966, 2.1–4, 159)

(As if I were naked / or on the verge of being born or dying, / in the terrible net of [the] spiritless air, / in the thirtieth year of my youth.)

In addition to the contrary-to-fact positionality of "Como si estuviera desnudo" ("As if I were naked") of the opening line of

verse, this framing technique is underscored by the expression
"al borde de" ("on the verge of") as well as the undecidable
liminality of "de nacer o de morir" ("of being born or dying").
The suspended animation of this opening strophe is even more
clearly enunciated by the absence of a principal verbal structure;
furthermore, in a sense the speaker's own expression/representa-
tion is caught in the ambiguous and "terrible red del aire detenido" ("terrible net of [the] spiritless air"), since there is an
undeniable, stuttering repetition of the same sounds in the last
two lines of verse:

en la terrible red del aire detenido,

en el trigésimo año de mi juventud.

(in the terrible net of [the] spiritless air / in the thirtieth year of
my youth.)

Moreover, this last line of verse ultimately undermines itself, in
that the foregrounding of the speaker's years ticking off mocks
the very concept of youth that he is at pains to underscore.

In the succeeding strophe, the speaker depends upon a vocabulary referring to the painter's art in order to further substantiate
the frame of reference for this particular self-portrait:

> Como el modelo no es vida
> en el pincel, sino materia
> que aún no imita la vida, inmóvil
> permanezco dentro
> de mi propia visión,
> reconocible apenas
> para quienes me aman,
> sentado o súbitamente en pie,
> y sobre un fondo gris
> una ventana abierta
> en que no se distinguen
> un paisaje o el mar.
>
> (Ibid., 2.5–16, 159)

(Since the model is not life / in the paintbrush, but rather material
which does not yet imitate life, immobile / I stay within / my own
vision, / hardly recognizable / to those who love me, / seated or sud-

denly standing, / and on a grey background / an open window / in which one does not distinguish / a landscape or the sea.)

The speaker captures himself who is Other within his mind's I/ eye, and freely concedes that the power of the image resides in what it is *not:* "el modelo no es vida" ("the model is not life), "no imita la vida" ("it does not imitate life"), "reconocible apenas" ("hardly recognizable"), "sobre un fondo gris" ("on a gray background"), and "una ventana abierta / en que no se distinguen / un paisaje o el mar" ("in an open window / in which one does not distinguish a landscape or the sea"). This play of presence and absence evokes the well-known metaphor of the painting and its "supplemental" frame: the painting is (de)limited and defined by what it is not, what is exterior to itself. The reader may question at this juncture what are the specifics to which one may make reference, in order to counterbalance the negation and absence communicated by the previous section of the text. But the speaker continues to define the Self in terms of an Other utilizing the same strategy of negation with which he started. But here the painting metaphor is transformed into the creativity of the word: "Bien podía latir el corazón, / pero no hablo del corazón, / y la palabra bien podía cantar, / pero no hablo de la palabra" ("The heart could well beat, / but I am not talking about the heart, / and the word could well sing, / but I am not talking about the word") (Ibid., 2.17–20, 159–60). He once again returns to the visual metaphor to emphasize the lack, the space, the absence, the Otherness, that is the center of identity and representation: the frame is and is not supplemental to the definition of its contents. Poetry utilizes ekphrasis as a strategy to overcome a lack, a space, a supposed deficiency in the power of its own discourse, but this same strategy also shows the lack in the visual discourse. The poetic text repeats in its form the message that the speaker conveys through the power of his words and images, whether verbal or visual, since the center of his gaze is communicated at the very center of this partcular poetic text of seventy-two lines of verse:[14]

> El centro está en lo gris
> y en la inmovilidad, no en la acción.
> El centro es el vacío.
> 　　Objeto
> ciego de mi propia visión, petrificado
> perfil de niño tenebroso,
> el hombre que contemplo no desciende

de su memoria sino de su olvido.

(Valente, 1966, 2.33–40, 160)

(The center is in the grey area / and in immobility, not in action. / The center is the void. / Object / blind to my own vision, petrified / profile of [a] gloomy boy, / the man that I contemplate does not descend / from his memory but from his forgetfulness.)

It is fascinating to note that lines 35 and 36 visually depict the speaker's lemma that "El centro es el vacío" ("The center is the void"), since space / nothingness / absence / lack surrounds, defines, and IS the "object" of the speaker's artistic desire in those very lines of verse. But in the very act of stating this position, the speaker's statement is subverted; by this act of naming, by putting into words the concept of emptiness, what is inside and outside the frame of reference, that very frame of reference no longer applies.

By taking advantage of the painting metaphor with its inherent set of boundaries—inside/outside, foreground/background, presence/absence, action/immobility, reality/representation—the speaker attempts to communicate the simultaneous success and failure of all artistic creativity and activity. The object of artistic desire is present only ephemerally, in the ebb and flow of suggestion, allusion, the presence of absence, the description of what it is not. The speaker's description of the Self that is Other is communicated not through what is remembered, but through the echo of what has been forgotten or left out, that which has not been possessed in the paltry approximation of Truth and Beauty that we define as the art object. As he so eloquently states,

Lejos estoy del hombre que contemplo,
autor de breves
composiciones o supervivencias,
inmóvil frente al muro
secreto que separa
lo que no he conocido de cuanto desconozco.

(Ibid., 2.60–65, 161)

(I am far from the man whom I contemplate, / author of short / compositions and survivals, immobile facing the secret / wall that separates / what I have not known from how much I fail to recognize.)

In the act of portraying himself, the speaker inevitably must come to terms with the obverse of the image that is present/

absent before him, and admits that the contemplated surface renders quite literally only "half of the story." As in the case of "El espejo" ("The Mirror") the metapoetic dimension of this text makes possible a reading where the speaker's attempt to capture his self-portrait in words takes on the power of the heroic struggle to gain sovereignty over the obstreperous Other, where the Other stands for all artistic creation. The Other is forever present/ absent from the Self's grasp and gaze, forever inside/outside the frame of artistic reference and representation. The crafty and artful (dis)guise of the Other reflects the image and visage of the Self, who (un)knowingly views the Other. Or is it the Self?[15]

The speaker closes in a manner similar to how he began, by making reference to those ambiguous and undecidable limits, and thus the very nature of art, representation, and ultimately, life and death:

> En el umbral del año,
> en la explosión del límite,
> el alba es un comienzo,
> nunca un adiós.
> Aguardo,
> zarpa cruel de la esperanza, un día
> tu bautismo sangriento.
>
> (Valente 1966, 2.66–72, 161)

(On the threshold of the year, / in the explosion of the boundary, / the dawn is a beginning, / never a good-bye. / I await , / cruel [feline] paw of hope, one day / your bloody baptism.)

The last few lines of verse plaintively echo the previously noted "centro" ("center") as "vacío" ("void"), in that the speaker pays tribute to the hope that is present in the darkness, the emptiness, the Otherness, the void that is and is also just before the dawn of a new day. This void surrounds the word "Aguardo" ("I await"), the typography repeating the speaker's existential and artistic positionality. Day and night frame each other, the seeming hopefulness of a new day subverted by the suggestion of horrific initiation to life and/or annihilation of death of "tu bautismo sangriento" ("your bloody baptism").

In his ten-line poem entitled "Retrato del autor" ("Portrait of the Author") (Valente 1970, 337) of El inocente (The Innocent [One]) the poetic speaker celebrates the act of self-portraiture and that of framing in a slightly different fashion. In contrast with the previously considered texts, he uses a totally different

tone, and very playfully underscores the problematic relationship between creator and created, peppering this self-portrait
with self-deprecating humor in the act of creating it:

> Digo a mi perro:
>   Je suis un poète.
> J'ai quarante ans
> et je sui content.
>   Mi perro me contempla
> con la fijeza de la incomprensión.
> Hay, existe, se ha manifestado
> el milagro del público lector,
> mon semblable, mon frère.
>   ¡Hurra!
>
>   (Valente 1970, 337)

(I say to my dog: / *I am a poet.* / *I am forty years old* / *and I am content.*
dog contemplates me / with the steadfastness of incomprehensioi
There is, [it] exists, [it] has manifested itself / the miracle of
public reader [m.] / *my likeness, my brother.* // Hurray!) (Verse line
cursive were in French in the original.)

In this poetic text the speaker emphasizes the inside/outside dichotomy of the frame and the distancing effect that it accomplishes by naming the senders and receivers of textuality—the
poet himself, his dog and his reader—, by switching codes at
key places in the text between Spanish and French, and also by
leaving a significant space between his description of creation
and reception, and between his own commentary on that relationship. In this manner he suggests the endless concatenation
that constitutes the process of signification, and comments upon
the receiver's role and how it is similar to that of the poet himself.
The speaker punctuates the supposed difference between the
poet and his public by using three distinct verbs, "Hay, existe, se
ha manifestado" ("There is, [it] exists, [it] has manifested itself")
to mark the boundary or frame between the poet's wor(l)d and
"el milagro del público lector" ("the miracle of the public
reader") but then goes on to subvert that very distinction by
confessing to their shared likeness, "mon semblable, mon frère"
("my likeness, my brother").[16] Ironically, the speaker points out
this similarity in French, which he has also used to speak of
himself; on the other hand, he uses only Spanish to refer to his
faithful canine companion. For his reader, he uses both Spanish
and French. Spanish, the native tongue of the poet named José

Angel Valente, identifies and describes the faithful hound, who listens in a state of rapt attention and incomprehension. It is evident that his master is "speaking another language," but it is not clear whether that incomprehension is because of the switch from French to Spanish, whether the canine prefers some other genre over poetry, or simply that the language barrier between species was too great to overcome.[17] Implicitly with this nod to the state of courteous but nonetheless total incomprehension of his text's receiver, the speaker acknowledges the difficulty and imperfection of the communicative process in a text's reception and interpretation.

This reader was reminded of the original RCA advertisement, where a perky little mongrel named Nipper listens intently to an old-style phonograph, and underneath appears the slogan "His Master's Voice." Presumably the receiver of that advertisement is to understand that the truthfulness of the sound delivered by the record player attains such a level of approximation that the dog believes that he is actually hearing the familiar voice of his human companion. The dog's attentiveness and body language communicate this message, and repeat in visual imagery the slogan of the advertisement. He believes he is hearing the truth, and we, as readers of the advertisement, ought to believe the dog, not to mention RCA and Madison Avenue. But as human beings, we have the capacity to perceive what is real versus what is an illusion, and how the two do and do not coincide. An implicit message of this famous piece of commercial propaganda is that illusion may indeed give the illusion of reality, and we have the power to choose.

In Valente's poem, the speaker likens himself to his audience, who "me contempla / con la fijeza de la incomprensión" ("contemplates me / with the steadfastness of incomprehension"), his first audience being of course the loyal cur at his side. But the frame is both repeated and ruptured, since the readers of his poetic text, in turn, must also enter into the process of contemplation and simultaneous comprehension and incomprehension: we take on the role of both the poet and his faithful dog, by silently receiving the text, as does the dog, and also by continuing the creative process of assimilating its images and continuing the sequence of reception and (in)comprehension. One cannot ignore the tongue-in-cheek posture that the speaker adopts in this self-portrait, nor the ironic and self-deprecating humor that permeates its message. In a wry manner, the poetic speaker admits his own ignorance and incomprehension, and willingly

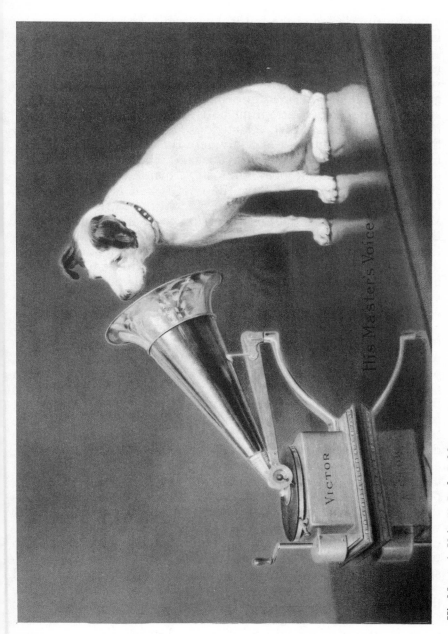

His Master's Voice © Jack Golden.

takes on the stance of the faithful, adorable, adoring, and totally
uncomprehending hound. Similarly, the typography repeats in
"graphic" fashion the inside/outside dichotomy that the speaker
is at pains to underscore. By the variance of the left margin in
succeeding lines of verse, the speaker acknowledges and typographically takes on or mimes the shifting positionality of the
sender and receiver, adopting both positions at different moments in the subject-object dialectic. The portrait of the author
that emerges at the end is one where the focus changes yet remains the same: the poet is the speaker, who is his dog, who is
the reader, who is the poet, who is. . . . Inside is and is not outside; Self is and is not Other; the poet is and is not the poem;
the frame is and is not a defining aspect of the work of art. Thus,
Valente's "Retrato del autor" turns out to be a mirror in which
there is reflected the duplicitous image of Self and of Otherness
that is all artistic creativity. This poetic text offers a portrait of the
dynamics and ongoing process of representation and reception,
of the changing yet constant duality of inside/outside, of fixed
yet broken borders, the reality of illusion, and the "point of danger" that the presence of Otherness presupposes (Meltzer, 215).

One final example deserves mention in regard to Valente's efforts in the matter of (self-)portraiture. The portrait that he offers
up for consideration is not that of a conventional human being,
but rather that of a plaything. The poem is entitled "A Pancho, mi
muñeco" ("To Pancho, My Doll") (Valente, 169–71) and proceeds
from the collection La memoria y los signos.[18] A doll does not
fall within the conventional category of portraiture, in a traditional sense.[19] But in this text, the poet utilizes the image of the
doll as a humanly created object that mirrors the human image,
a soft sculpture of sorts.[20] This elevation of the doll to an art
object—and object of the poem's focus—subverts the doll's supposed minor importance, frames, distances, and defamiliarizes
the speaker's portrait of himself, and provides the reader
with sufficient space to consider the issues of identity, Self/Oth-
er(ness), and representation. The doll as sculpture analogy also
permits the reader to frame the text within a postmodern perspective, since this analogy bring to the forefront the combined
celebration and subversion of artistic goals and ideals in the
figure of the doll. Here, the child's plaything simultaneously is
and is not itself, holding within its soft folds, bulges, and creases
an evocation of classical sculpture. Sculpture's power to represent aesthetic ideals and human (im)perfection is inscribed
upon the doll by the speaker who projects his own misgivings

and humanity's foibles onto it. In turn, the doll sustains sculpture's representational power in ironic fashion, since its pliant substantiality refutes the rigidity of stone but at the same time aptly reflects the human condition. The carnivalization of sculpture in the form of the doll also calls into question the inside/outside dialectic of conventionalized art, and the boundaries that simultaneously keep in and keep out certain forms as either acceptable or unacceptable, according to well-established cultural parameters. Defamiliarization occurs at yet another level and from a different perspective, since a doll would not be considered the traditional play object of a male speaker; it would be more readily identified with a female counterpart.[21] Thus, gender also plays a suggestive role in the reader's consideration of the relationship of the speaker to this particular art object, one that would suggest a questioning of the power, dominance, and control normatively manifested as a replication of the typical and patriarchal order of things. This issue of power and order will take on singular importance in the inversion and subversion that occurs with the portrait and poem's unfolding.

The speaker breathes life into this replica of human nature by opening the poem with an apostrophic apology, one that simultaneously asks forgiveness of, and concedes life to, a seemingly inanimate double of the human being. The use of apostrophe is subversive, in that it calls to the reader's attention the similarities and differences between Pancho and the speaker, and suggests that Pancho's lifelessness may well be a reflection of the speaker's existential plight:[22]

> Perdona, viejo Pancho, el no ser por mi culpa
> más que esto que eres,
> el muñeco de un hombre.
> (Valente 1966, 2.1–3, 169)

(Forgive [me], old Pancho, your not being through my fault, / more than this that you are, / the doll of a man.)

It becomes abundantly clear that the speaker feels dissatisfaction and discomfort in the superior/subordinate type of relationship that is inherent to the human being/doll configuration, and attempts to rationalize his treatment of Pancho, because of his own guilt in regard to such an arrangement:

> Yo te he librado de una muerte temprana
> (Perdóname de nuevo)
> entre la ingenua flor de la juguetería.

Te he librado por pena,
acaso por terror,
acaso por creer
(comprendo que no es cierto)
que me pertenecías.

(Ibid., 2.7–14, 169)

(I have freed you from an early death [Forgive me once again] / among the naive elite of [the] toydom. / I have freed you because of sorrow, / perhaps because of terror, / perhaps because of believing [I comprehend that it is not true] that you belonged to me.)

Pancho is the "person"-age to whom he dedicates his verse, and in the process is the one whose image he attempts to capture: "escribo este poema, copiándote de cerca, del natural. ¡A ti!" ("I write this poem / copying you [fam. sing.] up close, / from life. You! [fam. sing.]") (Ibid., 169). He intuits Pancho's disappointment, for the speaker is certain that the doll would have wished another for his companion, "Esperabas los ojos asombrados de un niño" ("You hoped for the astonished eyes of a little boy"), and the accompanying "grito de alegría" ("shriek of happiness") (Ibid., 170). And he plaintively questions the doll, "¿Pero acaso—contesta— / no me has hecho mirarte / con los ojos remotos de otro niño olvidado?" ("But perhaps—answer [me]—/ haven't you made me look at you / with the eyes of another forgotten little boy?") (Ibid., 170). The doll responds enigmatically with unbroken silence, and the speaker must sadly admit Pancho's wisdom, and his unremitting destiny, which is to exist within a (con)text based on time and work over which he has no control:

Aquel niño no existe.
Acompañas a un hombre
que te obliga a durar
entre papel y días
y libros y sus sueños.

(Ibid., 2.41–45, 170)

(That little boy does not exist. / You accompany a man / who obliges you to endure / among paper and days / and books and his dreams.)

The passage of time marks the doll's faithfulness to his own fate, and to that of the speaker's:

> Qué historia, viejo Pancho,
> durar a duras penas
> de un lunes a otro lunes,
> de un otoño a otro otoño,
> mudar la risa en llanto,
> el llanto en vida nueva,
> los días en más días.
> Te digo que estoy vivo,
> en suma. Ya me entiendes.
>
> (Ibid., 2.46–54, 171)

(What a story, old Pancho, to endure with great difficulty / from one Monday to another Monday, / from one autumn to another autumn, / to change laughter into tears, / tears into new life, / days into more days. / I tell you that I am alive, / in short. Now you [fam. sing.] understand me.)

The speaker then provides a visually oriented image of the doll, one that directs the reader to the metaphorically telling details of the doll's physical presence, including a detailed and feminized glance over the doll's formal attire:

> Tú tienes tu casaca
> con un remiendo sólo,
> tu cuello almidonado
> con su lazo impasible,
> el gorro siempre puesto
> (no te descubras nunca)
> la negra piel de trapo
> y los brazos abiertos
> casi crucificados.
>   Porque también a ti
> te hicieron (¡tan grotesco!),
> hermoso Pancho mío, a nuestra imagen.
>
> (Ibid., 2.55–66, 171)

(You have your long coat / with only one patch, / your starched collar / with its impassive bow, your cap always on [don't ever remove your hat {make your presence known}] / [the] black skin [made] of rag / and [your] arms open / almost crucified. / Because also you [fam. sing.] / they made you [fam. sing.] {so grotesque!}, / beautiful Pancho of mine, in our image.)

The doll's outward clothing stands visibly tattered, the neck is stiff, the head covered, and the speaker admonishes the doll never to reveal himself. The skinlike rag of the body is sullied, and the arms are spread wide, as if in the cruciform manner. The speaker directs his final comment to Pancho, but the reader of the poet-speaker's text feels their impact, since Pancho's image likens itself not only to that of the speaker, but to all those who have been a witness to, or receiver of, the doll's description. The portrait that the speaker has offered of the doll becomes ultimately his own, and that of the reader as well. Pancho stands in as a human effigy and reflects the all-too-human foibles and weaknesses of the human condition. With this closing statement, it remains up to the reader to either open further the frame of reference, namely, to reread the poetic text and ponder the similarities between Pancho and humanity's estate and concomitantly those between the poet/speaker/creator and the other Creator we know as God.[23] The portrait of Pancho may now be viewed as a meditation on the concepts of power(lessness) and (lack of) status that obtain between creator and created, from a verbal as well as existential perspective. The "otro niño olvidado" ("other forgotten little boy") may well take on the identity of the speaker himself, abandoned by an uncaring God, in whose image he himself had been made, a child lost in an uncomprehending and incomprehensible world. The distancing that takes place in the "framing" of Pancho as the powerless *and* powerful Other serves to underscore the problematical inside/outside dialectic that is both affirmed and denied in the process of poetic creation. If at the text's beginning, Pancho as created object plays out a submissive role under his creator's watchful eye and hand, mimicking the traditional (im)balance between the Judeo-Christian God and the created world, at the poem's closing the creator's own self-doubt, feelings of culpability, and worthlessness, cast Pancho's enigmatic silence into the more powerful of the two possible positions. The speaker's meditation on the traditional order of things between dominating and dominated recasts the equation within an entirely reworked existential perspective, where the role of dominated achieves and enjoys moral supremacy. Pancho's silence is framed by the speaker's textuality, but the doll's silence also frames the speaker's text with a distinct moral and existential positionality. Thus, inside becomes outside, and vice versa. The roles of creator and created, subject and object, dominating and dominated, textuality and silence, elide one into another and back again. In the metamorphosis of Self into Other, that which comes to the forefront is the relativity of the inside/outside opposition, and the simultaneous acknowledgment and rupture of the frame of reference and referentiality.[24]

In the texts that have been considered here José Angel Valente confronts the "point of danger" named by Meltzer as inherent to the portrait in a literary text in a manner that is at once similar yet distinct from that of Jaime Gil de Biedma. While Gil de Biedma mimics in linguistic fashion a "trompe d'oeil" painting or allows his textual Self and Other to speak for themselves in a verbally distinctive and descriptive manner, Valente evokes much more distant and enigmatic portraits of the Self/Other dialectic, whether in the temporally framed mirror image, the silent birthday (self-)portrait, or the inanimate Pancho, the softly sculptured innocent reflection of the human condition. But most significantly, it is in and through the description of the piercing silence that permeates the three, that Valente's distanced images "speak for themselves," and for the frames of reference that both separate and unite that which is inside the frame from/to that which is outside. Each poet acknowledges within the framed (self-)portrait the delicate, stressed balance of lack and desire, presence and absence, power and pleasure, surrender and sovereignty, that is played out in the duel of verbal and visual discourse with the verbal and visual image.

6

Pop Goes the (W)Easel: Portraits by and of María Victoria Atencia and Ana Rossetti

As was suggested in the introductory chapter, when an artist, whether verbal or visual, paints a portrait, there comes into play a series of tensions, one of the most important of which is gender. As several critics have already noted, the I/eye of the text traditionally has been male; the so-called male gaze defines the sensory as well as the philosophical point of view of the art piece, and decides the aesthetic and erotic value as well. A male viewer looks upon a passive and mute object of beauty, very often represented by a female, silent, naked body. This naked, silent, female body frequently comes to symbolize art, with its power, its (im)-perfections, and its ineluctable but rancorous, devious, and only momentary submission to the will of the (male) artist and/or viewer.[1] But what happens when the artist is female? How does the concept of the gaze change? There are several possible responses to this query, and all involve the inversion and/or subversion of the traditional patriarchal point of view concerning the subject/object polarity.

When the artist or writer is female, the gaze changes accordingly; the traditional object of that gaze now occupies the position of the (male) subject, the position carrying subtle gender echoes of its former occupant.[2] Late twentieth-century female creators of texts, whether visual or verbal, enter into dialogue with the traditional patriarchal canon, but assert their presence by finding their own voice even in the silence imposed by that very canon. As we saw in the case of Gloria Fuertes and Carmen Martín Gaite, female creative artists have a different manner of seeing and saying, and enjoy "double vision," which leads to double voicing. Women as women, as alien "Other" creatures in patriarchal society, "see with their own eyes," but their place in society, that is to say either subtly or openly marginalized from the discourse(s) of power, forces them to see from the male view-

146

point as well. The female gaze is always and ever underwritten and framed by the male one, the dominant and dominating cultural force in society. This male gaze is ever-present even in its absence, and is inscribed in the decisions of the female writer in regard to the desired object, perspective, means, and codes of representation. Teresa de Lauretis speaks of the code of the cinema, and the problems of signification that ensue when the cinematographer's hand is that of a woman, and controls the camera; it is a female eye that trains a lens on an alien object: "The woman cannot transform the codes; she can only transgress them, make trouble, provoke, pervert, turn the represenation into a trap" (De Lauretis 1984, 35). The process is quite similar when the woman artist is a poet, one who chooses to portray, but from a female perspective. The lens of the mind's I and eye is shadowed by the codes of canonical acceptability, underwritten by the law of the patriarchy.[3]

The feminist critic Dale M. Bauer applies the Bakhtinian concepts of heteroglossia and dialogism to the problem of female writing practices in order to dismantle the tradition of the male gaze: she proposes that "the feminist voice (rather than the male gaze) can construct and dismantle the exclusive community and patriarchal critical discourse. With voice (and not with gaze), female writers can engage in the battle Bakhtin suggests is the basis for community. The opposition between the surveillant gaze and the disruptive (excessive or insistent) voice constitutes the structure of double-voiced texts" (Bauer 1988, 2). For Bauer, "women refuse to be silent bearers of meaning" (Ibid., 3). I believe that the attempt to read women's voice(s) back into a text is an effective strategy with which to confront ekphrastic texts written by women, and by extension, to all artistic texts produced by women.

From a quite different perspective, the male critic W. J. T. Mitchell proposes that the tradition of the male gaze finds a female permutation in the female narrator or speaker as a "painter or keen-sighted viewer, a 'seeing' as opposed to a speaking subject, a dweller in space rather than time" (Mitchell 1989, 97). He views the gaze's change from the traditional male one to an "Other" that is quite female, that permits an intrusion of what he terms an anxiety-ridden process full of ambivalence. Since the gaze of an artistic text has been traditionally male, when a female artist realigns the point of view to a female perspective, the focus necessarily changes. But the male gaze is still present in its absence, and is inscribed in the decisions of the female artist in regard to the desired object, perspective, and means of representation. Thus, the ambivalence. In point of fact, Mitchell sees the traditional male-female dichotomy of ekphrastic art—active, creative subject versus passive, silent, beautiful object—as a central rather than peripheral issue, an emblem of all the O/others that the reader must process completely, if that reader is to make peace with the issue of social and existential Otherness (Caws 1989, 6). Mitchell views ekphrasis as a means of transferring to the realm of literary art sublimated versions of our ambivalence about social Others, whether that Other be of a different gender (i.e., female), race, economic class, religion, social or cultural group (Mitchell 1994, 161–65).

The concept of the female gaze as it relates to portraiture is of interest for yet another reason, in that it brings to the surface the issue of representational convention and metatextuality. As Françoise Meltzer notes in her *Salome and the Dance of Writing*, "the portrait, because it is 'other' to the verbal economy of the text, functions as a good barometer for literature's views on itself, on representation, and on the power of writing" (Meltzer 1987, 1). Also, I might add, it offers an excellent metaliterary commentary on the issue of gender, given that the female gaze is inscribed over the male one. Since women are so often the object of the male gaze in portraits, when a woman takes the place of the traditional male viewer in relation to the view finder, the rules and codes of representation are brought into focus as much as the object of her gaze.

As will be shown in the consideration of poetic texts of María Victoria Atencia and Ana Rossetti, the portrait that a woman artist paints—whether with oil or with words—makes reference to the objective world, to the underlying codes of representation, and to her position as a woman and an artist within that world and within those codes. In other words, through their poems the reader as voyeur / voyeuse flirts with a "bird's-eye view" (bird : slang for "woman") of the poet herself, how she perceives herself as attached or detached from that world, and how she both sees *and* tells of woman's place as simultaneously inside and outside the frame that patriarchal society has constructed for her, as a woman and as a writer, and as the traditional object of male desire and of the male gaze. Spanish women poets of the twentieth century enter into dialogue with the traditional patriarchal canon, but assert their presence by finding their own voice, even in the silence imposed by that very canon.

As several feminist critics have noted, a woman's biography, and most especially the biography of her development as a writer/artist, more often than not cannot be rendered in straight lines and in the direct flowering of creative urges, since a woman's biography is so often attuned and tied to the rhythms of domestic and familial concerns. Thus, her distinct life rhythms may put her out of synchrony with other (male) writers of her chronological and biological generation. The two poets whose work is to be considered here—María Victoria Atencia (b. 1931) and Ana Rossetti (b. 1950)—began to publish with a steady cadence in the mid-1970s, although Atencia is at least a generation older than Rossetti. In their poetry each gives special attention to the visual/verbal connection, providing for their readers portraits of varying styles and formats.[4] And each sets about breaking the frame in regard to the concept of ekphrasis itself, by positing new ways for the verbal to arrest the spatiality of the visual and to transmute new visual realities of the current era into verbal approximations. María Victoria Atencia's portraits are deceptively straightforward, and belie the poet's inclination to see into, through, and beyond the surface object of her attention and desire. Late twentieth-century culture is the backdrop, frame, and focus of her poetic texts. Ana Rossetti, for her part, enters into the frame of reference of pop culture and advertising, dueling and dialoguing head-on with the images, verbal and visual, that are the norm for twentieth-century post-modern culture, in all its variation and self-parody.

In her recently published *Conversaciones y poemas: La nueva poesía femenina española en castellano* (1991), (*Conversations and Poems: New Women's Poetry of Spain in Spanish*) Sharon Keefe Ugalde identifies María Victoria Atencia as one of the "newer" lyric voices currently being heard in the Spanish-speaking world, in spite of the fact that this poet was born five years prior to the start of the Civil War. Atencia's work may be divided into two distinct epochs: the first is comprised of three early works, produced between 1953 and 1961, after which there is a pause of fifteen years. Her work began to appear again in 1976, with the publication of *Marta & María* (*Martha and Mary*).[5] Atencia herself noted to Ugalde that in a 1985 essay she was associated with the first generation of post-Civil War writers, while because of her age, it would seem to be more logical to group her with the second generation. But because of the style of her more recent work, she herself would tend to see some affinity with those poets of the "novísimos" generation.

In the interview conducted by Ugalde with Atencia, the poet

disagrees with Guillermo Carnero, who perceives what he terms "una persistente ocultación de las motivaciones reales y bio-gráficas" ("a persistent hiding of the real and biographical moti-vations").[6] Atencia counters that "es una ocultación que se limita a prescindir de la anécdota. Pero por un juego de espejos, siem-pre se me puede ver en el fondo del poema" ("it is a hiding that limits itself to dispense with anecdote. But by means of a game of mirrors, I can always be seen in the background of the poem") (Ugalde 1991, 15). As we shall see in looking at several of her poetic texts, the poet is indeed behind the glass of the mirror, behind the lens of the female gaze of her poetic texts, framed and reflected by her unique view of the world. The facet which intrigues most in regard to the poetry of María Victoria Atencia is that area which I will call her "portrait" poems, implicitly or explicitly ekphrastic in nature, where the poet attempts to cap-ture in words an image or portrait, much as the visual artist would do through a predetermined sitting, or merely a quick sketch, or a candid family photograph. Atencia noted in her con-versation with Ugalde that she has always been fascinated by painting:

Creo que a ella [la pintura] le debo un cierto sentido de la composi-ción, de las distancias, de la indagación de eso que llaman el "punto de fuga" (que en la poesía rara vez es uno solo), del color y de sus gradaciones, del equilibrio entre volúmenes. La pintura me enseñó y sigue enseñándome a mirar, para ver el conjunto como una in-stantánea manifestación perdurable. Muchos de mis poemas deben a la pintura ese aire como de *flash* (Ibid., 4).

(I believe that I owe to painting a certain sense of composition, of distances, of inquiry of that which is known as the "vanishing point" (which in poetry rarely is one alone), of color and of its gradations, of the balance between masses. Painting taught me and continues to teach me to look at, to see the entirety as a lasting instantaneous manifestation. Many of my poems owe to painting this look of [pho-tographic] *flash*.)

The "punto de fuga" ("vanishing point")[7] which Atencia sig-nals draws special attention to the concepts of perspective, fram-ing, surface perception versus concrete reality, illusion, and the relationship among the portrait, its producer, and its viewer. Moreover, Atencia's parenthetical comment that "rarely in po-etry is there only one [vanishing point]" emphasizes that in the contemplation of her poems the reader is free, and even encouraged, to use more than one perspective, visual or philosophical, to appreciate the subtlety of their construction and message. The suggestion of *flash* or freeze-frame instantaneity insinuates that the poet views her verbal portraits as a conflation of two distinct modes of portraiture, that of the formal sitting favored for painting, and the spontaneous or unposed image captured in candid photography and in film such as cinéma vérité. The suggestion of both photography and film invites a broadening of the term *ekphrasis* to include twentieth-century modes of artistic production, and these two media will be dealt with more fully in the final chapter on the poetry of Pere Gimferrer and Jenaro Talens.

Ugalde points out that several of Atencia's critics attribute the poet's singular feminine voice to what they term "el abandono del entorno doméstico a favor del cultural" ("the abandonment of the domestic milieu in favor of the cultural") (Ugalde 1991, 6). Atencia herself denies the apparent abandonment of the domestic sphere, preferring to see it as painted in more diluted hues. As will be demonstrated in the analysis of several of Atencia's poetic texts, the poet utilizes the female, domestic sphere as the point of departure (or as women's "vanishing point"?) for a consideration of a woman's place and voice; and of the conventions that determine human behavior, customs, and habits whether within the confines of the private or public domain. Thus, in Atencia's work, the domestic sphere overcomes its own cloistering, to take on a more highly charged value. The domestic acts as a catalyst for the poet to consider women's space and place, relative to all human existence.

A two-stanza poem entitled "Muñecas" ("Dolls"), taken from her pivotal *Marta & María* and which was reprinted in *Ex Libris*, is a case in point. In it the speaker, presumably female, offers a portrait of herself through the playthings of her childhood.[8] The setting is domestic, and the voice of the speaker projects a tone of intimacy by utilizing the dolls onto which she projects her innermost feelings. She speaks to them directly, opening the poem with "Tenéis un renovado oficio cada noche, / muñecas que pasasteis un día por mis manos" ("You [fam. pl.] have a renewed function each night / you dolls who passed one day through my hands.") Her description of the dolls at first glance seems to be based on sight and on the effect that this sight produces in her, when she compares them to "un vaso de fresca naranjada reciente" ("a glass of fresh, recent orangeade"). The speaker also makes note of their "tirabuzones lacios de estropajo teñido" ("languid corkscrew curls made of tinted rag") and "ojos de aguas azules"("eyes of blue waters"). Just as for other females who are praised for their physical beauty, the dolls call the attention of this speaker when she praises their hair and eye color, both (stereo)typical characteristics of female and feminine beauty. The speaker sees herself as having changed places with them, and wishes to recapture the sense of innocence and security of which the dolls are an emblem.

> Casi humanas y mías, mi juego de otro tiempo,
> soy vuestro juego ahora, casi vuestra y humana.
> Esto quiere la vida: más vida poseída,
> vivida, incorporada.
> Entregada a vosotras, pudierais trasladarme
> para siempre a los años del cine de Shirley.
>
> (Atencia 1976, 30)

(Almost human and mine, my game of another time, / I am your [fam. pl.] game now, almost yours and human. Life wants this: more possessed life, / lived, embodied. / Handed over to you [fam. pl.], you [fam. pl.] could transport [move] me / forever to the movie years of Shirley.)

There is quite an abrupt shift between the first and last stanza, in that the first strophe paints a portrait of warmth, caring, security, and shared identity between the speaker and the dolls, and underscores the affirmative aspects of the relationship. But in the second stanza the fact of possession takes on a more negative inflection. And the word "casi" ("almost") acts as a fulcrum upon which the balance shifts to the more negative connotation. "Casi humanas y mías" ("Almost human and mine") generously bestows humanity upon the dolls who in the past were the beloved playthings of the adult speaker, and thus they are able to to share an affirmative, vital part of the speaker's identity and being. But in the chiasmuslike inversion that follows, the statement "casi vuestra y humana" ("almost yours [fam. pl.] and human"), has the completely opposite effect, since it withdraws the same quality of humanness from the speaker. The ambiguous placement of "casi" inserts the suggestion of woman's reification, "soy vuestro juego ahora, casi vuestra y humana" ("I am your [fam. pl.] game now, almost yours [fam. pl.] and human"). The "almost" may refer to the inversion of possession—now the speaker is almost but not quite fully possessed by the dolls—and/or it may refer to the speaker being "almost" but not quite human. Simone de Beauvoir's oft-quoted statement comes easily to mind: "There are two kinds of people: human beings and women. And when women start acting like human beings, they are accused of trying to be men," the underlying message of course being that in the patriarchal view, women are not really totally human beings after all. They are just women.

The milieu that is depicted at the end of the text switches from the domestic to that of a wider and more public cultural sphere, that of the wonder years of Hollywood. The speaker of the text sees herself as handed over to the dolls, just as they were handed over to her when she herself was a child. The last intertextual reference to the world of cinema, I presume, is to the curly-haired darling of the silver screen, Shirley Temple, a perfectly manufactured (. . . and manufactured-ly perfect) female icon created by the movie tycoons of yesteryear. The girl-child Hollywood star of movie fame portrays and projects the patriarchally inspired image of the perfect female: innocence, beauty, childlike submission, perfect obedience, cheerfulness, nonthreatening sexuality, and lack of control over herself and her life.

In this poetic text there is a suggestive transparency evident in the portrait that the speaker offers to us. The female gaze is shadowed by the male one. For in the poem a woman looks upon her own youth, and demonstrates how it was manipulated by the images created for and of the girl-child and woman, through various cultural conventions and also through the lens of Hollywood. The final comment is ironic, since we as readers now view the female speaker as aware, whether in a conscious or subconscious manner, of the fact that her portrait of the dolls may also be viewed as a portrait of herself. Just as they were her playthings in fantasies of her own making, she in turn may be a plaything in someone else's celluloid fantasy, that someone else most probably male. We as readers are both inside and outside the several frames and codes by which the text, the speaker, and all women are bound.

The concept of the female gaze is played out on several different levels in a poem entitled "Godiva en blue jean" ("Godiva in Blue Jeans") taken from Atencia's *El mundo de M.V.* (*The World of M.V.*) (1978), which was reprinted in her *Ex Libris*.[9] Just as in "Muñecas," there is an incredibly beautiful interweaving of the domestic and a much wider cultural milieu, but here the speaker reaches back in historical time to a now legendary epoch, and allows two different temporal eras to coexist in one portrait. In the first strophe the speaker portrays and ultimately takes on the persona of the legendary and lovely Lady Godiva (1040–80), wife

of Leofric, Lord of Coventry, who meets the challenge of providing protection for those she loves in inimitable fashion:

> Cuando sobrepasemos la raya que separa
> la tarde de la noche, pondremos un caballo
> a la puerta del sueño y, tal lady Godiva,
> puesto que así lo quieres, pasearé mi cuerpo
> —los postigos cerrados—por la ciudad en vela . . .
>
> (Ibid., 79)

(When we pass over the line that separates / afternoon from night,
we will put a horse / at the door of sleep, and, just as Lady Godiva, /
since that is how you want it, I will show off my body /—the window
shutters closed—throughout the city at vigil . . .)

Popular legend claims that Lady Godiva met her husband's challenge and rode naked through the town of Coventry, to impel
him to lower the heavy taxes that he had levied on the townspeople. They were advised of her intentions in advance, and so
all closed their doors and shutters in order to protect their lady's
honor. Her nakedness was thus very creatively covered by an
inversion and subversion of the patriarchal order, in both senses
of the word. The only man who looked became known as Peeping
Tom. The speaker offers to the reader (Peeping Tom?) the tantalizing possibility of viewing her "forbidden" sexuality/textuality
by (un)covering her nakedness in much the same manner as Lady
Godiva; the speaker and her legendary role model both obey and
transgress the power of the word. The speaker is and is not Lady
Godiva, with the subversive "tal" ("just as") (un)covering the link
between them. Opening the text in first-person plural, the
speaker bids the receiver(s) of her version of Lady Godiva's exploits to enter into the oneiric, atemporal, fused world of past,
present, and future. This/these receiver(s) may be Lord Leofric
(Lady Godiva's husband), the speaker's own husband, Peeping
Tom, the townspeople, the speaker herself divided into I and
Other, the poet and her creative power as ally and alien Other,
or the reader(s) of the poetic text. The speaker makes oblique
reference to the act of framing in her mention of "los postigos
cerrados" ("the closed window shutters"), the voluntarily sealed
shutters which close in/out Lady Godiva in regard to her place
in her world, but in inverted, ironic fashion. For it is she who is
outside, naked, yet covered and protected, and inside, by her very
act of obedience to her husband's heavy-handedness. And in
her act of naked obedience, she covers and protects her beloved

people, circumventing the cloistering and powerlessness that are normally woman's lot. Her surrender to the rule and order of patriarchy, emblemized by her nakedness, (dis)covers her true sovereignty and nobility, that of her character, in that she was willing to entrust her honor to her vassals, those whom she herself was obliged to nourish and protect because of her elevated social status.

One possible reading is that the reader takes on the role of Peeping Tom, whose gaze is framed by the open/closed shutter; in the very act of reading the text, the reader eyes (I's and ayes) the inverted and subverted patriarchal order of creativity, where the poet and speaker are female, and look upon the naked female body of Lady Godiva and also upon the exposed body of the text, to give a new reading of woman as both subject *and* object. The woman speaker subverts the patriarchally imposed law of silence and obedience, merely by telling Lady Godiva's story of silence and obedience. Moreover, the speaker subverts yet another patriarchal order, by taking control of her poem, the body of her text, and the text of her body. She chooses to venture out at night, to become a "lady of the night" as it were, thus suggesting will, decisiveness, and the freedom to determine how she will live, including the way in which she will attain her sexual and textual fulfillment.[10] The speaker elects to invert the roles of both Lady Godiva and her husband in her poetic text. Lord Leofric did not want or expect his wife to obey his order; she did so anyway, sallying forth nude, and in broad daylight, in this manner manifesting explicit obedience as well as implicit disobedience. In contrast, the speaker first ventures forth at night, presumably with her husband's blessing, help, and encouragement:" . . . pondremos un caballo / a la puerta del sueño y, tal Lady Godiva, / puesto que así lo quieres, pasearé mi cuerpo /—los postigos cerrados—por la ciudad en vela . . ." (" . . . we will put a horse / at the door of sleep, and, just as Lady Godiva, / since that is how you want it, I will show off my body /—the window shutters closed—throughout the city at vigil. . . .). In the speaker's case (self-)[made] image and representation are the objective, and she obeys only her own creative urges.

After a pause, the speaker focuses on a different level of portrayal by both asserting and negating a level of metaphor of which the reader may or may not have been aware, when she states

> No, no es eso, no es eso; mi poema no es eso.
> Sólo lo cierto cuenta.
>
> (Atencia 1978, 79)

(No, that is not it, that is not it; that is not my poem. / Only certainty counts.)

With these evocative lines of verse, she simultaneously establishes and ruptures the frames of portrayal, representation, and textuality, and the codes which support those (denied) realities. With the "No, no es eso" ("No, that is not it") the speaker declares a divided and complex Self, who is part woman and part degendered poet.[11] There is also a suggestion of several models of femaleness and femininity, all of them validated within the poem: free-spirited sexual being, legend, woman of the night, (dis)obedient wife, poet, wife as equal partner, homemaker, liberated woman.[12] Seeing and telling of Lady Godiva's acts from a woman's perspective have meaning on several levels of interpretation, in what they (dis)cover about a woman's place and about a woman's power to exist both inside and outside the limits imposed upon her, whether in a domestic or public sphere, the world at large, or within the framework of her own (self-)[made] image and creativity.

The milieu shifts in the following lines of verse to a more contemporary venue, where the speaker seemingly disengages from her previous identification with Lady Godiva. But her disavowal only serves to strengthen the bond between the two creative women, one a Lady, the other a poet. In her own way, the latter repeats the acts of creativity and love of her legendary model. Like Lady Godiva she now ventures forth during the day, and provides for her loved ones a more "conventional" fare of "amor y pan y fruta"("love and bread and fruit"). And, I would add, poetry as well:

> Saldré de pantalón vaquero (hacia las nueve
> de la mañana), blusa del "Long Play" y el cesto
> de esparto de Guadix (aunque me araña a veces
> las rodillas). Y luego, de vuelta del mercado,
> repartiré en la casa amor y pan y fruta.
>
> (Atencia 1978, 79)

(I will go out in cowboy pants [around nine / in the morning], "Long Play [brand] blouse and the basket / of esparto from Gaudix [although it scratches at times / my knees]. And then, upon returning from the market, / I will apportion in the house love and bread and fruit.)

The speaker insists on the sameness of her Otherness in regard to Lady Godiva, in a very "telling fashion," that of inversion and subversion. She has chosen a legendary, historical figure of English rather than Spanish origin, in order to ponder her own image and the image of women in general from a defamiliarized position; Godiva was a legendary noblewoman, whose life story would seem to have little applicability to twentieth-century women's concerns. And in this second half of the poem, she refers to herself as clothed rather than naked. The act of "clothing" is repeated in the form of the poem, in that the poet makes uses of parentheses in the second stanza; these marks of punctuation serve to close in as well as close out, much as Lady Godiva's nudity did in the first stanza. Just as the text of Lady Godiva's naked body was both read and not read by the townspeople and by Peeping Tom because of its lack of clothing, the reading of the body of the poet's text is also unsettled because of the rupture of the parentheses. But it is fascinating to note that the speaker refers to her own clothing in both English and Spanish. "Blue jeans" of the title is followed by "pantalón vaquero" ("cowboy pants"), which is followed by "blusa del "Long Play"" ("Long Play" [brand] blouse"), the last example being a combination of the two. In addition, she resolutely demythologizes her function as a woman and as a poet in a very postmodern turn, by positioning herself within the conventional framework of women's relationship to domestic tasks, in this case that of shopping for food. Also, the speaker places herself within a popular and trite boundary by her insistence on brand names, "blusa del "Long Play" and "cesto de esparto de Guadix" ("basket of esparto from Guadix") thus lending a quite postmodern cast to the body of her text and of the text of her body.[13]

Just like the fabled Lady Godiva, the speaker goes home after her adventure in and with the world, to parcel out according to her ability the stuff of life—love, bread, and fruit—all substances essential to a family and community's welfare. And by offering the present text to the reader, the poem's speaker extends the implicit gift of poetry as well, and thus subverts woman's traditional silent role as object of the male gaze enclosed within the domestic sphere. Just as in the case of her seeing and telling Lady Godiva's story, here the female poet subverts the patriarchal order simply by seeing and telling her own function and story inside and outside the domestic space. This poetic text communicates on a variety of levels, and its power resides in how the poet through her speaker puts into play the concept of the gaze from both a male and female perspective, in the problematic presence of women inside and outside the patriarchal order, as well as in how it reveals the rules and codes of conventional representation.

There is a powerful oscillation between male and female, subject and object, past and present, legendary and historical time, she and I, interior and exterior, domestic and official, noble and popular, private and public, covered and uncovered, sexual and textual. The portrait that the speaker presents explicitly establishes the relationship between the legendary figure of Lady Godiva and the laws which govern her behavior, and how she creatively subverts the laws of the patriarchal order simply by obeying them. Thus, the poem presents to the reader several different portraits at once: the female I/eye of the text gazes upon the winsome and spunky Lady Godiva, by gazing upon an image of herself in dream time as well as in her ordinary daily life. But it is also privy from a woman's perspective to a rendering of a portrait of female creativity, and the manner in which it reacts to, revises, inverts, and subverts the conventions of the patriarchy. The poet's portrait of Lady Godiva is also a portrait of the poet herself, in the act of creating the portrait of the Other, who is and is not the Self. As a consequence of this portrayal, the poet allows the reader, whether male or female, to ponder wider theoretical and philosophical questions concerning the social, cultural, and aesthetic codes that determine virtually all of our behavior whether public, private, or creative. In the process, she also allows the reader to catch a glimpse of the female hand and eye behind the framing of that portrait, and how the female hand and eye must first and foremost be fluent in two orders, both the patriarchal and secondly, the matriarchal. The female gaze then may be given voice; but once again, it is a double vision and voicing that (dis)covers the trace of the patriarchy by its very nature.

Atencia utilizes other strategies in order to highlight the female gaze in her other texts. For example, "Mujeres de la casa" ("Women of the House") also from *Marta & María* is reminiscent of "Muñecas" in that the speaker chooses an intimate domestic scene, and contrasts the present with the past from the perspective of a first-person speaker. But in this text, the speaker addresses older women who were a part of her girlish world:

> Si alguna vez pudieseis volver hasta encontrarme
> (bordados trajes, blancas tiras, encañonados
> filos para el paseo, palomas de maíz,
> 28 de noviembre, calle del Angel, I),

mujeres de la casa,
cómo os recibiría, ahora que os comprendo.

(Atencia 1984, 31)

(If some time you [fam. pl.] could return even find me / [embroidered gowns, white strips of cloth, fluted / edges for the promenade, pop-corn, / 28th of November, Angel Street, number 1], women of the house, / how I would receive you [fam. pl.], now that I understand you [fam. pl.])

She sets her decidedly female gaze upon the women who peo-pled her childhood, unnamed and heretofore unsung household women, framing them in several different ways. First she dis-tances them in time and memory, but the speaker remains mute on how the distancing took place. Did the women move on to other households or perhaps die off, or did the speaker herself "move away" in a physical, geographical and psychological sense? Secondly, the act of framing is underscored through the distinctive use of parentheses, within whose confines the speaker cloisters objects associated with their identity as women, and cloisters the women themselves within a certain house with a specific address and a calendar date to represent their specifi-cally domestic "place" in her life.[14] The portrait of the women is also framed by the speaker's admission of her own internal change, from a past distanced viewpoint, perhaps based on a rejection of these women's choices, priorities, and social reality, to present understanding of, and receptivity to, their given role in society in the final line of verse. There is a gentle inversion of roles here, since presumably, it is the speaker who "moved away," but now it is she who beseeches those selfless, loving, unnamed, and voiceless women of her youth to return to her. But in the text, she herself longs to return to them, in a specific place and time, to return to the security of childhood, but with a deeply felt appreciation for these women, garnered from her own experience as an adult woman.

In the second, closing strophe, the speaker acknowledges the value and importance of the anonymous women of her early life, those who willingly awakened from deep slumber

y espantabais mi miedo deslizando las manos
por mis trenzas tirantes, me limpiabais los mocos
y endulzabais mi siesta con miel de Frigiliana.

(Atencia 1984, 31)

(and scared away my fear sliding your [fam. pl.] hands / over my taut braids, / you [fam. pl.] helped me to blow my nose / and you [fam. pl.] sweetened my siesta with Frigiliana [brand] honey.)

Just as in "Muñecas" in the final verses of this text Atencia inverts the given order, to reveal a different portrait of the older women in the speaker's life and the speaker herself: "Dejadme ir a vosotras, que quiero, blandamente, / patear como entonces vuestro animal regazo" ("[You [fam. pl.] Allow me to go to you [fam. pl.], since I want to, tenderly, / tread as [back] then your [fam. pl.] animallike lap"). The adult woman reexamines the role of traditional women, and values what has not been given public value in patriarchal society, namely, the worth of nurturing, teaching, and keeping safe, healthy, and clean the developing child. Implicitly, she also makes reference to their role as Earth Mothers, in naming their "animal regazo" ("animallike lap"). The speaker longs to go to them, to leave behind her adult public, independent persona, to climb into their laps, and to feel the sense of security that they represent; and only now can she honestly admit this need. Once again, the poet reveals a much broader cultural milieu, by allowing a simple domestic scene to act as an emblem for a universal reality, that is, the devalued position and worth of anonymous traditional women. This is a complicated portrait of those women, the speaker herself, and how the speaker's female gaze finds a voice and struggles to speak out and come to terms with her own conflicted set of values in regard to the changing role of women in modern society.[15]

The collection *El mundo de M. V.* includes a poem of the same title which may be found in the section named "Tiempo para tejer, tiempo para destejer" ("Time to Weave, Time to Unweave"). This rubric suggests a constellation of intertextual possibilities, such as the story of Penelope and her suitors, the divinely allotted Fates' office of weaving and cutting off of humanity's destiny, the mythical weaving contest of Minerva and Arachne, or of Ariadne's gift of a ball of thread to Theseus, which when unrolled, would aid him in escaping the Minotaur's maze.[16] In the poetic text entitled "El mundo de M. V." the poet is only spectrally present in the suggestive initials of the title; the first-person speaker weaves herself, her I/eye, her gaze, her voice, into various art forms, including that of tapestry, which she names directly in the closing lines of the first stanza:

puedo llegarme al verde y al azul de los bosques
de Aubusson y sentarme al borde de un estanque
cuyas aguas retiene el tapiz en sus hilos.

(Atencia 1984, 63)

(I can arrive at the green and at the blue of the forests / of Aubusson
and sit down on the edge of a pond / whose waters the tapestry retain
in its threads.)

Aubusson, a town in central France, was famous for its tapestry
and carpet manufacture dating from the fifteenth century. The
speaker posits an inversion in that she is not looking at a tapestry
which holds within its threads the image of the shimmering
blue-green shades of water; rather, she seats herself in a bucolic
scene which conjures up the image depicted on a tapestry. Thus,
the speaker is thrice framed: once within the pastoral scene of
woods and water, secondly within the tapestry's evocation of that
pastoral vision, and third within the speaker's own imagination.
But the speaker takes the representation one step further, in that
the tapestry in and of itself becomes a metaphor of woman's
creative capacity framed by the domestic sphere. The anonymous act of weaving—her story (truth and/or fiction?), her fate,
her destiny, her salvation—opens a space for female individuality and originality, framing and legitimizing it within a domestic
milieu. The speaker states in the second and final stanza:

Me asomo a las umbrías de cuanto en esta hora
dispongo y pueda darme su reposo: también
este mundo es el mío: entreabro la puerta
de su ficción y dejo que sobre este añadido
vegetal de mi casa, por donde los insectos
derivan su zumbido, se instale una paloma.

(Ibid.)

(I look out to the shady places of all of which at this hour / is at my
disposal and can give me its repose: also / this world is mine: I set
ajar the door / of its fiction and I allow upon this vegetable supplement to my house, through where the insects / derive their buzzing,
that a dove install itself.)

Once again, the domestic is imbued with a metaphoric and a
more highly charged cultural value. In this text, the domestic
encourages and supports a metapoetic interpretation. The

speaker takes in her world and by taking it in visually and mentally, naming it, also participates in creating it anew through language, weaving it into a personal, female worldview. Many elements are intimately connected to the traditional female sphere of earth and domesticity, such as "casa" ("house"), "puerta" ("door"), "me asomo" ("I look out"), and the vegetable class. The flight of (female) creativity is portrayed by the beautiful dove who alights and is woven into the speaker's gaze and voice. The speaker evokes the graceful dove as an emblem of female creativity, and also puts into practice her own creative nature by that very act of naming, the act of weaving her own story into the fabric of poetic verse from the point of view of a first-person speaker. This speaker casts her glance upon the dove from the vantage point of her "casa," her space, her place in the world, from where she gazes upon the public world from the female perspective, separate yet related to the domestic sphere.

The final two poems, "Museo" ("Museum") and "'Eva'" ("'Eve'"), from Atencia's *Pared contigua* (*Adjoining Wall*) (1989) play on and with the female gaze through yet other verbal strategies. In the first, "Museo," the speaker's muse and the speaker herself "muse" upon the persona of the museum exhibit "object"; through this object she inverts and subverts the traditional Pygmalion ploy of the male artist who brings the (female) object of his desire to life. In this text, it remains unclear whether the speaker is solely the observer, or whether the I/eye of the text takes on and metamorphoses into the "she" of the museum object herself. Both readings are possible, subverting yet reinforcing each other, Self eliding into Other and back again in the two elongated sentences of which the entire poem is composed. Whichever the reading, the Woman brings *herself* to life, abruptly awakening to her own desire, to her artistic surroundings, and to the heavy burden that beauty imposes upon those who possess it, from the perspective of those who have beauty as a personal characteristic, and of those who appreciate it and thus want to make it their own and control it in others:

> El zaguán conocido, las muelles escaleras
> de olorosa madera antigua que hago, silenciosa, crujir
> —esquivada la guardia de abotonadas botas—,
> su luz velada ofrecen a quien no la precisa;
> a quien supo ya el dulce pesar de la caricia que la
> hermosura deja
> y—despierta de súbito—deseante se viste e

interrumpe la noche
se echa a la calle, avanza, y vuelve a aquel museo en el
que estuvo expuesta.

(Atencia 1989, 42)

(The known portico, the luxurious steps / of fragrant antique wood
that I [fem.], noiseless, make to creak /—dodged the guard of but-
toned boots—, / they offer their veiled light to the person who does
not specify [need] it; / to the person who found out already the sweet
sorrow of the caress that / beauty leaves / and—suddenly awake {the
[fem.] person}—full of desire she clothes herself and / interrupts the
night / she bursts onto the street, advances, and returns to that museum in which / she was exhibited.)

It is fascinating to note that once again Atencia draws the reader's
attention to the spaces of female enclosure, here, for example,
choosing to focus on a museum's architectural details—"el za-
guán" ("the portico") and "las muelles escaleras / de olorosa
madera antigua" ("the luxurious stairs / of fragrant antique
wood")—to suggest how female beauty is both exalted yet imprisoned by patriarchally imposed standards.[17] The female I of the
first part of the text gazes upon this engineered beauty in silence,
but the speaker's description of that silence in and of itself subverts the message's intent. This I/eye of the first half of the poem
gazes upon and may (or may not. . . .) depersonalize herself into
becoming the female object of artistic desire in the second half.
Another possible reading is that the female speaker portrays
women's existence as a containment made bearable by the imagination. For example, a female museum-goer enjoys the female
version of Walter Mitty's daydreaming, by imagining the escape
of the imprisoned art object into the night. She thus projects her
desire to escape her boundaries onto the (in)animate object.[18]
   In an alternate reading, the (un)reified woman, as both (art)
object and subject, brings herself to life, clothes herself, and escapes from the framework of her patriarchally structured existence. The speaker is silent concerning what ensues between exit
and reentry to the patriarchal order, but the verbs "se echa"
("she bursts out"), "avanza" ("she advances"), and "vuelve" ("she
returns") all suggest will, decisiveness, and freedom of movement. Significantly, the term "deseante" ("full of desire") opens
the poem to the idea of sexual freedom and fulfillment. The
object of beauty escapes into the night to possess it and to be
possessed by it fully, of her own volition, and for her own pleasure. This desire and decision to "take back the night" evokes

the traditional spaces of the "fallen woman," spaces such as cafés, follies, theaters, and brothels (Pollock 1978, 72 and ff.) The after-hours museum escapee subverts the patriarchally imposed negative connotation of the fallen woman, by rising to the challenge of self-determination.

The object of artistic desire ultimately returns to the very site/ sight in which she was framed in the first place: "vuelve a aquel museo en el/que estuvo expuesta" ("she returns to that museum in / which she was exhibited"). The speaker slips and slides in (im)perceptible dreamlike fashion between a perspective of "I" and "she," and of course brings to the forefront the concepts of framing, woman as object, and the codes and conventions of power, conduct, portrayal and representation. There is an undercurrent of conflict and transgression(s), since the female gaze, attitude, and subject/object of this text challenge the male one to which it responds. The challenge resides in the female object bringing herself to life, clothing herself and thus denying voyeuristic, impersonal pleasure to those who wish to possess her through the gaze, purposefully overstepping the boundaries of her enclosure, going out into the world, and then returning on her own terms. The female nude who brings herself to life may indeed also be a metaphor for the independence of any art work: the artist cannot retain possession, since the act of creation is only the first step in the process of reception and interpretation that exists between that artwork and its observer. The artwork takes on an independent life, once freed from the gaze and hand of its creator.

In the final poem, the title "'Eva'" appears within quotes, with a reference to Auguste Rodin as an epigraph set off to the right margin. Thus "Eva" is the object of the patriarchal gaze, from both a biblical and sculptural perspective. But Atencia once again revises the patriarchal code, by telling and retelling Eve's story, framing her anew within a text of her own creation, yet simultaneously liberating her from her representation as "Other" from the male perspective.[19] Atencia continues the tradition of framing Eve with the distinctively typographical annotation of the title; but the poet's frame also makes reference to Eve as the subject of Rodin's object of art . Traditionally Eve had been framed—in both senses of the word—by her role in the male version of the creation story. Here the poet takes on a first-person persona, and rewrites the story of Eve, "her story"/"herstory" and frees her from captivity in stone, that of patriarchal tradition and that of Rodin's sculpture:

Huyo y viene conmigo la misma lumbre cómplice
o sombra de aquel árbol interpuesto a unos ojos
que aguardaban mi paso como desconociéndome,
y era yo tan sabida, tan usual, tan propia
que he de fingir pudor y sorpresa: ocultándome
    para que no cesara
aquella luz que hacía deseables mis pasos
hacia un lecho de doblegadas hojas.

(Atencia 1989, 43)

(I flee and the same complicit glow comes with me / or shadow of that tree interposed to some eyes / which awaited my step as if disavowing me, and it was I [fem.] so clever, so usual, so my own / that I am to feign modesty and surprise: hiding myself / so that it does not cease / that light that made desirable my steps / toward a bed of bent leaves.)

One reading of this text is that Eve herself is the first-person speaker who flees (women have so much from which to flee) and is accompanied in her quest by a complicitous shaft of light or darkness, depending on the angle and/or gender of the gaze. The speaker casts a new light on her own story, (dis)covering a different version of her Otherness, simultaneously both inside and outside the official frame of reference. The text is saturated with feminine and female "norms," such as flight, modesty, and the show of emotion; these are subverted by the speaker's admission of feigning, thus giving credence to her own will and determination to circumvent patriarchal enclosure and domination in whatever way she can. The woman flees from the imprisonment of monological representation, and through the text, the poet allows the Rodin sculpture titled "'Eva'" to speak for itself/herself, to find a safer, hidden, protected place, to work out her own story, with her own light, within the self-imposed boundaries of her own sexuality/textuality. But in so doing, she underscores the presence of several frames that both include and exclude "Other" versions of the original Woman. The portrait of Eve/Everywoman once again gives a glimpse of the creative woman behind the portrait. The representation of the woman, or simply Woman, (which one??? Eve? which Eve? the speaker? the poet? the female artist? the female model for the artist? the female reader?) points to the frames and their fissures, in the very act of portraying the woman/Woman who flees enclosure in a portrait that portrays her as "Other."

Both the power and pleasure of María Victoria Atencia's portrait poems reside in the manner in which they are able to both obey and transgress the patriarchal rules for the representation of woman as object, woman as Other. In the process, the domestic and the popular take on the value of metaphor, so that the poet may ponder much broader and more profound issues, issues that pertain to the cultural and social milieu of the waning years of the twentieth century. In addition, the portraits of women and of Woman that this female poet offers to her readers ultimately may be read as a portrait of the poet herself as artist, who through her texts gives vision and voice to her own struggles with the subject/object dialectic, creativity, originality, submission to conventions of any ilk, and to the re-vision and subtle subversion of those same conventions. Similarly, the poet contemplates simultaneous models and patterns of female and feminine identity, and allows the reader to draw private conclusions about those models and patterns, and how they do or do not coincide with the ones determined by the patriarchy for women. Her texts thus reveal an alluring and enigmatic blend of the premeditated and staged portrait in oil and the freeze-frame flash photograph. The "vanishing point" is to be found in the reader, who must (dis)-cover and resolve the distance between the two radically opposed forms and views of portraiture, both of which are informed and framed by the male gaze. In the final analysis, Atencia's verbal portraits of women within their designated domestic sphere represent the power of representation itself, and how the choices that obtain in the act of representation communicate an ideology of power, both in what is portrayed and what is left out.

While María Victoria Atencia utilizes the domestic sphere in order to contemplate other existential issues and the power of representation, Ana Rossetti resolutely undertakes the task of dismantling and subverting several modes of discourse sacred to Western culture.[20] The portraits that Rossetti offers both of herself as artist, creator, and woman, and of others also participate in the dialogic struggle of power and pleasure as well as surrender and sovereignty, and typify clearly the previously stated proposition of Teresa de Lauretis in regard to the female gaze: "The woman cannot transform the codes; she can only transgress them, make trouble, provoke, pervert, turn the representation into a trap" (de Lauretis 1984, 35). Rossetti's texts enact the game of ambush and entrapment, and are deliciously wicked in their mode, purpose, perspective, and framing of image and representation, since they depend upon a double vision and a concomitant double voicing in order to simultaneously celebrate and call into question prevailing standards of beauty, culture, sacredness, sexuality, and textuality.[21] As has already been noted by several other critics, Rossetti's poetry is characterized by a bipolar movement, wherein her speakers simultaneously approach yet alienate themselves from traditional positions and modes of discourse (Ugalde 1989–90, 24).[22] In this regard, her most outstanding topoi are the languages of visual art, mysticism, and popular advertising. In her poetic texts that treat each of these, alone or in combination, Rossetti's speakers refuse to represent women as being "silent bearers of meaning" (Bauer 1988, 3), but rather exercise women's newly achieved freedom to take on the more active role of the controller of the gaze, the "keen-sighted viewer" suggested by Mitchell (Mitchell 1989, 97).[23] And these speakers demonstrate a resilient fluid identity, so that desire may be articulated in a variety of forms and formats, without regard to the normative predispositions that proclaim the cultural standard of only male/female attraction, with the male being the pursuer, and the female being the object of that pursuit. As Mirella Servodidio and Marcia L. Welles comment, "All manners of desire are figured: woman for man, man for woman, man for man, woman for woman, older lovers for younger (of the same sex or the other) and with no restrictions of gender in the representation of a subject/object, passive/active, voice/body binarism" (Servodidio and Welles 1983, 320). Andrew P. Debicki has noted the decidedly postmodern bent of Rossetti's very cheeky verse style and focus, in that her texts celebrate indeterminacy by allowing several differing readings at once, play upon previous discursive conventions and intertexts, and foreground the speakers' apparent lack of self-consciousness (Debicki, 48).

In response to a question posed in an interview with Sharon Keefe Ugalde, Rossetti responded that painting was one of several art forms that had left its mark on her poetry (Ugalde 1991, 158). Painting's effect may be perceived in her precise attention to visual detail, the inside/outside polarity of the framing technique, her expert manipulation of perspective whether visual, philosophical or sexual, and her brazen expression of subversive *jouissance* with regard to several traditional themes of painting, such as religious art or the celebration of beauty, whether physical or spiritual.[24] The poem "A Sebastián, virgen" ("To Sebastian, Virgin") of *Los devaneos de Erato* (*The Delirium of Erato* (Muse of Elegeic Poetry)) recalls many Renaissance and baroque paintings of the martyred saint, whose innocent body is pierced by arrows; his uplifted face is bathed in ecstasy as his mortal eyes fade, but those of his soul catch a glimpse of the eternal reward reserved for martyrs.[25] This vision of intense human, physical suffering and sacrifice was to serve as a worldly reminder of divine love and redemption. The body's mortification leads to the spiritual discourse of mysticism.

In Rossetti's poem, the speaker's sense of sight is initially projected onto the "arquero divino" ("divine archer"), who lusts after (the spirit or the flesh? of) the innocent young man. This sense of sight is titillated by that of touch, in that the unmediated gaze of the "arquero" ("archer") of the opening verse pierces and violates Sebastián's corporal presence in much the same way as the arrows of his tormentors and as the divine desire to possess Sebastián:[26] "Temblábanle los pulsos al arquero divino, / sus ojos fornicaban por tu espalda" ("The pulse beats of the divine archer trembled, / his eyes fornicated through your [fam. sing.] back"). In these opening lines, Rossetti's text first adopts the perspective of a distanced viewer/speaker, and evokes in baroque fashion divinity's desire for the saintly youth, who is framed and stilled by his martyrdom in a static pose of spiritual ecstasy. There is a significant inversion triggered by this opening gaze which sets the tone for the entire text, in that the movement of the arrows finds expression in the synecdoche of the archer's fluttering pulse and "knowing" eyes.[27] But the speaker of indeterminate gender then switches to a more intimate first-person perspective, indicating that the divine archer's eyes "fornicaban por tu espalda" ("fornicated through your [fam. sing.] back"). Saint Sebastian's image of purity and saintliness purposefully becomes tinged with the unsettling hues of both hetero-and homoeroticism, bestiality, sadomasochism, bondage, fellatio, and a vampirelike perversion of the Christian rite of drinking the blood of the Savior. The speaker feminizes Sebastián himself under the surveillant gaze emphasizing that his body is a receptacle with "inviolada urna" ("inviolate urn"), he is "virgen siempre virgen" ("virgin always virgin"), and "ninguno te inseminará tu vientre" (not one [masc.] will inseminate your [fam. sing.] womb"); the speaker also suggests the physical release of orgasm in the "sudor que precede al espasmo" ("sweat that precedes the spasm") and notes a maternal presence in "la maternal noticia / del beso ritual caído en el embozo" ("the maternal notion / of the ritual kiss that falls on the cloak's edge"). And his "cuerpo entreabierto" ("half-opened body")—by phallic arrows. . . .—mimics female sexuality and its receptive form to the penetrating male presence.

There is a suggestion of female genitalia in "carne desgranada" ("toothless flesh"), followed by the speaker's action of "Recojo con mi lengua los rubiés, / perro manso que bebe en tus heridas" ("I collect with my tongue the rubies, / tame dog that drinks from your wounds"), perhaps a veiled reference to cunnilingus during menstruation. And finally, the immaculate youth's deflo-ration could come at the hands not of the Christian God (as with the Virgin Mary) but of the Greek Eros with his overpowering "dardo" ("dart"), that is, penis: "Hermoso maniatado, si Eros de ti / se desenamorara, / su intencionado dardo pudiera desflorarte" ("Beautiful manacled one, if Eros with you / fell out of love, / his intentioned dart could deflower you").

In this text Rossetti blithely manipulates and takes full advan-tage of the highly stylized visual and verbal discourses of the baroque tradition in regard to hagiographic iconicity as well as to the corporal/spiritual dialectic of mysticism, while at the same time revising and subverting those very modes of discourse. The ungendered speaker gazes upon and gives voice to the mute art object that is Saint Sebastian's corporal image, not with the in-tention of being reminded of his saintliness, but rather to charge that saintly corporality with a dangerous, forbidden sexuality and perversion.[28] The spirituality of Saint Sebastian's image, which is in direct counterpoint to his carnality, becomes thus the catalyst that increases the perverse pleasures of desire and corruption. If Sebastian were not so pure, so innocent, so virgin, the desire and subsequent pleasure of the flesh would not be as great. The discourse of spirituality thus forms the basis for the speaker's intense desire of the youthful saint's carnality, instead of the other way around, as in traditional mysticism. In this man-ner the poet re-imagines and rewrites the life of this saint, by rewriting the outcome, the "coming out," and the just plain "coming" of his body . . . to a new frame of reference, one that is both inside and outside the economy of the corporal/spiritual dialectic. Moreover, the ungendered I/eye of the text restructures the gaze so as to allow for an and/or reading of the male/female opposition in regard to both the subject and object of that gaze.

The focus of Ana Rossetti's gaze—her (re)vision of culturally pervasive male icons—also falls upon the world of popular cul-ture, as embodied in the discourse of commercial advertising. As several critics have already noted, Rossetti utilizes this particular "language" and thus, according to Debicki, "challenges old no-tions of what is "proper" for literature" (Debicki, 48). Her poems entitled "Chico Wrangler" ("Wrangler Boy") and "Calvin Klein,

Underdrawers" use as their point of departure the visual advertisement campaigns for men's clothing, whether exterior or interior.[29] In both cases, the I/eye of the text makes use of the gaze
as the principal structuring device, and the impudent speaker
goes about revising, inverting, and subverting the patriarchal order, in that the object of desire is now the male body swathed in
tight-fitting clothing, whether the suggestive sheathing of white
underwear of "Calvin Klein, Underdrawers" or the form-fitting
blue jeans of "Chico Wrangler." In both cases, what is not so
discreetly (un)covered is the male penis and the speaker's desire
for it. The penis is present/absent in the manner in which it is
(dis)covered and (un)named. (Im)modesty allows IT to be (un)-
seen in and on the body, whether of the male model, of the poetic
text, or of the visual one of the ad campaign.[30] In "Calvin Klein,
Underdrawers," the male organ is variously metamorphosed into
"un lirio" ("a lily"), "el más severo mármol Travertino" ("the
most severe Travertino marble"), or possibly "redondos capiteles." Two possible readings are that the "redondos capiteles"
(round capitals") refer either to the speaker or to the male body's
buttocks or testicles:

> Fuera yo como nevada arena
> alrededor de un lirio,
> hoja de acanto, de tu vientre horma,
> o flor de algodonero que en su nube ocultara
> el más severo mármol Travertino.
> Suave estuche de tela, moldura de caricias,
> fuera yo, y en tu joven turgencia
> me tensara.
>   Fuera yo tu cintura,
> fuera el abismo oscuro de tus ingles,
> redondos capiteles para tus muslos fuera.
> Fuera yo, Calvin Klein.
>
>   (Rossetti 1980, 68)

(Would that I were as snow-covered [white] sand / around a lily, /
leaf of acanthus, of your belly [the] mold, / or flower of [the] cotton
plant that in its cloud would hide / the most severe Travertino marble. / Soft sheath of cloth, molding of caresses, / would that I were,
and in your young turgescence / I would make [myself] taut. / Would
that I were your waist, / would that I were the dark abyss of your
[fam. sing.] groin, / round capitals for your [fam. sing.] thighs, would
that I were. / Would that I were, Calvin Klein.)

The speaker's gaze and voice mimic the intimate article of clothing, in that this speaker desires to be metamorphosed into an
element that will enjoy the pleasure of close physical contact
and (un)cover the male model's sexuality in precisely the same
way as the intimate apparel. The gaze and voice of the speaker('s
text) (dis)covers the sexuality/textuality of the object of desire.
The metaphorization converts the pointedly ungendered speaker
at various moments into "nevada arena" ("snow-covered sand"),
"hoja de acanto" ("leaf of acanthus"), "horma" ("mold"), "flor de
algodonero" ("flower of [the] cotton plant"), "suave estuche de
tela" ("soft sheath of cloth"), and "moldura de caricias" ("molding of caresses"). The speaker's choice of metaphor on the one
hand suggests the feminine, in that softness, whiteness, roundness, and cleavage are qualities archetypally female. But on the
other hand, the ungendered I/eye of the text subverts this very
feminization by using these same qualities to convey the archetypally male qualities of tautness and erectness as well as the
activities of covering, penetration, and domination, as with the
phallo/gynocentric "lirio" ("lily") or "flor de algodonero que en
su nube ocultara" ("flower of [the] cotton plant that in its cloud
would hide"). The speaker puts into undecidable oscillation a
masculinist and/or feminist reading of the text. There is feminine
and masculine presence implied in much of the imagery, such
as the act of surrounding an inserted element, as with "alrededor
de" ("around"), "horma" ("mold"), estuche" ("sheath"), or
"moldura" ("molding").

After the (un)named climactic moment of "fuera yo, y en tu
joven turgencia / me tensara" ("[that] I were / and in your [fam.
sing.] young turgescence I would make [myself] taut") and a pregnant pause, the two,—subject and object, viewer and viewed—
become as one, in that the subject through desire now "comes"
and becomes the object of that very desire: "Fuera yo tu cintura, /
fuera el abismo oscuro de tus ingles, / redondos capiteles para
tus muslos fuera" ("Would that I were your waist, / would that I
were the dark abyss of your groin, / round capitals for your thighs
would that I were"). The problematic last line of verse, "Fuera
yo, Calvin Klein" ("Would that I were, Calvin Klein") presents
the possibility that the speaker is communicating directly to the
designing and advertising wizard, Calvin Klein, thus projecting
the speaker's own (homo?)erotic desire onto a public (or pubic?)
persona. The speaker thus markets the view for possible pub(l)ic
consumption that (homo?)erotic desire may be a (dis)cover(y)

about to come . . . undone. What a blow (job). Or alternately, the fashion mogul's name is a metonymic emblem of the underwear lionized in the poem, and is a handy cover-up with which to clothe the speaker's own gender-indeterminate lust for the nubile youth's very appealing masculine sexuality. In either case, this text as well as "Chico wrangler" serve to verbally articulate the speaker's desire to possess the alien object of desire, to "get into his pants."

Ana Rossetti pushes the limits of texuality in yet another fashion (with a nod to Calvin Klein. . . .), in that she also published this poetic text inscribed on the visual advertisement itself with the slightly modified title of "Calvin Klein Underwear,"[31] thus allowing space for a very popular and unconventional form of ekphrasis to come into being, one defined by the joining of a written text and by a visual one taken from the popular, determinedly un-literary world of marketing and advertising. There is a yet a third text present, since the visual and verbal ones are accompanied by scribbles and doodles which add to/detract from the viewer's/reader's focus and pleasure. But in another sense, Rossetti very cleverly gives new meaning to the feminist perspective on "writing the body," since the graphemic and graphic elements of her written/drawn text is inscribed upon the visual reproduction of the male body glorified in the ad campaign.[32] As Mary Makris comments, "In this graphic text which leaves everything and nothing to the imagination, one questions whether the poem illustrates the photograph or if the photograph illustrates the poem. When confronted with such an ekphrastic text, the reader stands before a pair of texts and must read in parallel, responding to and deciphering both verbal and visual signs and establishing correlations between them" (Makris 1983, 246). Moreover, I would add that the reader must read simultaneously the *trio* of texts—the photograph, the graffiti, and the poem—all with *and* against one another, the graphemic/graphic texts acting as both a supplement and defacement of the advertisement's photograph. Rossetti's multicolored doodles, scribbles, scrawls, arrows and kisses undercut and "underwrite" in the mode of graffiti the classical cast of the visual text, with the male model's Adonis-like body leaning against a postmodern version of a Corynthian column. Thus, Rossetti incorporates her bipolar approach to discourse from a completely different perspective in this text, in that her handwriting and her "hand (in the process of) writing" writes the body of the male model and of the visual text in a unique and very postmodern manner. The reader/viewer of this text is encouraged to participate in the exchange of power and pleasure and in the play of surrender and sovereignty from a decidedly unconventional perspective. The hybrid nature of this singular ekphrastic text of the late twentieth century foregrounds the concept of play so central to the postmodernist undertaking: it celebrates, derides, parodies and quite literally "rewrites" the classical, patriarchal tradition upon which it is based.

In this very "seeing," "touching," and "telling" text, Rossetti commemorates, calls into question, revises, and finally subverts the patriarchal organization of reality, by invalidating a plethora of culturally ordained oppositions such as male/female, active/passive, inner/outer, covered/uncovered, classical/popular, named/unnamed, literature/advertising, writing/graffitti. She pokes fun at the standard that in the past put a silent woman on a pedestal, an out-of-reach romanticized ideal, a being out of touch with the reality of the here and now. By choosing the Calvin Klein advertising campaign as the basis for her own verbal text, Rossetti's bipolar perspective creates for the reader an interpretive space that permits multiple readings without an overtly self-conscious speaker. The power of this text resides in its "graphic," verbal, and visual virtuosity, in its playfulness, as well as in its silence.

In the case of "Chico Wrangler" the speaker alludes to the male's sexual capacity by the speaker's own sexual awakening in the opening line of verse:

> Dulce corazón mío de súbito asaltado.
> Todo por adorar más de lo permisible.
> Todo porque un cigarro se asienta en una boca
> y en tus jugosas sedas se humedece.
> Porque una camiseta incitante señala,
> de su pecho, el escudo durísimo,
> y un vigoroso brazo de la mínima manga sobresale.
> Todo porque unas piernas, unas perfectas piernas,
> dentro del más ceñido pantalón, frente a mí se separan.
> Se separan.
>
> (Rossetti 1980, 99)

(Sweetheart of mine suddenly assaulted. / All in exchange for adoring more than is permissible. / All because a cigar perches on a mouth / and in its juicy silks becomes damp. / Because a stimulating undershirt signals, / from its chest, the oh so hard shield, / and a vigorous arm from the minimal sleeve juts out. / All because some legs, some

perfect legs, / within the most tight-fitting pair of pants, right in front
of me separate. / They separate.)

As Debicki comments, this first verse line "could well appear in
a cliché sentimental poem, and may evoke for us "traditional"
love poetry, or perhaps the stereotype of the poem we might
expect a cliché "poetisa" ("poetess") to produce" (Debicki, 48).
With an unabashed wink and nod at Sigmund Freud,—"Todo
porque un cigarro se asienta en una boca" ("All because a cigar
perches on a mouth")—the once again ungendered speaker then
allows her/his gaze in salacious fashion to fall upon, take in,
devour in a visual and implicitly oral sense, and finally possess
in a sexual/textual manner the male model's body and clothing,
with its sexual potency very suggestively (un)covered for the
voyeuristic pleasure of the viewer. The speaker mentions "una
camiseta incitante" ("a stimulating undershirt"), "su pecho, el
escudo durísimo" ("its chest, the oh so hard shield"), and "un
vigoroso brazo de la mínima manga sobresale" ("a vigorous arm
from the minimal sleeve juts out"). The phallic presence and the
speaker's desire are (un)named and (dis)covered in the rhythmic
repetition of "todo" ("all"), "piernas" ("legs"), and "se separan"
("they separate").

As in the case of "Calvin Klein, Underdrawers," this poetic
text is structured by the power of the gaze; Rossetti both celebrates and subverts the patriarchal norm of male voyeuristic
power and pleasure by focusing on the suggestively sheathed
male body in casual attire rather than the female one in more
formal, stylized garments. This ungendered speaker exercises
sovereignty over the passive male, held in a trance by the photographer's lens as well as by the eye-catching appeal of advertising,
and calls for the model's surrender to the viewer's gaze. The
model does capitulate with legs spread wide, adopting the (female) pose fantasized in the stereotypical (male) wet dream. In
addition, I think that Rossetti offers a specific intertextual reference that is revealing in its playfulness: this particular text could
be making reference to the Calvin Klein ad campaign that pictured the Hollywood starlet Brooke Shields in a similar type of
Madison Avenue *lay*-out: in it, her rounded rump and spread
legs decked out in very tight-fitting blue jeans fall within the
central focus of the ad, while she coyly looks into the camera
over a bare shoulder, and over a very naked torso. The ad's coy-
ness and lack of full frontal nudity is in direct contrast to Rossetti's unabashed (un)covered verbal virtuosity, and its (in)direct

reference to human sexuality. The campaign's slogan at the foot of the ad stated Nothing comes between me and my Calvin Kleins. With this possible intertext, Rossetti also may be making very sly reference to commercial competition, in that in her po-etry as well as on Madison Avenue, there are two brands of blue jeans—Calvin Kleins and Chico Wrangler—, and gaze—male and female—that vie for the reader's/viewer's attention.

Much has been stated, debated, written, and refuted in regard to the difference and *differánce* between what is written by men and women. I would propose that the act of writing is the same. But what *is* different is the manner of seeing, and how the per-ceptions by men and women are translated and transmuted into written form. It is my contention that women writers—poets, novelists, dramatists, essayists—suffer from / enjoy what I would term *double vision,* which leads to *double voicing.* By this I mean that women as women, as alien "Other" creatures in patri-archal society "see with their own eyes," but their place in soci-ety, that is to say marginalized from the discourse of power, forces them to see with the eyes of an/the "Other." The female gaze is always and ever underwritten and framed by the male gaze, the dominant and dominating cultural force in society. Nowhere is this "double vision" so prominent as in the case of women's ekphrastic literature, where the portraits that are summoned up by the verbal creativity of such poets as María Victoria Atencia and Ana Rossetti reflect an image not only of the outer objective world but of the inner subjective one of the poet as well. More-over, in the inscription of the female gaze upon the male one, that which is portrayed is the process of representation and the codes that govern all behavior and all creativity, whether male or female. In the case of the two poets whose work has been considered here, they have at their disposition a variety of strate-gies with which to evoke and then break the frame of conven-tional representation imposed upon them by patriarchal norms. María Victoria Atencia uses the domestic sphere and women's traditional enclosure as a point of departure from which to con-template her own positionality and her own soaring creativity. For Ana Rossetti, her double vision and double voicing emanate from her bipolar perspective in regard to the traditional topoi of erotic love, religious discourse, and the very postmodern popular culture. Both poets enter into active dialogue with the limits imposed upon them, creating an original duet from their familiar position as alien, not-so-silent Other, in combination with the centrality of the patriarchal discourse of power.

7

Pere Gimferrer and Jenaro Talens on [the] Camera, or The Lens and the I's/Eye's Obscure Object of Desire

THE theorization and evaluation of both photography and cinema as art forms have been a twentieth-century concern, since these two media as intersections of aesthetics and technology were created and developed in the contemporary epoch. Both these forms, as image producers and reproducers, necessarily underscore the problems of image value and production, and call into question central aesthetic issues such as those of authorship, authority, power, authenticity, and signification. Walter Benjamin, the eclectic cultural critic, aesthete, and literary theorist, perceived the import and complexity of these new forms of representation, and correctly stated the relationship between them, that photography was the forerunner of film. Furthermore, he detected that these technologically based methods of imagistic representation in and of themselves pressure the concepts of authorship and power, and implicitly demand a reconsideration of the relationship of art to society and to cultural tradition. As he stated in his famous "Work of Art in the Age of Mechanical Reproduction," "That which withers in the age of mechanical reproduction is the aura of the work of art. . . . [T]he technique of reproduction detaches the reproduced object from the domain of tradition. By making many reproductions it substitutes a plurality of copies for a unique existence" (Benjamin 1969, 221).[1] This plurality of copies brings to the forefront the change in the object's value and authenticity, and necessarily contextualizes the art forms so reproduced within a specific historical, social, and economic framework.

Because of the aesthetic relationship that has been forged and cemented over the twentieth century between art and the camera in regard to image production, representation, and reduplication, it is then not surprising that both the power and problematic authority of the two art forms that are irremediably associated with the camera lens, whether cinema or still photography, will be appropriated by contemporary poets through the discursive strategy of ekphrasis. Such is the case with Pere Gimferrer (b. 1945) and Jenaro Talens (b. 1946), both of whom, in addition to their poetry, have written extensively on literary theory and criticism, the relationship between culture and sign production, and the cinema. Gimferrer published his *Cine y literatura* (*Film and Literature*) in 1985, and Talens, his *El ojo tachado: "Un chien andalou" de Luis Buñuel* (*The Branded Eye: Luis Buñuel's "An Andalusian Dog"*) in 1986. Significantly, the camera makes itself manifest in various ways in these writers' poetry as well.[2] Gimferrer's *La muerte en Beverly Hills* (*[The] Death in Beverly Hills*) (1967) and *Los espejos /(Els miralls)* (*[The] Mirrors*) (1970) come easily to mind. Talens, for his part, published two poetic collections in the same time period as *El ojo tachado*, *Tabula rasa* (1985), a collection that utilizes ekphrasis from the perspective of the camera, among others, and *La mirada extranjera* (*The Foreign Gaze*) (1985), for which he joined artistic forces with the photographer Michaël Nerlich to produce a verbal/visual text composed of poems and photographs.[3] With this chapter, I propose to establish for these two poets a firm relationship between their poetic production and their individual theories related to the camera, whether photography or cinema, and will demonstrate the camera's presence not only as an image and a theme, but also as a catalyst for perspective, form, and structure, whether of individual poetic texts or of collections of poems. I will return later to a consideration of Gimferrer's *Cine y literatura* and Talens's *El ojo tachado* and to the theoretical implications of their individual stances toward the camera's art for their poetry; a brief review of the method, use, history, transformation, and theoretical implications of photography and thus cinema will provide a point of departure and frame of reference for the two poets' work, both theoretical and poetic.[4]

What is a photograph? According to *The Columbia Viking Desk Encyclopedia* (1960), it is the "science and art concerned with forming and fixing an image on a film or a plate made sensitive to light. Earliest known form is the camera obscura described by Leonardo da Vinci but generally credited to Giambattista della Porta. Development of light-sensitive surface which would retain an image stemmed from the discovery in 1727 that light causes darkening of silver salts" (20: 1043).[5] With this definition, traditional concepts of art were changed forever, in that technological and scientific discoveries facilitated as well as complicated the creative process and the artist's authorship and authority. For with the advent of the camera obscura the creative artist who chooses this medium will subsequently and necessarily be forced to express his creative urges not so much with the hand but rather with the eye, the camera lens being the creative vehicle and the mechanical metaphor of the artist's vision, both neurological and aesthetic.[6] And as a consequence of this epistemological and physiological shift, the I/eye that looks through the camera lens is one that seems simple—single, bare, unadorned, unimportant—but in truth is the surface sign for multiplicity, fragmentation, and deceit. This multiplicity ineluctably leads to the problem of the subject, a central concern of the twentieth century. In the case of photography, and the artist's creative journey from mental image to photographic one will be mediated by, among other things, the camera's technical and calibrational capacity, the time of day or the efficacy of flash equipment, the quality of the film and the development chemicals, the developer's art and skill, the time lapse between plate or film and resulting photograph, and the paper's constitution upon which the photograph is printed. These components, for their part, also presuppose the intervention of other authors and creators, those who invented, engineered, or produced them from a technical perspective.

In regard to the art of cinema, the process of creativity postulated by the cinematic I/eye is mediated and dispersed to an even further extent than that of photography, for now there are at least two cameras, one that makes the film and another that projects it. The qualification "at least" exerts itself here, since the conventional full-length feature film reflects the presence of many cameras, whose purpose resides in the multiplicity of shots required to capture the many angles of a given scene. Moreover, that mental image created by the problematic "author" of a film (writer? scriptwriter? cinematographer? producer? director?) must acknowledge and absorb the presence, the movement, and play of actors, film editor, light and sound technicians, multiple camera operators, and even the lowly projectionist at the local Bijou movie house, to name only a few. In turn each of these participants' perspectives, choices, and motions are mediated by the material, mechanical, technical apparatus, and its creators. And while aristocratic forms of art such as the portrait or sculpted piece were to be created and enjoyed by a small segment of society, these newer forms of visual art appealed to and were readily more available to wider circles of society. As Benjamin had already commented in his seminal essay, art forms in the age of mechanical reproduction would produce shock waves on society and directly affect culture and its definition(s). One need only take note of more recent forms of imagery and representation such as MTV, video, cybernetics, computer mania, virtual reality, the information superhighway, and the like to perceive the change and impact upon society and culture in general.

Keeping in mind Benjamin's comments about how mechanical forms of reproduction problematize art and its value, let us now turn to a consideration of the filmic media beginning with photography, in order to contemplate its uses and functions. The relationship of photography to other forms of pictorial and representational art reveals that while the former's codes of visual composition were orginally based on those of painting, the uses to which photography has been put have gone far afield of painting's aesthetic, representational, and sociopolitical goals. John Tagg, in his *Burden of Representation: Essays on Photographies and Histories* traces the evolution of photography's purpose from its beginning as a bourgeois or working class substitution for the aristocratic portrait, miniature or full size, which he defines as "a sign whose purpose is both description of an individual and the inscription of social identity" (Tagg 1988, 37). Moreover, technological advances in film processing "ended the trade in reproductions of portraits of topical or celebrated public figures. No longer would it seem remarkable to possess an image of someone well-known or powerful. The era of throwaway images had begun" (Ibid., 57).

This throwaway rendition was just one of photography's functions, in competition with that of photography as an art form. A third function of photography posited by Tagg revolves around the concepts of evidence, surveillance, legal truth, and social order; with the creation and growth of government at various levels both in the United States and in Western Europe in the late nineteenth and early twentieth centuries, photography quickly became a potent tool of social, political, and legal power and control. Photographs swiftly integrated themselves as an obligatory component of police records, court evidence, and as a means of justification of sometimes questionable social goals. For example the city of Leeds, England, in the late 1800s used photographs to justify the need to destroy a portion of the city's slum dwellings, as a means of controlling outbreaks of typhus fever, cholera, and lung disease. This action displaced thousands of slum dwellers, mostly poor immigrant families; no effort was made until well into the twentieth century to resolve the desperate housing situation that the wholesale destruction of neighborhoods had caused (Ibid., 121–26). And in the United States, photography and newsreel cinema of the 1930s and 1940s played a preeminent documentary role in Franklin Roosevelt's drive for congressional and popular acceptance of his so-called "New Deal" reformist social policies (Ibid., 153–83).[7]

As Tagg and others have noted, the appeal of photography, whether in its function as throwaway image, art form, or implement of social, political, and legal control, is its basic and undeniable illusion of realism and objectivity, the (mis)conception of it as an unmediated purveyor of truth. But what is at issue, of course, is power. Tagg comments:

> Power, then, is what is centrally at issue here: the forms and relations of power which are brought to bear on practices of representation or constitute their conditions of existence, but also the power effects which representational practices themselves engender—the interlacing of these power fields, but also their interference patterns, their differences, their irreducibility one to another. (Ibid., 21)

The illusion of realism, whether in photography or cinema, bequeathes the power to represent Truth, a truth that seems more compelling than even that of painting, since the latter medium's cultural and economic value, history, and aesthetic contextualization remove it from the vision of all but the cultured class. Cinema and photography's realistic illusion in turn effectively filters out the receiver's awareness of mediation of any kind, and encourages that receiver to identify with and appropriate the gaze of the photographic or cinematic text's I/eye and version of Truth. But as we previously have seen, the I/eye of the filmic text would be less comparable to the human model, and more akin to that of the common housefly, with its anatomically determined multifaceted structure and intake capacity.[8]

Roland Barthes's posthumously published *Chambre claire* (*Camera lucida*) (1981) is the French author's meditation on, and interpretation of, the science, art, and meaning of photography.[9] His study both suffers from and revels in a dual stance on this technologically produced medium of representation. For on the one hand, Barthes expresses a decided nostalgic position in asserting the camera's capacity to produce "realistic" images, as evidence of Truth; but on the other, he emphasizes the photographic image's undecidabilty, in the play of presence and absence in the photograph's competing codes of signification.[10] As Barthes comments, the viewer tends not to see the photograph itself, only what it attempts to represent (Ibid., 28). It is fascinating to note that his definition of photography reflects an open-ended process, in that he utilizes the verb "to become" rather than "to be": "The Photograph then becomes a bizarre *medium*, a new form of hallucination: false on the level of perception, true on the level of time: a temporal hallucination, so to speak, a modest, *shared* hallucination (on the one hand "it is not there," on the other "but it has indeed been"): a mad image, chafed by reality" (Ibid., 115). In the end, Barthes's essay on photography is underwritten by, and a response to, death, the ultimate presence of absence. The meditation and the process of converting it into written form are a means of confronting and ultimately framing his mother's life and death, a means of letting go and of immortalizing "a just image" of her (Ibid., 70).

In addition to the rich possibilities of slippery signification that accompany the play of presence and absence in photography, there are two key concepts that Barthes develops that will be useful in the relation of the filmic media to ekphrasis. One of these is what he terms the *wound*, an opening or a space of rapprochement of filmic text, sender, and receiver. As Barthes comments: "I see, I feel, hence I notice, I observe, and I think" (Ibid., 21). Barthes couples the *wound* with the *punctum*, "sting, speck, cut, little hole"; he defines the second term as "that accident which pricks me (but also bruises me, is poignant to me)" (Ibid., 27).[11] The images and conceptualizations of these two terms, *wound* and *punctum*, are striking, in that they link the technical process—light's inscription or wounding of the chemically treated surface—with the spectator's perception and subsequent reaction to a filmic image. Just as light (particle or wave?) penetrates a camera and engraves an image upon a receptive surface within the camera's dark interior, so too that filmic image, aided by light that penetrates the eye's lens, first impresses itself on the eye's interior structure of rods and cones, then once again "impresses itself" on the consciousness of the I in the mind's eye. And I would suggest that this image of wounding in addition recalls the medium of writing, with the writer's pen opening a furrow and then inscribing a message on the blank page, a message that communicates deferral, undecidability or perhaps implicit presence/absence of signification. To my mind, the concept of "wound" or "wounding" contains within it traces of both the feminine and the masculine, since the opening of the skin or tissue, whether it be broken, cut, pierced, or torn, is generally produced by the penetration by a foreign object. The erotic suggestibility becomes readily apparent.[12]

As I have demonstrated in each of the preceding chapters, ekphrasis as a discursive strategy attempts to appropriate the representational codes of visual art forms, to transmute these into linguistic code, and then to inscribe them through language upon the literary genres we know as poetry or narrative, for example, which themselves are known primarily through writing.[13] By having recourse to the discourses of other visual media, the literary text reveals its opening, lack, or wound, implicitly surrendering to the latter's sovereignty. These, in turn, wound the literary text by producing an opening in the literary text's frame as well as by weakening the literary text's authority.

But in using the filmic media of photography and cinema as the implement for the literary text's rupture or wounding, the wounding of the signifying process intensifies, because of the mediation by so many other agents of *author*-ity and of *author*-ship of the filmic I/eye that were discussed earlier. The presence/absence of the filmic text within the literary one complicates and disperses the image and *mirage* of power not only by reference to that very image, but also by the contextualization of the filmic representation within its own dispersed frames of reference as throwaway, art, evidence, documentary, a means of sociopolitical control and/or subversion, or merely as entertainment, as well as by film and photography's innate questioning of artistic value. To educated and artistically inclined viewers, does a promotional photo of Marilyn Monroe have as much commercial and aesthetic value as a painting of her? The supposed response is "Probably not." What of the June 1995 issue of the U.S. Postal Service commemorative stamp of the famed actress? What of its image value to those who use it merely as a thirty-two-cent stamp, to the Postal Service, which wishes to profit from the sale of the gummed sheets of paper upon which it is printed, or to the collector in years to come? And what of Andy Warhol's "pop art" painting, of Marilyn Monroe, where the actress's photographic image is reproduced in prismlike fashion over and over again on the painter's canvas? Referentiality is in doubt, and so self-referentiality, as the I/eye of the text is blinded and enlightened by the multiplicity of (de)valued images and of the (de)valued images of multiplicity. The literary text, implicitly or explicitly, must enter into dialogue with the filmic image that wounds, as well as that image's function and frame of reference, and how the latter reveals the presence/absence—the Derridean trace—of the remaining categories which do not characterize it. In other words, a photograph or cinematic shot that is artistic in nature, by its presence, has inscribed upon it the absence—the difference, the *differánce*—of/from the photograph or film shot as throwaway or evidence, for example. The reassuring indeterminacy of Manuel Machado's "Felipe IV" from chapter 2 now seems familiar and even comforting, in light of the defocalization engendered by examples of ekphrasis based upon the filmic media. The power of these filmic media to simultaneously capture and disperse an image's authority with its equivocal objectivity and realism destabilizes even further the inside/outside dialectic that is the basis for the discursive strategy known as ekphrasis. The tension between surrender and sovereignty as well as pleasure and power plays itself out not only between the literary work and its reference to photography or cinema, but also within the I/eye of the filmic text itself. Moreover, the problematization of authority and authorship, the underlying fragmentation of the filmic media's focal point, lends itself easily as a postmodern image and metaphor.

It is not surprising then that photography and cinema are the visual media chosen with such frequency by Pere Gimferrer and Jenaro Talens, two Spanish poets of the postmodern era, of the so-called "novísimos" generation.[14] Many critics have already noted that the principal characteristics of the "novísimos" group define the work of these writers as an explicit and indisputable example of postmodern poetry: their view of the literary text as an open-ended system, their expressed skepticism concerning poetic language as an efficacious means of representing reality, their questioning of genre definitions, the simultaneous celebration and rupture of frames of all types, their overt display of the process of poetry and self-referentiality, and their generational fascination with pop culture and mass media.[15] The well-known Catalan writer, Pere Gimferrer, a member of the "novísimos" generation of Spanish poets, has written of his debt to cinema's art, function, and power.[16] And in several interviews as well as in the 1979 edition of his collected poetry to date, *Poemas 1963–1969* (*Poems 1963–1969*) he acknowledges his debt to the filmic art of the silver screen in the writing of his collection of poetry entitled *La muerte en Beverly Hills*.

Este período cubre desde enero del 66 a julio del 67, en que inicié la redacción de *La muerte en Beverly Hills*. Este libro—el más lenta y cuidadosamente elaborado de los que he escrito, pese a su brevedad—es en realidad un solo poema, y como tal lo sentí mientras lo iba escribiendo. Principalmente, era un esfuerzo por liberarme de *Arde el mar* e incorporar a mi generación. Es mi libro más triste, en la sensibilidad, narrando a través de ellos—como yo mismo a veces creo de los gustos de ricos o culturales—una historia íntima. (Que el mundo elegido fuera el cine americano de los años dorados y que este mundo estuviera de moda no fue sino una coincidencia que prueba, como mucho, que no estoy tan distante como yo mismo a veces creo de los gustos de mi generación.) Es mi libro más triste, en la medida en que su tema es la nostalgia y la indefensa necesidad de amor. Desde otro ángulo, puede verse también como un juego de múltiples máscaras o espejos, es decir, como un libro irónico. No creo que una interpretación excluya a la otra: se complementan. (Gimferrer 1967, 12–13)

(This period covers from January 1966 to July 1967, in which I began the writing of *[The] Death in Beverly Hills*. This book—the most slowly and carefully elaborated of [all] those that I have written, in spite of its brevity—is in truth only one poem, and I perceived it as such while I was writing it. Principally, it was an effort to free myself from *The Sea Is Burning* and to incorporate [myself] into my generation. It is my saddest book, in sensibility, narrating through them—as I myself at times believe of the tastes of the rich or cultural elite—an intimate [personal] story. (That the chosen world was American movies of the golden years and that this world was in fashion was nothing other than a coincidence which proves, at most, that I am not so distant as I myself believe from the tastes of my generation.) It is my saddest book, in proportion to [the idea] that its theme is nostalgia and the defenseless need of love. From another angle, it can be seen also as a game of multiple masks or mirrors, that is to say, as an ironic book. I do not believe that one interpretation excludes another: they complement each other.)

Gimferrer's assertion that his choice of film as the "imagined world" of this book of poetry as a mere coincidence notwithstanding, I would like to propose that the Hollywood context of artifice and unabashed dedication to make-believe, and film's undecidable readings of (ir)reality are a useful and revealing code which the poet utilizes in order to convey the story of his ongoing dialogue with poetry as a creative process and with language itself. Moreover, his interest in, and theories about, the cinematic medium are reflected in his poetry not only in theme and surface content, but in the very structure and chronology of the various phases of his poetic production. In other words,

Gimferrer appropriates, consciously or unconsciously, film's coding, conceits, narrative strategies, artifice, and artificiality as he interprets them, in order to reflect and reflect upon the story of his own poetry's evolution, the (im)possibility of referentiality and representation through language, and ultimately the uncertain value of any sign system. Film's transparency as undecidable image of duplicitous reality thus becomes the basic metaphor of the poet's own struggles with the relationship among language, poetry, and reality. The use of the filmic medium is "doubly" ekphrastic, since cinema's presence/absence within the poetic text breaks the frame of the lyric genre as well as the narrative one of Gimferrer's development as a poet. And since cinema simultaneously is and is not a mute art object that must be encouraged to "speak for itself" within Gimferrer's poetry and the narrative that his poetry tells, the poet effectively breaks the frame of ekphrasis itself. Both silent films and "talkies," art forms that contain movement and then sound, challenge and then subvert the traditional time/space dialectic—the still movement—posited by literary ekphrasis in all of its previous manifestations throughout literary history, and a few examples of which we have seen in previous chapters.

In his *Cine y literatura* Gimferrer celebrates the work of D. W. Griffith, whom the poet signals as the "fundador del lenguaje cinematográfico" ("founder of cinematographic language") (Gimferrer 1985, 6), whose theories have shaped filmic history, production, and realization from Georges Méliès's *Faust et Marguerite* (1897) to Steven Spielberg's *Jaws* (1975) and beyond.[17] Griffith, director of *The Birth of a Nation* (1915) was the one who, according to the poet, established cinema's major function and model. This American director and producer posited that film's function was to tell stories, and its model was to be sought not in the theater, but rather in the configuration of its story according to the laws of the form of literary expression and narration that Griffith and others considered to be the optimal, that of the nineteenth-century novel (Gimferrer 1985, 7). According to Gimferrer, "A partir de Griffith, el cine se convierte en un lenguaje narrativo estructurado según los módulos de la narrativa decimonónica, en el que el montaje alterna las diversas posibilidades del plano, desde el primer plano hasta el plano general. La movilidad de la cámara . . . crea un espacio que, al permitir la máxima nitidez en los segundos términos del encuadre, crea un espacio visual donde el movimiento puede orientar hacia el fondo, y no sólo hacia los laterales, la mirada del espectador"

("Starting with Griffith, film changed into a narrative language structured according to the modules of nineteenth-century narrative, in which the montage alternates the diverse possibilities of the surface, from the foreground to the general distance. The mobility of the camera . . . creates a space which, in permitting the maximum clarity in the second grounds of the focusing, creates a visual space where movement can orient the gaze of the spectator toward the background, and not only toward the sides") (Ibid., 11). And interestingly enough, the Catalan poet views film as a means by which the spectator can be made to rediscover reading. As he states it, "La imagen [cinematográfica] reinventa las palabras, hace leer de nuevo" ("The [cinematographic] image reinvents words, it makes [us] read anew") (Ibid., 18).

Gimferrer then goes on to explicate some of cinema's most outstanding techniques and strategies, in its singular adaptation, via various cinematographers, producers, and directors, of the nineteenth-century novel's narrative style: contemplation of characters' behavior, the physical presence of objects and accesories and the actors' conduct in relation to them, the lack of discussion about what happens, filmic ambiguity, superimposition of one image over another, self-referentiality, and the unfolding of the self into various fractured but no less valid versions of the self. In reference to Ingmar Bergman's Persona (1966), Gimferrer comments that the major character(s) is/are "un ser que ni es enteramente nadie ni enteramente deja de ser alguien; una existencia a medias, no por incompleta, sino por desdoblada en dos mitades que se unen con esa inquietud última que queda siempre tras una fisura a punto de abrirse quizá nuevamente cuando menos se espera" ("a being that neither is entirely no one, nor does [the major character] stop being someone; an existence by halves, not on account of [being] incomplete, but rather on account of the unfolding in two halves that are united with that final inquietude that always remains behind at a fissure just about to open again when it is least expected") (Ibid., 34). It is noteworthy that Pere Gimferrer devotes precious little space to the work of Luis Buñuel, the internationally known Spanish director and cinematographer whose work began to appear in the late 1920s. Moreover, Buñuel's ground-breaking Un chien andalou (An Andalusian Dog) (1929), the film based on the script that Buñuel and Salvador Dalí had written, is not even mentioned. This curious decision of omission is in fact based on Gimferrer's own conceptualization of film and of its origins in the nineteenth-century novel. He recognizes Buñuel's originality, in that the film director's work was "uno de los intentos más claros de buscar una forma de narración enteramente libre de todo tributo al modelo novelesco que Griffith propuso e implantó para el cine, basada, por lo contrario, en el poder inmanente de asociación de las imágenes—por relaciones de afinidad, contigüidad, rechazo o complementariedad—con independencia de cualquier nexo lógico encaminado a respetar las leyes del relato tradicional" ("one of the clearest attempts to search for a form of narration entirely free of all tribute to the novelesque model that Griffith proposed and introduced for film, based, on the contrary, on the immanent power of association of images— through relations of affinity, contiguity, rejection, or complementarity—with independence from whatever logical link directed toward respecting the laws of the traditional story") (Ibid., 12). Buñuel's competing model of cinematographic form and function will be taken up later in this chapter, since it is ekphrastically present/absent in the poetry of Jenaro Talens, once again, not only as theme and content, but also in his poetry's structure and relative chronology.

Returning now to Gimferrer's own description of *La muerte en Beverly Hills*, his comment that "es en realidad un solo poema" ("it is in truth only one poem") and that "[e]s mi libro más triste, en la sensibilidad, narrando a través de ellos . . . una historia íntima. . . . Desde otro ángulo, puede verse también como un juego de múltiples máscaras o espejos, es decir, como un libro irónico" ("[i]t is my saddest book, in sensibility, narrating through them . . . an intimate [personal] story. . . . From another angle, it can also be seen as a game of multiple masks or mirrors, that is to say, as an ironic book") (Ibid., 13) reflects his theorization regarding cinema as being based on the aforementioned nineteenth-century novel.[18] This type of novel's narrativity makes itself manifest in the collection having been organized and written as one long poem; and its "historia íntima" ("intimate [personal] story") pays homage to the novelistic likes of *Madame Bovary*, *La Regenta* (*The Regent* [fem.]), or *Fortunata y Jacinta* (*Fortunata and Jacinta*), but the collection uses Hollywood as the backdrop, and creates a convincing "movie set" within which the spectator/reader can execute what T. S. Eliot referred to as a willing suspension of disbelief (Holland 1968). The alternate but equally defensible reading that Gimferrer offers of this collection of poems, as "un juego de múltiples máscaras o espejos, es decir, como un libro irónico" ("a game of multiple masks or mirrors, that is to say, as an ironic book") also may allude to this type of narrative's power and authority, in its questioning, reflection of, and reflection about, the (im)possibility of reality and representation, its metaliterary inclinations. While I agree to a certain point with Timothy Rogers that Gimferrer's *Muerte en Beverly Hills* may produce a collage-like effect upon the reader because of the poet's use of snippets of language and imagery garnered from movies, comic strips, second-rate detective stories, and other examples taken from various forms of pop culture, the overall organization of the collection is narrative, its milieu is Hollywood of the 1940s, and its meticulous attention to minor details of color, design, backdrop, sound, and focus are cinematographically inspired, pure "tinsel town." Each poem of the collection attempts, on the one hand, to re-create in verbal form, individual filmic scenes, or "camera takes," with their visual and sound effects—close-up, pan, cross-cutting, split screen, superimposition, accelerated montage, flash frame, fade-out, for example—, and on the other to advance the trite story line of love and loss championed by movie companies such as Metro Goldwyn Mayer or Paramount of the 1940s and 1950s, in their unending search for blockbuster hits at the box office.

The collection as a whole is divided into eight sections; the last section, carries the title of "Elegía" ("Elegy") within parentheses. The opening scene of the cinematic poem establishes the speaker-character's milieu in melodramatic and very visual terms, as the camera's I/eye takes in both backdrop and individual details of chromatic, textured, and aural nature:

Mimbre, bebidas de colores vivos, luces oxigenadas que chorrean
    despacio.
bañando en un oscuro esplendor las espaldas, acariciando con
    fulgor de hierro blanco
unos hombros desnudos, unos ojos eléctricos, la dorada caída
    de una mano en el aire sigiloso,
el resplandor de una cabellera desplomándose entre música
    suave y luces indirectas,
todas las sombras de mi juventud, en una usual figuración
    poética.
                                                    (Gimferrer 1967, 53)

(. . . Wicker, drinks of lively colors, oxygenated lights that gush /
slowly. / bathing in a dark splendor the backs, caressing with / [the]
brightness of white iron / some naked shoulders, some electric eyes,
the golden way of hanging / of a hand in the secretive air, / the

splendor of a head of hair cascading between soft / music and indirect lights,/ all the shadows of my youth, in a usual poetic / figuration.)

In the second segment, the first-person speaker bifurcates into two, in that he is both the movie's protagonist as well as the enraptured spectator eating popcorn in the first row of the darkened movie theater, who awaits the grand entrance of the likes of Marilyn Monroe, Bette Davis, or Joan Crawford. Alas, he is star-struck by the blond bombshell beauty of his leading lady, a celluloid reflection of Jean Harlow, and her mogul-manufactured image of the feminine ideal, as well as by the seedy Art Deco ambience suggestive of Miami, Florida:

> Debo de parecer un loco batiendo palmas solo y cantando en
>   alta voz en este cuarto de hotel.
> Con un seco frenazo se ha detenido un coche fundido en luz
>   y resplandor de plata.
> ¡Sonrisas de Jean Harlow! El bungalow al alba y el mar
>   centelleante.
> Música por toda la olvidada estación del deseo. Palmeras,
>   giratoria luminosidad de la playa encendiéndose
> sólo para estos ojos tras un cristal ahumado.
>   ¡No me mires más, Némesis!
> Ya conozco tus uñas pintadas de rojo, el óvalo hechicero de tu
>   cara, tu sonrisa pastosa y húmeda de nymphette,
> estos vestidos negros, estas mallas, tus guantes hasta el codo,
>   el encaje en los pechos,
> esta espalda que vibra y palpita como una columna de mercurio.
> Cuando amanezca me encontrarán muerto y llamarán a Charlie
>   Chan.
>   (Ibid., 55)

(I must seem like a madman clapping [my] hands alone and singing / aloud in this hotel room. / With a dry slamming of brakes a car has stopped cast in light / and [the] splendor of silver. / Smiles of Jean Harlow! The bungalow at dawn and the sea/shimmering. / Music for all the forgotten season of desire. Palm trees, / girating luminosity of the beach kindling itself / only for these eyes behind a smoked pane of glass. / Don't look at me anymore, Nemesis! / I already know your finger nails painted red, the bewithching oval of your / face, your pasty and humid smile of [a] nymphet,/these black dresses, these tights, your gloves up to the elbow, / the lace on your breasts,/this back that vibrates and palpitates as a column of mercury. / When dawn arrives they will find me dead and they will call Charlie Chan.)

As the poem(s)/story/movie unfold(s) there are suggestions of unsolved Hollywood-style murders, the recollection of the room where Proust wrote, Las Vegas and life's games of chance, and mysterious telephone calls. And in the tattered lines of verse, the speaker/protagonist/spectator of the poem(s)/story/movie makes use of virtually all of the cinematic techniques and strategies codified by D. W. Griffith that Pere Gimferrer would enumerate in his *Cine y literatura*: contemplation of characters' behavior, the physical presence of objects and accessories and the actors' conduct in relation to them, the lack of discussion about what happens, filmic ambiguity, superimposition of one image over another, self-referentiality, and the unfolding of the self into various fractured but no less valid. versions of the self. The visual/verbal movie "takes" of each of the collection's eight sections reproduce for the reader through language the equivalent of the vaseline-smeared camera lens, that is, a gossamer, out-of-focus image that does and does not communicate an artificially created and perceived (ir)reality, and communicates as well the imperfections of the system of signs at various levels that are being manipulated to communicate that blurred image. In other words, because of the slightly out-of-focus image, the spectator/viewer/reader of the poem/story/movie is encouraged to read the text mimetically, semiotically, and ironically, and ponder not only the trite and corny Hollywood goings-on with a jaded I/eye, but also with the message that the systems of communication and representation (im)perfectly reflect an artificial image and an image of artifice of a given milieu and also of representation itself, whether it be poetic, cinematic, novelistic, linguistic, or any other sign system.

The section entitled ("Elegía") ("Elegy") closes the collection/story/movie; the camera's I/eye takes in the panoramic view as well as the individual detail that lends focal interest to the scene at hand:

> En invierno, la lluvia dulce en las parabrisas, las carreteras
>   brillando hacia el océano,
> la viajera de los guantes rosa, oh mi desfallecido corazón, cla-
>   vel en la solapa de smoking,
> muerto bajo el aullido de la noche insaciable, los lotos en la
>   niebla, el erizo de mar al fondo de un armario,
> el viento que recorre los pasillos y no se cansa de pronunciar
>   tu nombre.

(Ibid., 64)

(In winter, the sweet rain on the windshield, the highways / shining toward the ocean, / the traveler [fem.] with the rose-colored gloves, oh my swooning heart, car-/ nation in the lapel of [the] tuxedo, / dead under the wail of the insatiable night, the lotuses in the / mist, the sea urchin at the back of a wardrobe, / the wind that traverses the halls and does not tire of pronouncing / your name.)

And with the use of italics the speaker/protagonist brings the reader's attention to the text as a verbal, written, and printed artifact, once again allowing for metatextual considerations:

> *Todas las noches, en el snack,*
> *mis ojos febriles la vieron pasar.*
> *Todo el invierno que pasé en New York*
> *mis ojos la buscaban entre nieve y neón.*
>
> (Ibid.)

(*Every night, in the snack bar, / my feverish eyes saw her pass by. / The entire winter that I spent in New York / my eyes searched for her between snow and neon.*)

This time, the shadowy femme fatale escapes not into an Edward Hopper painting that we saw in the case of the Carmen Martín Gaite text of chapter 4, but rather into a movie, or rather, a movie set, both set and character having been artificially created in order to communicate only an image of (ir)reality. The poem/ collection/story/movie ends with an ambiguous shot—camera as well as gun—, simultaneously closing/opening it for the speaker/ protagonist/spectator/reader's thoughtful consideration, as reference, textuality, and artifice fall under the spotlight of the artist's (poet? director? film editor? cinematographer? reader?) moving— mobile as well as affecting—gaze and watchful I/eye:

> Los asesinos llevan zapatos de charol. Fuman rubio, sonríen.
>   Disparan.
> La orquesta tiene un saxo, un batería, un piano. Los can-
>   tantes. Hay un número de strip-tease y un prestidi-
>   gitador.
> Aquella noche llovía. El cielo era de cobre y luz mag-
>   nética.
> ¡Focos para el desfile de modelos, pistolas humeantes!
>
> (Ibid., 65)

(The assassins are wearing patent leather shoes. They smoke American cigarettes, they smile. / They shoot. / The orchestra has a sax,

percussion, a piano. The sing-/ ers . There is a striptease number and
a magi-/ cian. That night it was raining. The sky was of copper and
mag-/ netic light. / Spotlights for the parade of models, smoking
pistols!)

Certainly Gimferrer's *Muerte en Beverly Hills* poses questions
concerning the I's/eye's fragmented gaze and thus the dispersion
of power, authority, and authorship within the framework of
ekphrasis in singular fashion, and allows the reader to focus on
(although not very clearly! . . .) representational authenticity
and value, as well as frames and their rupture from a clearly
postmodern perspective. But the presence/absence of the cinematic art piece within poetry is only an illusion and ultimately
leads to a consideration of the very definition of ekphrasis itself,
since cinema's resolution of the time/space dialectic literally and
figuratively keeps moving, and moving out of, away from, and
beyond its enclosure within its own given frame of the camera
as well as that of the poetic text of Pere Gimferrer. The poet, only
one of the many magicians knowledgeable in illusion/allusion
and sleight of hand and eye whose art and craft(iness) are evident
in this fine example of filmic poetry, puts into practice a simultaneous surrender to, and sovereignty over, the novel—new as well
as narrative—cinematic form in a highly original manner. His
poetic text underscores both the triumph and failure of "borrowed" representation through ekphrasis, since the new art form
moves fleetingly, illusorily, into, out of, and beyond its poetic
"urn," reminiscent of as well undercutting the still movement
celebrated by Keats in his poem. Yet because of cinema's definition as an art form with movement and then sound, both of which
subvert the "still" of the still movement of ekphrasis, the melding
of cinema and poetry calls for a reconsideration and an expansion of the definition of ekphrasis itself.

Two other collections of Gimferrer that I would like to mention
briefly manifest at least some of the filmic strategies that were
mentioned earlier in regard to their structure, organization, and
underlying narrativity, while only sparingly making use of the
filmic ambience of Hollywood as the locus and focus of superficial theme and imagery that were seen in *La muerte en Beverly
Hills*. The first of these is *Els miralls/Los espejos*, the first of his
many poetic works to be published in Catalan or in bilingual
editions of Catalan and Spanish; it first appeared in 1970, later
was anthologized with two other of his later works in the collection *Poesía 1970–1977* (*Poetry 1970–1977*), and was again put

into circulation by Visor in 1978. The collection's title of *Els miralls/Los espejos* may be an allusion to the secondary reading of *La muerte en Beverly Hills* that the poet offered, namely, "un juego de múltiples máscaras o espejos" ("a game of multiple masks or mirrors") (Gimferrer 1970, 13) or indeed may also be making oblique reference to the camera's interior construction replete with mirrors, which aid in the production of artificial images of (ir)reality and real images of artifice. Indeed authorial voice and gaze, authorship, authority, and power are overwhelmingly dispersed by not only the poet's choice to produce a bilingual edition, but also to serve as his own translator and critic. In the translator's note he states: "En este caso el traductor es el autor; debe pedir, pues, doble indulgencia para su trabajo. O tal vez no, en rigor; apenas he pretendido traducir, si por tal cosa se entiende recrear el original, crear un poema equivalente" ("In this case, the translator is the author; he should, then, ask for double forbearance for his work. Or perhaps not, strictly speaking; I have hardly attempted to translate, if for such a thing it is understood [not] to re-create the original, [but] to create an equivalent poem") (Ibid., 29). That is, the poet indicates that the two versions, one in Catalan, and the other in Spanish, are each original poems. The poet then continues with "El texto castellano que ofrezco al lector no pretende, pues, otra cosa, que ser un calco fiel del texto catalán, y facilitar su lectura a quienes no conozcan dicho idioma"("The text in Spanish that I offer to the reader does not seek, then, other than to be a faithful tracing of the text in Catalan, and to facilitate its reading to those who are not familiar with said language") (Ibid., 29). Thus, it is clear, based on his own explication, that the poet's intent is to foreground the original Catalan version of his work. But in the refracted image of the translated text, the reader is brought face-to-face and I/eye to I/eye with the impossibility of that task, and with the impossibility of the perfection of the oneness of the sign. It should be noted that the author himself goes agains his own statement about the primacy of the Catalan version. On the front page the Spanish title *Los espejos* appears at the top of the page, while the Catalan title *Els miralls* appears in parentheses. Also, the Spanish version of each poem is located on the right-hand page, the better to catch the reader's eye, while the Catalan text is on the left. Or, this arrangement may reflect a split-screen image, where the reader's I/eye must choose or choose not to choose either or both of the systems of representation. In addition, the poet also declares that he has made several corrections

to the Catalan version of the poems, and thus, "esta edición bi-
lingüe es, pues, por ahora, la edición definitiva de mi poesía
posterior a 1969" ("this bilingual edition is, then, for now, the
definitive edition of my poetry after 1969") (Ibid., 30). In so describing his position, the poet effectively establishes the mirror-
image text—in Catalan and Spanish—as the *author*-itative one,
but also undermines that very authority with the phrase "por
ahora" ("for now"). The image of/in the mirror becomes that of
mirage. The poet—in (his own) word(s) and deed—points to the
mutability of the linguistic sign, in spite of his own protestations
to the contrary. He declares the primacy of one version over
another, yet installs the supplement in a central position. And in
so doing, he also points to the metapoetic cast of this collection, a
mode that will be developed in several poems from a variety of
perspectives.

The opening poem of this collection, entitled "Paranys"
("Snares") in Catalan and "Celadas"("Snares") in Spanish, does
in point of fact indeed establish a series of snares for the reader
as the title would indicate. This single opening text duplicates
the edition as a whole, as well as the function of the poet-transla-
tor-commentator. It has a bipartate or split-screen structure,
wherein the poetic voice offers a vision of the artistic task at
hand in the first part, only to comment upon it and to ultimately
put that vision in question in the second. The poet creates a
reflected or refracted image of other authors in the process of
creating, and draws upon examples taken from many sources.
Thus, within Gimferrer's poetic text, the piercing gaze of many
other I's/eyes become evident. Apollinaire, Juan Gris, Goethe,
Hölderlin, Rimbaud, Pavese, and Yeats are named directly, while
other authors and texts are re-created in oblique fashion. The
speaker juxtaposes different worlds, such as that of Orpheus and
his love, Eurydice, with a more contemporary and rather jarring context:

> El mundo de Orfeo es el de detrás de los espejos: la caída
>   de Orfeo,
> como el retorno de Eurídice de los infiernos, las bicicletas, los
>   chicos que venían de jugar al tenis y mascaban *chewing*
>   gum
>
>   (Ibid., 41)

(The world of Orpheus is the one behind the mirrors: the fall / of
Orpheus, / as the return of Eurydice from the nether world, the bicy-

cles, the / boys who came from playing tennis and were chewing
chewing / gum)

What is the reader to make of this? How is the Orphic world of
mythical time related to the contemporary one represented by
the clatter and crack of bicycles, tennis-playing boys, and chewing gum?

The image of reflection and the reflection of images plays a
central role in the questioning of the value of language and representation, and in truth, sets a snare for the unwary reader, who
is encouraged to partake in this game of creative play signaled
by Debicki (Debicki 1988, 40).[19] The poetic speaker makes reference to various art forms, verbal as well as visual, in a kaleidoscope of forms, colors, and perspectives reminiscent of surrealist
art, and particularly of the cinema; he is well aware of the quick-
sand upon which it is based. At the close of the main section
of the poem, the speaker elaborates upon some lovely fictional
characters, and then stops to comment upon the questionable
author-ity of his posture. The speaker now not only fulfills the
function of poetic voice but also that of commentator as well, by
which he directs his comments directly to his audience, in the
form of "vosotros" ("you"[fam. pl.]), and thus implicitly makes
reference to the textuality of his work. In essence he lays bare
the frame of his composition, by placing himself outside that
frame of reference, even removed in time, and comments upon
the linguistic reality that he has created in the collage of his own
creation and in those of other arts, whether verbal or visual. But
in so doing, he undermines and ultimately relinquishes
his authority over textuality. In the decentering of discursive
power—from the speaker's text to outside a frame of his own
making and then back again—this speaker points to the pitfalls
of linguistic representation. The reality reflected is that that is
to be found only within the text; moreover, the speaker must
cede his authority to the overriding presence of the mutable sign.
Thus, the poetic voice and gaze become ensnared in a trap of
their own making. By placing himself outside his text in order
to comment upon it, the speaker foregrounds the primary role
of the sign in shaping not only meaning, but also the reader's
perception of the speaker himself.

In part 2 of this opening poem, the speaker continues his questioning stance in regard to textuality, but views the text from yet
another entirely different perspective, namely, as a product that
fulfills distinct functions for very different kinds of receivers. He

also repeats the technique of self-commentary or documentary evaluation, but now his focus is on the poetic text from the perspective of product, rather than from the signifying object:

> Este poema es
> una sucesión de celadas: para el
> lector y para el
> corrector de pruebas
> y para
> el editor de poesía.
>
> (Gimferrer 1970, 41)

(This poem is / a succession of snares: for the / reader and for the / proofreader / and for / the publisher of poetry.)

Here the text is viewed not so much as an artistic product but as a social or even commercial one that simultaneously entraps and is entrapped by a series of snares, only glancingly manifest on the surface level of the text. All those receivers named by the speaker—reader, proofreader, publisher—are readers of the same text, but they each produce a different text, each interpreting the text's signs from a different perspective. Once again, the reality to which the speaker refers is ephemeral, since this reality is linguistic and textual, in both the literary and coldly commercial sense. The text is only an object, to be held under the refracted gaze of whichever reader or to be held in that person's hands; this limited and more limiting perspective could be construed as a very pessimistic stance toward textuality, but the speaker transforms this seemingly negative perspective into something totally different and unexpected. The poem closes with the speaker emphasizing his lack of power and authority in the process of signification. The poetic voice recognizes the snares of textuality at its many levels but is unable to disentangle itself from their grasp. His final attempt at explication is to make reference to yet another mirrored art form,—"el dibujo del tapiz" ("the figure in the carpet [the tapestry drawing]")—, only to admit that to see what lies behind and beyond the "celadas" is an impossible task.[20]

One could view this opening poem of *Els miralls/Los espejos* from a pessimistic perspective and arrive at the conclusion that the poet views artistic creation as totally derivative at best, or completely moribund at worst. But this view, I believe, is off the mark. Rather, both the structure and the content of this poetic text may be viewed as the poet's narrative and commentary about art within its contemporary social, political, and cultural context, and is similar to the comment that he made about *La muerte en Beverly Hills*. Art, whether it be painting, photography, cinema, literature, or other uncanonized forms from pop culture, no longer need be fettered by artificial frames of reference, whether temporal, prescriptive, or referential, nor be limited to one monolithic, authoritative voice or gaze. The snares of the title serve as signposts to the creator(s) and receivers of the text and mark the points at which the functioning of intertextuality and thus the dispersion of the text's and texts' I's / eyes are at their most obvious, where the presence of Otherness may be most deliberately noted. The snares inherent in discursive space point to the Otherness of language, the slipperiness of the sign which is not content to remain attached to one particular meaning. And the poet views this state of affairs as positive rather than negative.

Based on this perspective, the reader is given an opportunity to view the text in a new light. Rather than being a closed system, the text is now viewed as a concourse of voice, gaze, and threads of signification which reflect, echo, parody, and otherwise repeat in a refracted and dispersed manner each other and their entire cultural context, similar to what we saw as the basis for the filmic media. Keeping this in mind, the reader can then proceed to the succeeding poems of the collection, and look upon them as yet other perspectives in the poet's meditation upon poetry and other art forms as differing yet connected reflections of and upon a much larger system that we know as culture. The trade-off is obvious: even though textual authority is decentered, the gain is that the text is enriched by an ever-widening gyre of signification. One final example of the many that find expression in this pastiche of highly original collection of poetry is a text entitled "Interludi/Interludio" ("Interlude") from the collection *Los espejos/Els miralls*. The speaker offers an enigmatic message of ekphrastic inclination to the reader, where the allusion is to detective fiction as well as to cinema. The entire poem reads as follows:

> Construir un montaje
> > un film de espías
> > > Sherlock Holmes en el bosque
>
> Amigo Watson
> > me han herido
> > > dame la mano
> > > > amigo Watson
> > > > (Gimferrer, 55)

(To construct a montage / a spy movie / Sherlock Holmes in the woods / Friend Watson / they have wounded me / give me your hand / friend Watson)

The speaker constructs his own visual and poetic montage from the bits and pieces of cinematic as well as narrative discourse, similar to the technique that Gimferrer used in *La muerte en Beverly Hills*. The words on the printed page faintly resemble the film advancing through the camera, and evoke the fictional characters of Sir Arthur Conan Doyle, the English detective Sherlock Holmes and his sidekick Dr. Watson. The poetic voice and gaze are decidedly decentered: they may pertain to the poet-speaker, who contemplates making a film based on a fictional narrative, that of a spy thriller whose central character is the colorful and rather eccentric fictional English detective, Sherlock Holmes; or in the second half, the poetic voice may be that of the fictional character himself. It is significant that Gimferrer has opted to include a reference to spying, since this activity slyly represents the redoubtable presence of a perceptive Other, one who witnesses, one who gazes, and who gathers information that might justify action through surveillance. In either case, the wound to which the speaker refers is symbolic of the opening— as verbal noun—of the textual body by an alien Other, be it the body of the fictional Sherlock Holmes or that of the text (poem, novel, or film), by the spy, the detective, the poet, or the reader. (Or are they one and the same???) He, Holmes or poet/speaker, asks for a hand from Watson, the reader/receiver/supplement in support of his endeavor to find a cure for the textual body's involuntary and inevitable penetration by the Other, in this case the filmic medium, in his desire to be helped along the way in the process of signification, to counterbalance the loss of wholeness and oneness. Thus, the speaker (Holmes or the poetic voice and gaze) becomes one more reader of his own text, as well as a variety of other texts. Implicitly, he also asks the reader to participate in this process of creation, emission, reception, and evolution of text and sign. There can be no Sherlock Holmes without the supplemental presence of Watson, just as the poet's supplement is to be found in all the other art forms that fall under and are incorporated into the gaze of the textual I/eye, and finally into the reader. And the textual wound is the site at which their complementary yet subversive roles are simultaneously reflected. Poetry is wounded by the presence/absence of the filmic medium. Each is and is not the Other; neither can exist without the Other within the frame of this particular text; the penetrating wound effects the cure. Oneness is illusory, for its image is always reflected in the Other. And the mirror, whether of language or within the camera, is the creative membrane that joins one and Other in fragile, complementary, and subversive unity.

One other collection of poems by Pere Gimferrer that needs to be mentioned in regard to the decentralization and dispersion of the textual I/eye reminiscent of cinema is *El vendeval* (*The Gale*), first published in 1988 in Catalan, and then in 1989 in a bilingual Catalan/Spanish format. The I/eye of this text is dispersed in a new and creative way, in that the poet requested that other poets,—Octavio Paz, Antonio Colinas, Juan Ramón Masoliver, Justo Navarro, Francisco Rico, Jaime Siles, and Ramón Xirau—effect the translation process. Moreover, at times one poet would translate a text and another translation by another poet of the very same poem would appear. Alternately, two poets worked together to produce in collaboration their translation of one poem, or one poet alone would translate a series of poems within a given section. In the introduction to the collection, Gimferrer implicitly subverts his previous translations of his own poetry when he explains to his reader:

> Tiene sin duda derecho el lector a preguntar, ante todo, por qué en esta ocasión no he traducido yo mismo mi poesía y, en segundo lugar, por qué la tarea se ha repartido entre siete traductores. No he traducido yo mismo mi poesía no sólo porque íntimamente no me satisfacen del todo mis autotraducciones anteriores, sino también porque, en los últimos años, mi trabajo se centra de modo tan específico sobre la materia verbal, que carezco de la distancia suficiente para repetir la operación sobre el mismo cañamazo; más fácil me sería escribir cualesquiera otros poemas en castellano ex novo.
> (Gimferrer 1988, 13)

> (*The reader has without a doubt the right to ask, above all, why on this occasion I myself have not translated my poetry, and in the second place, why the task has been parceled out among seven translators. I myself have not translated my poetry not only because my previous self-translations do not entirely satisfy me, but also because, in the last few years, my work has centered in such a specific manner on the substance of language, that I lack the sufficient distance to repeat the operation on the same canvas; it would be easier for me to write any other poems in Spanish ex novo [from scratch].*)

In this very brief introduction, Gimferrer opens the frame of reference to the continuing narration of the story that his poetry tells, from his earliest collections to the most recent: the poet's (mis)adventures with the linguistic sign and, by extension, all systems of representation, his refusal to exercise singular and monological authority and authorship, and his celebration of the text's ability to take in and project the seemingly monologic gaze of the multiple I/eye, such as is the case in cinema. The poems of this collection focus on the (im)possible task of representation, whatever the medium, and the bilingual format as well as the decentered translation structure continue the poet's saga.

The authority of the three poetic collections of Pere Gimferrer considered here, *La muerte en Beverly Hills*, *Els miralls/Los espejos* and *El vendeval* are all ironically founded upon the power that they derive from the decentering of authorial voice and gaze, from the breaking of limits, and from the questioning stance that they communicate in regard to the language of any art form as a closed system. Cinema and specifically the mirror's presence encapsulate the ambiguity, duplicity, and power that the poet recognizes in language, and in any sign system. The camera and/or the mirror represent(s) an object, but do(es) not hold the object in its/their power. The representation of the object by the camera/mirror is veridical, but only if perceived in a certain fashion, that is, visually rather than tactilely.[21] The image produced by the camera/mirror is more a "reflection" of the nature of the camera/mirror than that of the object itself. Likewise, in these collections, Gimferrer offers his views on,—tells his story of— the ambiguous power of language. Language represents/creates an object, but it is not the object beheld by the refracted gaze of a multiplicity of textual I's/eyes; rather, the object created is linguistic in nature. The linguistic object is veridical, but refers to itself rather than to objective reality. And lastly, this linguistic object reflects the nature of the sign—mutable, elusive, expanding—rather than objective reality. By appropriating, consciously or not, film's coding, conceits, and narrative strategies, artifice, and artificiality as he interprets them on the basis of the nineteenth-century novel, Gimferrer's poetic texts reflect and reflect upon the narration of his poetry's evolution, the (im)possibility of referentiality, and representation through language. The celebration of, and rupture within, the poet's discourse(s) simultaneously, subversively both wound and cure the I's/eye's story of the unending search for signification of and through the Other.

Let us now turn to Jenaro Talens, the second poet to be considered within the ekphrastic frame of poetry and the filmic me-

dia.[22] This Spanish poet of the twentieth century has theorized
a competing model of film, one that is based on the work of the
famed writer, director, and cinematographer, Luis Buñuel. As in
the case of Gimferrer, Talens's filmic model of choice will also
appear in his poetry, not only in images that appear at the level
of content, but also in the structure, organization, and presentation of his collections of verse. It should be remembered that
Gimferrer stated in his text on film and literature that Buñuel's
work was one of the clearest attempts to break away from the
narrative form based on the nineteenth-century novel; his cinematic syntax was based on the immanent power of association
between images, through relations of affinity, contiguity, complementarity, or inversion, thus freeing itself of whatever logical or
rational link that tied it to the aforementioned style of cinematic
narrative (Gimferrer 1985, 12). Talens, in his book on Luis Buñuel's *Chien andalou* (*Andalusian Dog*) entitled *El ojo tachado*,
utilizes as his point of departure the opening scene of Ramón del
Valle-Inclán's *Cuernos de don Friolera* (*Horns of Don Friolera*),
where Don Estrafalario claims the right to view the world from
a different perspective, much as the dead look at the world of
the living. Talens goes on to cite the last lines of Buñuel's autobiography, *My Last Sigh*, in which the cinematographer evokes a
similar image:

> Frankly, despite my horror of the press, I'd love to rise from the grave
> every ten years or so and go buy a few newspapers. Ghostly pale,
> sliding silently along the walls, my papers under my arm, I'd return
> to the cemetery and read about all the disasters in the world before
> falling back to sleep, safe and secure in my tomb (Talens, 1993, 256).
>   (xiii)

These comments, reminiscent also of those of Roland Barthes
in his treatise on photography and on its relationship to (his
mother's) death, for Talens preserve the essence of Buñuel's art,
to look at the world from a perspective alien to the conventional
subject/object of the gaze. As the poet describes it, "For almost
half a century from *Un chien andalou* (*An Andalusian Dog*) to
That Obscure Object of Desire, Buñuel's films have attempted,
with admirable constancy and radicality, to question not only the
cinematic apparatus itself—the mise-en-scène of a supposedly
neutral and objective gaze—but also the incoherent logic that
the imperialism of reason imposes on the real" (Ibid., xiii). He
also emphasizes that Buñuel's "work as a filmmaker centered on

a systematic attack of the optimism that founds the bourgeois
vision of the world," as well as that "his work focuses less on
the supposed contents of each film than on the rhetoric of the
discourse itself" (Ibid., xiii). Thus, it is obvious that Talens considers Buñuel's films to be primarly about how films mean, how
they are "metafilmic" as it were, and secondarily about a particular story or narration. Moreover, the distinction between fiction
and nonfiction becomes irrelevant, in that the problem that the
Spanish director's films present "is not so much *to show the
world* but *to analyze how this world is looked at* (that is, *constructed*) by the cinematographic apparatus" (Ibid., xvi) (Talens's
italics). In regard to the film discourse of *Un chien andalou*,
Talens proposes that it "gathers, problematizes, and finally denies the canonical workings of traditional artistic discourses by
conflicting with the epistemological system that supports them,
and thus to read this film also presupposes to deal with the more
general problem of *how to read*, that is, *how to produce sense
from a given text*" (Ibid., xxiv) (Talens's italics).

    In his first chapter, "Discursive Strategies and Production of
Sense" Talens sets about defining the role of the reader or receiver of Buñuel's nontraditional discourse, not only from the
perspective of the semiotics of imagery, but also from that of
textual space. Implicitly he recognizes the difficulty for the
reader/viewer in arriving at interpretive meaning, and obliquely
makes reference to the dispersion of the filmic I/eye: "Director,
producer, scriptwriter, editor, actors, light technicians, and
others compete for a privileged position that ultimately belongs
to all of them without exception and to no one in particular,
because it is the articulation of each of their discourses that
ultimately constitutes the speaking subject" (Ibid., 7). He is in
agreement with Gimferrer's views about the relationship between film and literature, in that Talens also underscores the
reflexive relationship between them: "film analysis lets scholars
return to literary texts with new instruments for reading that
have made it possible to see those mechanisms in a new light"
(Ibid., 8). Thus, the major question for Talens's reading of Buñuel's films is as follows: "From where does a film speak?" The
poet's answer is to be found in his theorization about reading as
the construction of the filmic object, and in the distinction that
he makes between what he terms film's possibility of "poetic
discourse versus narrative discourse." It is his position that Buñuel's films utilize "poetic discourse" rather than the narrative
one.

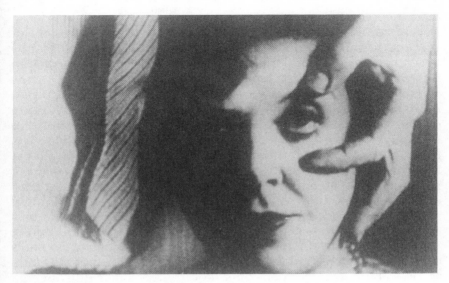

Un chien andalou © Luis Buñel.

His definition of what he terms film's *poetic discourse* as prac-
ticed by Buñuel calls for the cancellation of temporality, causality, sequentiality, and psychological motivation. Rather, it is
based on the (re)presentation of a series of fragments which are
not subordinated to the confines of space and time. As a consequence, "sense is produced . . . through the elaboration of the
nonmeaning of absent elements, that is, by means of the fissures
between links" (Ibid., 22). And for Talens, this process of signification ultimately leads to subversion, with its motor being "not
abstract thought, but desire; a desire understood not as *lack of
being* but as *provocation to action*" (Ibid., 23). Buñuel's *Chien
andalou* for Talens is the perfect example of the subversiveness
of this poetic discourse; that which is underscored is the multi-
plication of the text's signifying possibilities, with the inscription in the film of the equivocal ambiguity of its own interpretive
codes (Ibid., 25). This process of inscription presupposes an active role for the reader/viewer, who must be simultaneously inside and outside all of the interpretive codes which are at play
in this sort of filmic text.

Let us now turn to the poetry of Jenaro Talens with his film
theory in mind, and consider the three collections that appeared
within approximately the same temporal framework as *El ojo
tachado*. They are *La mirada extranjera*, *Tabula rasa*, and *Purga-*

torio (*Purgatory*) (1986). The first, *La mirada extranjera*, is a
hybrid collection in that the text as well as authorship is multiple; the poems of Talens are accompanied by the photographs
of Michaël Nerlich, or perhaps it is the other way around, that the
photos are accompanied by the poems; photographs and poems
construct a textual space based upon complementarity and simultaneity.[23] The cover of the collection captures the attention
of the reader, since there is a black-and-white photograph that
depicts the trunk of a naked woman in repose, whose body seems
to be painted with undulating stripes. The right breast is almost
totally out of view, while the left seems to be supported by a
piercing shaft of darkness that extends under the breast and
around to the center between the two. This image is strikingly
reminiscent of another that shocked early audiences of the cinema, in that there is a strong resemblance between it and one of
the opening shots of *Un chien andalou*, the one where a woman's
eye is held open, and a man's hand grasping a straight-blade
razor is about to cut it open. This shot from Buñuel's film appears
on both the front and back cover of Talens's *Ojo tachado*, and,
for this reader, serves as a metaphor of Buñuel's filmic discourse
by which the cinematographer looks at the world from an alien
perspective. The penetrating male hand wounds the space and
process of seeing, the site/sight of visual perception. The female
eye represents the locus of elision between subject and object,
and the discourse that will communicate that space and process.
In other words, the man's hand writes a new story directly on/
about the eye, about the process of seeing, about how to see, and
by extension, how to read. The act of wounding effects the cure
necessary to detach the see-er/seer from the conventional and to
see in a new and original manner.

The resemblance between Buñuel's cutting image of cutting
and Nerlich's equally disquieting one is not based on the superficial similarities,—a woman's naked body in one case, a
woman's head with a man standing behind her ready to mutilate
her left eye in the other—, but rather on form, organization, composition, and the distribution of light and dark in each of the
two shots. In Buñuel's shot, the dark shaft covers the right side
of the woman's face, while in Nerlich's it creeps around and
vaguely supports her left breast. The dark spot that is circled by
light in Buñuel's shot is the woman's left eye about to be slashed,
whereas in the cover photograph it is the woman's left nipple.
The man standing behind the woman in Buñuel's shot is wearing
a tie with diagonal stripes, the light stripes being wider than the

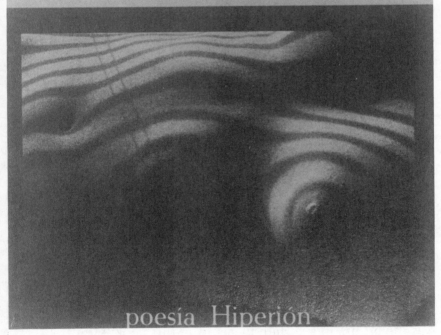

La mirada extranjera © Michaël Nerlich.

dark ones; his shirt has faint vertical black and white stripes. In the Nerlich cover shot, the woman's body seems to be painted with fluttering black-and-white stripes that follow her curves. There are two narrow black stripes that are vertical, and cut through the undulation of the body stripes, which faintly recall perhaps both the man's necktie and the faint vertical stripes of his shirt. Thus, the allusion in Nerlich's shot to the (in)famous one of Buñuel bases itself not on the superficial similarity of the two figures, but rather on the discourse of composition of the various fragments that make up the two very different shots, one by Buñuel in his ground-breaking movie, and the other by a photographer presumably inspired by the same iconoclastic mode of composition based on lines, light, and shadow.

And in point of fact, in the prose prologue to the collection entitled "Del azar como aventura y extraterritorialidad" ("Of Chance as Adventure and Extraterritoriality") Talens indeed makes reference to his work, to its chronology, and to its relationship to that of Luis Buñuel. The subtitle of his section of the prologue carries the title of "Historia de un libro, o de cómo el azar puso entre paréntesis la narratividad" ("History of a Book, Or of How Chance Put Between Parentheses Narrativity"). Buñuel's imprint is evident from several different perspectives: " . . me había planteado la posibilidad de elaborar un discurso poético no narrativo, cuya estructura no necesitara de apoyo anecdótico, ni hubiera de recurrir a una articulación de pensamiento para desarrollarse. Un discurso poético capaz de elevarse sobre sí mismo, sin perder, por ello, su transitividad" (". . . [the possibility had come to me of elaborating a poetic discourse that [was] not narrative, whose structure does not need anecdotal support, nor would it have recourse to an articulation of thought in order to develop [itself]. A poetic discourse capable of arising above itself, without losing, because of it, its transitivity") (Talens 1985, 12) . . . ". . . tenía que preparar un *Workshop* sobre *Un chien andalou* lo que hizo que me decidiera a terminar mi tantas veces propuesto libro sobre Buñuel. Esa extraña casualidad originó, en cierta medida, este libro" (" I had to prepare a *Workshop* on *An Andalusian Dog*, which made me decide to finish my so many times proposed book on Buñuel. This strange coincidence was the origin, in a certain measure, of this book") (Ibid., 14). . . . "*La mirada extranjera* y *El ojo tachado* fueron posibles el uno por el otro. Si, como afirma Lacan, es cierto que el encuentro de dos objetos en el tiempo y en el espacio es cuestión de azar, pero que todo lo que ocurra después está ya determinado por este

encuentro, esta inesperada aventura venía a confirmármelo"
("*The Foreign Gaze* and *The Branded Eye* were possible, the one
giving way to the other. If, as Lacan affirms, it is certain that the
encounter of two objects in time and in space is a question of
chance, but that all that occurs afterward is already determined
by this encounter, this unexpected adventure came to confirm it
to me") (Ibid., 15). As he sees it, the hybrid text of photography
and poetry is a sort of love story that rejects narrativity in the
nineteenth-century sense, and is told from the perspective or
gaze of a foreigner, and is constructed around the twin cities of
Minneapolis/St. Paul, Minnesota, using poetry and the visual
media of photography and cinema. The final product's description is eerily in harmony with *Un chien andalou*: "Las piezas
sueltas se negaban a contar una historia, pero dibujaban, en su
negativa, un mosáico con más lógica de la previsible. Desde una
idéntica vivencia del exilio y la extraterritorialidad, nuestro propuesto recorrido narrativo-turístico se había convertido en una
suerte de viaje interior" ("The loose pieces refused to tell a story,
but they delineated, in their negation, a mosaic with more logic
than anticipated. From an identical lived experience of exile and
extraterritoriality, our proposed narrative-touristic journey had
changed into a kind of interior journey") (Ibid., 16).

In the second half of the prologue, entitled "La mirada amor-
osa" ("The Loving Gaze"), the photographer Michaël Nerlich recounts his own version of the fortuitous meeting between
himself and Talens in Minneapolis, and his explanation for the
hybrid text that the reader is attempting to comprehend. His
verbal text contradicts several points emphasized by Talens—in
regard to chronology, intent, and motivation. But he too underscores his perspective as that of outsider: "El mundo no deja de
sorprenderme. Siempre lo miré con ojos de extranjero, y extranjero seguiré siendo, dejando algo de mí por donde pase, por
donde paso, llevando conmigo recuerdos, olvidos, imágenes ex-
trañas" ("The world does not stop surprising me. I always looked
at it with [the] eyes of a foreigner, and [a] foreigner I will continue
being, leaving behind something of myself through wherever I
pass, carrying with me memories, things forgotten, strange images") (Ibid., 17). The two are in agreement that their hybrid text
tells but one story in the fragments, conjunctions, and contigu-
ities, of which it is composed. As Nerlich states at the end of the
prologue, "Jamás mis imágenes han sido otra cosa que cantos de
amor (Y en eso se confunden poemas y fotografías)" ("Never have
my images been other than songs of love [And in that poems

and photographs mingle one with another]") (Ibid., 19). Thus *La mirada extranjera* by Talens and Nerlich transmutes the style and technique of Buñuel: the two artists use a conjoined yet disparate perspective that is alien to a poetic text on Minneapolis, in that they both are foreigners to the place itself, and choose not to (re)present their image via a discernible and conventional love narrative. Their love story is one of disjunction, fragmentation, defamiliarization, desire, and alienation. Because of the text's hybrid nature, they encourage the reader to focus more on the rhetoric of discourse, and to develop reading strategies to suit the complementarity of poetic text and photographic image, to arrive at interpretation(s) based upon the implicit power of association between images and the signifying presence of reason and logic's absence. Temporality, causality, and sequentiality fall under the reader's auspices, since the visual and verbal fragments form an uneasy collage of multiple interpretive possibilities. Moreover, the "love story" may be an affective one of interior emotions, but may as well refer to a fascination with an exterior object, one constructed by human intervention to serve either an aesthetic or practical purpose. In an overwhelming majority of the photographs that make up the filmic component of the hybrid text, architectural details of the Minneapolis environs and skyline fall within the focus of the camera I's/eye's gaze.

Each segment, composed of verbal text and photograph, is preceded by a title page that carries two titles, one in large block print and the other in italics. It is up to the reader to decide which title is for which communicative text, or perhaps one is the title and the other, the subtitle, for both. The opening poem begins with "Qué extraño ese viajero" ("How strange that traveler") (Ibid., 26), and the speaker continues with a third-person description that attempts to represent not only physical detail and movement, but also sentiment, absence, and the speaker's own difficulties in representing: "Difícil describir / tanto silencio junto" ("Difficult to describe / so much silence together") (Ibid.). It is only close to the end of this opening text that the speaker reveals a perspective that includes another person, the "tú" ("you" [fam. sing.]), to whom the description is addressed: "A lo lejos se ven las montañas del sur, / como un perfil borroso / donde a veces la lluvia y los tornados / son como tú, suceden" ("Afar the moutains of the south are seen / as an illegible profile / where at times the rains and the tornados / are like you [fam. sing.], they happen") (Ibid.). This opening text closes with an enigmatic statement, in that the speaker seems to affirm his / her version of the truth, but puts into question the (re)presentation by the use of a subversive negative:" No dudes / de mí. Yo no podría / imaginarte, ahora, / cuando la noche sólo ha comenzado" ("Don't [you (fam. sing.)] doubt / me. I could not imagine you [fam. sing.], now, / when the night has only begun") (Ibid., 29).

Each of the textual segments opens itself to further dispersion and fragmentation, since the titles and texts make reference by way of allusion and illusion to many other forms of textuality. For example, "LA FIGURA EN EL TAPIZ / DÓNDE BUSCAR TU IMAGEN / RIVERVIEW TOWER, MINNEAPOLIS" ("THE FIGURE IN THE CARPET / Where to search for your [fam. sing.] image / Riverview Tower, Minneapolis") may be making intertextual reference to the story by Henry James, "The Figure in the Carpet," which also appeared in Gimferrer's Els miralls/Los espejos, and most assuredly refers to the well-known postmodern architecture of the city of Minneapolis. The accompanying photo is a partial head and shoulder shot of the enigmatic woman whose body graces the cover of the collection. Black-and-white stripes trace her face, neck, and shoulders, and there are three perfectly straight white stripes evident on the wall behind her, which are perhaps a veiled reference to the skyscraper horizon of the northern city that she and the poet's/photographer's gaze attempt to frame and possess. The poetic text of this segment communicates the desire to know and possess as well as the ultimate failure in the attempt:

> Dónde buscar tu imagen, su volumen,
> el subterfugio de decirte con
> palabras que no dicen, se disgregan, y
> eliden piel, y cuerpo, y no conocen,
> casi como si un aire, o si fragmentos, o
> tal vez memoria, que fue tuya, que
> no dice cómo, ni por qué, ni dónde.
>
> (Ibid., 53)

(Where to look for your [fam. sing.] image, its volume, / the subterfuge of telling you [fam. sing.] with / words that do not tell, they break to pieces, and / they elide skin, and body, and they do not know, / almost as if an air, or if fragments, or / perhaps memory, that was yours [fam. sing.], that / does not tell how, nor why, nor where.)

Media of many forms and discourses make a fleeting appearance as well; there are references to flashes, perhaps photographic as well as inspirational, stage directions, biography, aperture (archi-

tectural, of a camera lens, ways of seeing, or existential stance?),
limits of representation, as well as the female nude. The collection's closing segment is entitled "Quelqu'un a parlé de magie
moderne (Stronger than geometry)" ("Somebody Has Spoken of
Modern Magic [Stronger than Geometry]") (Ibid., 151), and is
accompanied by a photograph of the enigmatic female nude's
lower back, buttocks, and thighs. Once again her body carries
the telltale (tail?) stripes that were visible in previous photos. In
the background there are both vertical and horizontal stripes
which seem to be enclosed by strict, enclosing frames. The closing verbal text is not a poem but rather a quote from Louis Aragón (1918):[24]

> Hemos seguido demasiado tiempo a nuestros hermanos mayores por
> encima de los cadáveres de otras civilizaciones. Ved cómo llega el
> tiempo de la vida. Ya no iremos a conmovernos a Bayreuth o a
> Ravena. . . . Más hermosos nos parecen los nombres de Toronto o
> Minneapolis. Alguien ha hablado de magia moderna.
>
> (Talens 1985, 151)

> (For too long we have followed our older brothers over the cadavers
> of other civilizations. (You [fam. pl.]) See how the time of life arrives.
> We will no longer be moved to go to Bayreuth or to Ravena. . . .
> The names of Toronto or Minneapolis seem more beautiful to us.
> Somebody has spoken of modern magic.)

This final intertextual reference by Talens to Aragón concerning
two major North American cities brings into focus their importance as centers of postmodern architecture and culture, with
postmodernism's tendency to playful self-reference, and the
timeless simultaneity of past, present, and future.[25] La mirada
extranjera of Talens and Nerlich enters into an ekphrastic relationship with the cinema, in that Buñuel's model of filmic construction   (architecture?)   inspires   this   multimedia   text's
(re)presentation of an "unstoried" story, and utilizes the Buñuelian technique of a decentered, detemporalized, and (il)logi-
cal gaze that pauses on both exterior and interior visions of
reality. In turn, this problematic gaze forces the reader, just as
the spectator of Un chien andalou to ponder the rhetoric of this
particular text and of all discourse, as well as the more general
question of "how to read." But this text is much more complicated from an ekphrastic perspective than, for example, La
muerte en Beverly Hills of Gimferrer, in that Buñuel's cinema
provides the theoretical / architectural model of construction,

but the two artists,—Talens, the poet and Nerlich, the photographer,—use their respective artistic material to further disperse the gaze. The gaze of this hybrid text reflects a postmodern turn, in that all the art forms that inform the creative process and product influence the focus, ambiguity, and dispersion of the textual I/eye. The simultaneous presence/absence of cinema, photography, and architecture stretch to the limit and beyond the new definition of ekphrasis that was called for in the case of Gimferrer's text. Here, the "still movement" is subverted not only by photography's moving out of and beyond the camera's frame, by Buñuelian cinema's action, sound, construction, theory, and escape from logic, but also by postmodern architecture, its simultaneity with, and complementarity to, Buñuelian cinema, and its tendency to break the frame of temporality, sequentiality, and causality.[26] In a deconstructivist move, the I/eye of this hybrid text becomes synonymous with the gaze of the Other, who resembles yet differs from/defers to the I/eye of the text(s) under consideration. The exchange of power and pleasure for all the creative artists and readers of La mirada extranjera results from the simultaneous and complementary surrender and sovereignty of the various art forms, the celebration and rupture of frames as one discourse cedes to another and back again, as each participant ponders not only this text, but also textuality, discourse, referentiality, and the power/impotence of the allusive/elusive sign in the high stakes yet playful game that is called postmodern representation.

Two other poetic collections by Jenaro Talens merit brief mention at this juncture, not because they use photography and cinema as their focal points of departure, but rather because they also use a multimedia approach to ekphrasis. The collection entitled Tabula rasa has a simple line drawing of a female nude on its cover reminiscent perhaps of those of Picasso in his Vollard Suite. The collection's title reminds the reader of the blank page or the film within the darkened camera, both of which await differing/deferred types of inscription.[27] And in the opening text, "El estado de las cosas" ("The State of Things"), the speaker makes reference to the gaze, creation, and difficulty of achieving the representation of a perceived object by means of language:

> Díme cuál es mi nombre, cómo
> son estos ojos que te miran,
> devueltos a su viejo territorio,
> con algo de un saber que no es cansancio

sino sólo el residuo que perdura
después de haber mirado tanto tiempo
las mismas cosas. Díme, dí quién soy,
esta voz que antecede a un habla muda,
y brota y te acaricia y no te toca;

(Talens 1985, 9)

([You {fam. sing.}] Tell me which is my name, how / are these eyes
that look at you [fam. sing.] / returned to their old territory, / with
something of a knowledge that is not fatigue / but rather only the
residue that lasts / after having looked for so long / at the same things.
[You {fam. sing.}] Tell me, [you {fam. sing.}] tell who I am, / this voice
that precedes a mute language, / and gushes out and caresses you
[fam. sing.] and does not touch you [fam. sing.])

In succeeding poems, the speaker makes reference to poetry,
narrative, architecture, portraits and still lifes, sculpture, dramatic performance, music and its lyrics, among others. For example in "*It takes two to tango* (Louise DeMint Zahareas)" the
title refers to music and dance as well as to the popular proverb
in English; the epigraph is from the English sculptor Henry
Moore, which states "Sculpture is like a journey. You have a
different view when you return" (Ibid., 23. Zahareas is a sculptor.). And in the poetic text, the speaker begins with the first-
person plural form of "nosotros" ("we") to compare and contrast
the mortality of humanity and the supposedly inanimate but
immortal sculpture, "Comparado con nosotros, este trozo de
bronce es inmortal" ("Compared with us, this bit of bronze is
immortal"), a direct reference to the plastic art. Thus, at its start
this particular poetic text purports to base its ekphrastic gaze on
two figures cast in metal. But the sculpture's artistic frame is
subtly broken in the closing lines of the text when the speaker
states:

. . . Míralos, abrazados
en una eternidad que no conocen,
cómo mis ojos funden su presencia escindida,
su sola forma de permanecer.

(Ibid.)

(. . . [You fam. sing.] Look at them, embraced / in an eternity that
they do not know, / how my eyes smelt their split presence, / their
only way of remaining.)

The object of the speaker's desire and gaze could well be an intertextual reference to Keats's young lovers of his famous "Ode on a Grecian Urn," one of the most outstanding and oft-cited examples of ekphrastic poetry. Thus, the poet-speaker's lens falls upon a sculpture and is described in poetic form through the speaker's voice. This sculpture may in turn be a revision of Keats's own poetic text. In the final two lines of verse, the speaker restricts his line of vision, which now falls upon himself, "cómo mis ojos. . . ." ("how my eyes. . . ."). In these closing lines, the speaker through his poetic text, bequeathes immortality upon the un-dead, in the act of seeing them in a new light, those for whom "su mutismo no es muerte, sino el murmullo sordo / de un corazón que ignora cómo latir" ("their muteness is not death, but rather the deaf murmur / of a heart that does not know how to beat"). But the bronze sculpture, immortalized in this poetic text, also concedes immortality to the very mortals who have created the immortal piece(s) of art; the sculptor, and the poet(s), Keats and Talens. The sculpture and the poetic texts remain, framed by and framing the three artists, whose shadows appear indelibly etched on the surface levels of their own creations.

And in "Ideas acerca de la confusión en Cherokee Avenue" ("Ideas Concerning the Confusion on Cherokee Avenue"), a long poem divided into five parts, the speaker rambles as if in a documentary film along the streets of St. Paul as well as in his own memory and consciousness in order to discover his own identity, his present, his past, and his sense of connectedness. Ekphrastic references are many, to poetry, painting, architecture, film, and lyrics of songs only half-remembered. At the end, the reader is encouraged to reread the entire text, since the poem closes with "El sueño es dulce cuando estás dormida" ("Dreaming is sweet when you [fam. sing.] are asleep") (Ibid., 30).

This collection has what Talens calls a neological "Postfacio" ("Postface")—in contrast with a "Preface"—in which he offers a defense of the collection, the process of its creation, and its place within his poetic trajectory as a whole, which he sees as "La búsqueda deliberada y constante de una escritura sin estilo, de un lenguaje que hiciese de la opacidad el no-lugar del síntoma, donde lo real pudiera inscribirse" ("The deliberate and constant search for a writing style without style, for a language that would make of opacity the symptomatic no-place, where the real could inscribe itself") (Ibid., 90). Within this framework, then, his use of other discourses, of other art forms, becomes the basis upon which he constructs a response to the "opacity of the no-place," the silence, the absence, the void that the artistic-creator attempts to confront and respond to through his or her art. Talens in this collection inscribes the other art forms as well as the fissures between them into the process of his journey, and conscripts the reader into the task of interpretation and signification. In the process of reading, the reader confronts not only the fissures of the text, but also the discourses of signification, as well as the reader's own means of constructing an individual process of "how to read." The breaking of various frames occurs not only through the use of ekphrasis, but also in the very structure of the collection itself, its refusal to closure with Talens's "Epilogue & after," as well as with his aforementioned "Postfacio," and finally with the "Apéndice" ("Appendix") provided by yet another author, Vicente Ponce. This final supplement leads the reader to consider, in Buñuelian fashion, not only the collection's poetry, but also the ruptured frame that (does not) fail(s) to enclose it.

In his "Postfacio" to Tabula rasa, Talens makes reference to yet another of his collections, Purgatori/Purgatorio (Purgatory) (1986), for which he collaborated with the artist Domènec Canet to produce a text that is similar to his Mirada extranjera, but in the case of Purgatori/Purgatorio the two media are poetry and line drawings instead of poetry and photography. But the textual gaze is dispersed even further in that the poetic texts that appear in the 1986 edition are in both Catalan and Spanish, Talens having produced the original versions in Catalan, and Antonia Cabanilles having served as the translator for the poems in Spanish, which is similar in composition to Pere Gimferrer's Vendeval. Also, the prologue for this collection was written by Sebastià Serrano, in which the poet Talens appears only as a third-person protagonist in the text of an/the Other. Similar to the statement made by Gimferrer concerning his Els miralls/Los espejos ([The] Mirrors), the first text to be published by Gimferrer in Catalan, Talens comments in regard to Purgatori:

> El extrañamiento de contar (¿me?) desde un espacio y una cultura diferentes comportaba la ruptura con el discurso personal de la memoria y el posible inicio de una escritura desde el vacío. Asumida la imposibilidad del silencio, quedaba, cuando menos, la voluntad de romper los espejos, acabando de una vez con ese juego solitario que consiste en ocultarse sin vacilaciones, bajo formas de desnudez, ("vuelto palabras claras y precisas"), en un dispositivo falsamente confesional.
>
> (Talens 1985, 90)

(The longing to tell [of myself?] from a different space and a culture bore the rupture with the personal discourse of memory and the possible initiation of a style of writing from the void. Having assumed the impossibility of silence, there remained, at the least, the will to break mirrors, finishing without more ado with that solitary game that consists of hiding oneself without vacillations, under forms of nakedness, ["turned into clear and precise words"], of a falsely confessional contrivance").[28]

As in the case of Gimferrer, Talens views his use of Catalan not only as a change in linguistic code, but also, and more importantly, as a means of exploring the Self, as viewing that Self as Other in a distanced yet familiar way, and as a means of approaching the void of silence within, of exploring the (im)possibilities of representation as well. Thus, breaking the frame through ekphrasis or through other rhetorical strategies, represents not a failure but an expansion of the (im)possibilities of representation, a celebration of the (failure of) language and discourse to represent and to communicate meaning, both of which remain as defining characteristics of the group of Spanish writers known as the "novísimos".

Similar to the stance taken by Gimferrer in regard to language, art, and the power of representation, that of Talens champions the breaking of frames not only through the presence/absence of the revolutionary Buñuelian filmic discourse but also the dispersion of textual authority in other ways, such as the presence of complementary drawings and photograph within or simultaneous with his hybrid texts. In so doing, Talens underscores his decidedly postmodern perspective, which reveals his unstoried story of rapprochement with the (im)possibility of the sign, and of the subsequent (ir)reality of silence. If Gimferrer narrates in nineteenth-century fashion his love story with poetry and other forms of textuality while using the discourse of the bygone days of Hollywood, then Talens does so with Buñuelian tatters of language and oblique forms of textuality that are pieced together into a disjointed, cinematic, moving collage of fragmented, timeless images, which the reader is at pains to (re)construct into a provisional whole that follows a logic evident only in the (de)-constructed fissures between the fragments.

The texts of both Gimferrer and Talens, much as those of photography and cinema upon which they are based, move out of and beyond the poetic frame that nominally encloses them, to celebrate the decentering of textual power and authority in a clearly postmodern manner. Their stance represents the poets' coming to terms with their own views on language—as slippery and deceptive, yet challenging and exhiliarating—and art's place in a much larger cultural system. By acknowledging the decenteredness of textual authority and opening up their texts to the presence of the alien Other with the wounding cure of ekphrasis, here manifested as the erotics of the gaze, a process of desire, penetration, and intersubjectivity between the I/eye and the Other, these twentieth-century poets reinforce the discursive power of their texts rather than dilute it. The gaze and voice of Jenaro Talens and Pere Gimferrer reflect not the nihilistic void posited by cultural doomsayers of the present day, but rather their sense of rapture in the presence of Otherness that is all language, all art, the essence of the sign itself. The obscure object of desire for both Gimferrer and Talens is the ongoing process of the subversive search for signification through, and simultaneously in spite of, language. Through their filmic poetry manifested in hybrid texts, each produces in unique fashion a moving picture that celebrates, questions, then moves out of, away from, and beyond the frames of discourse(s) upon which their system(s) of representation is/are based. Poetry and ekphrasis both are enriched by the still movement of their journeys.

Epilogue: Fade-out—or—Still Moving . . .

THE power of ekphrasis in twentieth-century Spanish poetry resides in its ability to speak to the issues of authority, authorship, value, ideology, and representation itself. As has been demonstrated in each of the preceding chapters, each poet allows an alien Other art object to "speak for itself" within the ruptured bounds of the poetic text. This art object, in speaking for itself, brings to the forefront the power and impotence of language or any other sign system to maintain its discursive integrity. Thus, ekphrasis moves far beyond mere description, to become the trope of tropes, the metaphor of language itself, a communicative system that both succeeds and fails to (re)present a reality outside of itself. This powerful literary strategy opens a text to the presence of the alien Other. The ruptured text, in turn, both celebrates and subverts the alien presence, by simultaneously giving voice to and effacing the trace of the invader. That which is ultimately revealed is the coding and conventionality of representation and signification itself.

In appraising the rapprochement of one form of art with another, each poet, beginning with Manuel Machado at the beginning of the century and continuing on until the closing years with Pere Gimferrer and Jenaro Talens, works out individual strategies to negotiate the exchange of power and pleasure and the play of surrender and sovereignty that inevitably occur in their attempts to interpret the time-space dialectic between art and literature. In the process the reader is inexorably drawn into the tangle of textuality, and is witness to, and participant in, the act of reading and writing, since this reader must read the poet reading yet another artwork, and be complicitous in how not only the poet reads the art object, but also how the art object reads the poet and the core ideology that is at work in this reading process. Each poet develops a mode of dialogue with the alien Other art object, and communicates not only to/with this alien Other, but also about the social, aesthetic, historical, and cultural context that has been the backdrop to the poet's ideological formation. And in this dialogue between poet and art object,

217

the ekphrastic texts speaks about poetry itself, poetic discourse, and convention, and how the poetic text both asserts and concedes its authority to the art object in the process of description. This metapoetic aspect is especially obvious in the texts from the second half of the century, such as those of Gil de Biedma, Valente, Fuertes, Gimferrer, and Talens, and to a somewhat lesser extent those of Atencia and Rossetti. As was demonstrated in the last chapter, both Gimferrer and Talens's use of ekphrasis through the film media brings attention to poetic discourse and to its codes and conventions, as well as demands a new definition for ekphrasis itself, one that will effectively frame the time-space dialectic from a filmic point of view, and also allow for the subversion of the definition of ekphrasis that calls for the celebration of the "still movement" seen in previous examples and manifestations.

The I/eye in the ekphrastic poem simultaneously takes in and projects an image that is both interior and exterior to the poem's boundary. The gaze of the poetic I/eye reflects and reflects upon power, ideology, authority, authorship, gender, and genre, and draws the reader into the play of signifiers that results from the confrontation between the poem and the art object. With each new confrontation, each poet enters into dialogue with history, culture, and society, and invites the reader to contemplate and celebrate the surrender, sovereignty, power, and pleasure that this intersection of art and literature manifests. The rupture of boundaries that results because of ekphrasis opens all artistic discourse, whether literary or visual, to new and hybrid possibilities of enriched signification.

Notes

CHAPTER 1. GET THE PICTURE?

1. For a history of ekphrasis, its intepretation from a variety of perspectives, and its application, see especially the studies by Emilie L. Bergmann, Diane Chaffee, Jean H. Hagstrum, James A. W. Heffernan, Murray Krieger, Françoise Meltzer, and W. J. T. Mitchell.

2. In his *Museum of Words* Heffernan takes issue with Krieger's assessment and definition of ekphrasis. For his part, Heffernan prefers to define ekphrasis as "the verbal representation of visual representation" (Heffernan 1993, 3).

3. The nine Muses, daughters of Zeus and Mnemosyne, are the following: Calliope, Muse of epic poetry and eloquence; Euterpe, Muse of music or of lyric poetry; Erato, Muse of the poetry of love; Polyhymnia, Muse of oratory and sacred poetry; Clio, Muse of history; Melpomene, Muse of tragedy; Thalia, Muse of comedy; Terpsichore, Muse of choral song and dance; Urania, Muse of astronomy.

4. Mitchell's last chapter in his *Picture Theory* (1994) entitled "From CNN to JFK" discusses the newer forms of pictorial representation, their relationship to the reader/viewer, and the need for a balance of power and responsibility.

5. For a discussion of point of view in the interartistic text, see the studies by Christopher S. Braider and Claus Clüver.

6. For a discussion of the problematic role of language as mediator, see Michael Baxandall, *Patterns of Intention* (1985).

7. Erich Auerbach's *Mimesis: The Representation of Reality in Western Literature* (1946) is an excellent example of this mimetic orientation.

8. *Avant-Garde, Avant Guerre, and the Language of Rupture* (1986). In her chapter on "The Invention of Collage" in her *The Futurist Moment*, Marjorie Perloff explores this art form that clearly demonstrates the tensions suggested by Gustavo Pérez Firmat in his study on liminality.

9. See Charles Bernheimer, "Manet's *Olympia*: The Figuration of Scandal (1989)," who posits that the female artist or reader may subvert the concept of the male gaze by assuming a position of power by "render[ing] the *male's* insecurity about sexual difference problematic to him" (Bernheimer 1989, 274). (Bernheimer's italics.)

10. Terence Diggory, commenting on Marcelin Pleynet, views this relationship as one of "perpetually deferring closure, continually placing itself in a productive differential relation with what remains beyond its boundaries" (Diggory 1985).

11. See especially Mitchell's opening section of *Picture Theory*, where he discusses the relationships among text, image, power, ideology, and value.

12. Mitchell prefers the term *ambivalence* (Mitchell 1994, 163); Heffernan

agrees, and cites examples of ekphrasis that exhibit "veneration and anxiety" (Heffernan 1993, 7).

13. See also Wendy Steiner's *Pictures of Romance. Form against Context in Literature and Painting* as well as her "Causes of Effect: Edith Wharton and the Economics of Ekphrasis." In the latter she demonstrates how ekphrasis is the fulcrum upon which a narration may balance itself. In the Wharton text, it polarizes capitalist versus aristocratic ideals, is "the topos of the still, transcendent moment, [and] opposes the contingency of plot flow and temporal progression in the novel and hence plays a signal role in the confrontation between contextual and acontextual value" (Steiner 1989, 279).

Chapter 2. How Manuel Machado Did (Not) Get the Picture

1. Several critics already have noted Manuel Machado's "modernista" tendencies. The article by Enric Bou is especially significant, in that he uses the "poesía pictórica" ("pictorial poetry") as a basis for the development of his thesis. See also the two studies by Allen W. Phillips as well as those by Luis Antonio de Villena and Manuel Romero Luque.

2. Machado's interest in, and exposure to, the visual arts has already been well documented. See especially the studies by Bou, Gordon Brotherston, Alfredo Carballo Picazo, María Pilar Celma Valero, and Francisco J. Blasco Pascual, Gerardo Diego, Gillian Gayton, Franciso López Estrada, and Machado's own *Guerra literaria*.

3. For studies of ekphrasis in Spanish Golden Age literature, see the studies by Bergmann and David H. Darst.

4. All references are to Machado, *Obras completas (Complete Works)*.

5. Among the many studies of this poem the ones that I have found to be the most useful are those of Dámaso Alonso, Brotherston, Carballo Picazo, Miguel D'Ors, and Gayton.

6. Gustavo Agrait notes very perceptively that Machado solves the rhyme problem of the final tercet in a very creative way. Instead of electing to turn the final stanza into a quartet, so that all the verses would be connected by rhyme, Machado opted to utilize the internal rhyme of the famous "guante de ante."

7. In addition to "Felipe IV," several others of Machado's portrait poems inspired similar debates. D'Ors offers an extensive catalog of those poems that he believes do not coincide precisely with the representation offered by the visual artist, in addition to information concerning the polemic(s) surrounding each poetic text. See also the general discussion of Machado's "inexactitudes" ("inaccuracies") by Celma Valero and Blasco Pascual Ibid., 1981, and that concerning "La infanta Margarita" (Princess Margaret") in Gayton (150). None of these studies offers any conclusions in regard to the reason behind the inaccuracies.

8. Jorge Guillén takes a different tack in his collection entitled *Homenaje (Homage)*. In his poem entitled "Al margen del *Poema del Cid*" ("At the Margin of the *Poem of the Cid*"), the generation of '27 poet utilizes different speakers in order to (de)construct and break his frames.

9. F. J. Sánchez Cantón identifies this structure as a "Brunelleschi-style loggia" (Sánchez Cantón 1959, 80).

10. Available criticism of Machado's poetry acknowledges the various artistic and cultural forces that have influenced his work, but tends not to establish an underlying unity.

11. Much work still remains to be done in regard to Machado's attempts at the representation of the Self, as well as the dialectic of Self and Other, Self versus Other, and Self as Other in his work, especially in light of current theoretical debate concerning representation, autobiography, and the nature of the sign, as well as that concerning Spanish modernism.

12. I am indebted to the editors of *Hispania* for having pointed out this connection to me. See the excellent study of the modernist poets by Perloff, *The Poetics of Indeterminacy.* (1981)

13. A nascent version of this manuscript was presented at the American Association of the Teachers of Spanish and Portuguese meetings in Madrid, in August 1986.

CHAPTER 3. THE WRITERLY/PAINTERLY TEXT: RAFAEL ALBERTI AND PABLO PICASSO

1. For other views on Rafael Alberti's relationship to painting, see Carlos Areán, Angel Crespo, Salvador Jiménez Fajardo, Jerónimo P. González Martín, Luis Lorenzo-Rivero, Roberto C. Manteiga, Luis Monguió, C. Brian Morris, Fernando Quiñones, and Ana Maria Winkelmann.

2. Some examples of Alberti's poetry-painting hybrid texts are *Los ojos de Picasso* (*The Eyes of Picasso*), *Escrito en el aire* (*Written on the Air*), and *Buenos Aires en tinta china* (*Buenos Aires in India Ink*). Each of these texts combine poetic texts by Alberti and drawings/paintings/engravings by the poet or by some other visual artist. In 1969 Alberti had an exhibition of a series of his temperas titled *Lirismo del alfabeto* (*Liricism of the Alphabet*). González-Martín describes it thus: "En ella el pintor va estudiando cuidadosamente las posibilidades pictóricas de todas las letras, sugiriendo, a su vez, los motivos poéticos en que aquéllas se utilizan o podrían utilizarse. Se trata de un viaje a través del alfabeto, visto como orientador de la fantasía y expresado en signos y color" ("Alberti y la pintura" 12). (In it the painter goes about carefully studying the pictorial possibilities of all the letters, suggesting, in turn, the poetic motifs in which they are utilized or could be utilized. It is about a journey through the alphabet, seen as a guiding fantasy and expressed in signs and colors" (González Martín "Alberti y la pintura" 1972 12).

3. For a fine discussion of modernism and the avant-garde, see Perloff's *Poetics of Indeterminacy* and *The Futurist Moment.*

4. *A la pintura* is much more than an evocation of specific painters and their works. See particularly the studies by Douglas K. Benson, Jiménez Fajardo, Lorenzo-Rivero, Antonio Risco, and C. Christopher Soufas.

5. In his insightful article on Alberti's study of Velázquez's *Meninas*, Soufas demonstrates how within one poetic text the poet conflates the two different artistic perspectives to produce what Stanley Fish has termed a "self-consuming artifact."

6. Like El Greco's, Picasso's verbal text was entitled *El entierro del conde de Orgaz* (*The Burial of the Count of Orgaz*) (Barcelona: Editorial Gustavo Gili, S.A., 1969).

7. *La arboleda perdida* is Alberti's ongoing autobiography. It first appeared

in 1942, and subsequent expanded editions were released in 1959 and 1987. Volumes 1 and 2 were reissued in 1975.

8. Steiner explores a similar technique used by James Joyce in his *Ulysses* and parallels Joyce's work to Picasso's (Steiner 1988, chap. 5).

9. The edition of *Los 8 nombres* that I use in this study is the third edition.

10. In his *Conflict of Light and Wind*, Soufas holds that Alberti evolves a worldview in his later poetry that moves away from the visual to approach more closely the oral/aural. My own perspective is that in his more recent poetry Alberti allows the visual and aural senses to permeate one another, so that language may be perceived in a new, defamiliarized way, thus endowing it with expanded power to refer to not only the outside world, but to refer to itself with startling eloquence, uncommonness, and originality.

11. In regard to Alberti's propensity for the sense of sight, see particularly the studies by Areán, Manteiga, Risco, Pieter Wesseling, and Winkelmann.

12. The studies by Crespo, Jiménez Fajardo, and Risco explore Alberti's inclination to express ideas through objects.

13. For this reader, it was fascinating to note that Alberti did *not* elect to use the Spanish word "soñar" ("to dream") in this text. But I think the choice was a reasoned one: in Spanish, "soñar" sounds like "sonar" ("to sound like"), which does appear. Thus, the trace of "soñar" ("to dream") is present/absent in "sonar" by the latter word's sound, meaning, *and* graphic representation.

14. From this same collection, see the poem entitled "Garrotín del tarambana" ("Gypsy Dance of the Scatterbrain") (Alberti, 85–86) in which the poet experiments with the word "tarambana" ("scatterbrain") on the phonological, morphological, and semantic levels.

15. In the text "Picasso Antibes la joie de vivre" ("Picasso Antibes the Joy of Living") (Alberti, 52–53) of *Los 8 nombres* the poet juxtaposes the "possible worlds" of classical painting, implicitly paralleling them to Picasso's "possible worlds." The fourth of seven stanzas contains a reference to "los veleros de Ulises" ("the sailboats of Ulysses").

16. In his article on *Los 8 nombres* Luis Capparós Esperante attempts to identify by name all the Picasso paintings to which Alberti makes reference in this collection.

17. I am indebted to John Hollander's article on the refrain for this bipolar cubist reading of the final verse of each stanza.

18. There is a displaced presence/absence of Picasso's "Guernica" throughout *Los 8 nombres*, but no one particular poetic text is dedicated to it within Alberti's *Ocho nombres* (*8 Names*). The poet continually evokes Picasso's famous painting in a variety of ways. For example "De azul se arrancó el toro" ("The Bull Torn Out of the Blue") ends with "Una ola, otra ola desollada. / Guernica. / Dolor al rojo vivo. / . . . Y aquí el juego del arte comienza a ser un juego / explosivo" ("One wave, another brazen wave. / Guernica. / Pain in living red. / . . . And hear the game [play] of art begins to be a an explosive game [play]"). And in "Tú hiciste "aquella obra" ("You made that work") the reader must arrive at this long poem's sixth to the last line of verse to discover that "aquella obra" ("that work") refers to Picasso's antiwar painting.

19. Other images that Picasso shares with Alberti to which the poet returns again and again in this collection are bulls and the sea.

20. In *Los 8 nombres* Alberti makes intertextual reference to other poets and visual artists. In addition to Rafael and El Greco, the poet mentions Braque, Apollinaire, Homer, Michelangelo, and many others.

21. See also "Entre tanta pintura en soledad" ("Among So much Painting in Solitude") (Alberti, 123).

22. "No digo más que lo que no digo" appears as section 6 (poem 71) in *Los 8 nombres*. The poet himself indicated in a footnote on page 145 that this poem/section served as the "Prólogo al texto de Picasso *EL ENTIERRO DEL CONDE DE ORGAZ*, publicado por Editorial Gustavo Gili, S.A., Barcelona, 1969" ("Prologue to Picasso's text *THE BURIAL OF THE COUNT OF ORGAZ*, published by Editorial Gustavo Gili, S.A., Barcelona, 1969"). With this footnote, Alberti breaks the frame of his own poetic composition, by utilizing an organizational and informational element that is not generally associated with the genre of poetry. This footnote "breaks the frame" in yet another way, in that with the information provided therein the poet celebrates his own work's intertextuality, and the concatenation between his work and that of Picasso and El Greco.

CHAPTER 4. SHOT OUT OF THE CAN(N)ON: GLORIA FUERTES, CARMEN MARTÍN GAITE, AND THE PROBLEM OF LIMINALITY

1. In regard to the time-space dialectic of ekphrasis, see especially Krieger, Jospeh Frank, and Chaffee.

2. See the excellent article by Susan Gubar, "The "Blank Page" and the Issues of Female Creativity."

3. From this point forward, all textual citations will be referred to in the body of the text as *OI, Obras incompletas* (*Incomplete Works*) and *HG, Historia de Gloria: amor, humor y desamor* (*History of Glory [Gloria]: Love, Humor and Indifference*).

4. *A rachas* (*With a Gust of Wind*) first appeared in 1976, then was augmented and reissued in 1986; the latter edition is that which I used in the preparation of this manuscript. In 1993 Martín Gaite's poetry was again published, but with the slightly amended title of *Después de todo: poesía a rachas* (*After All: Poetry With a Gust of Wind*). This edition contains a new section of fourteen poems, under the title of "Después de todo" ("After All").

5. For a feminist perspective on the history of the concept of virginity, see Jean Markale, *Women of the Celts*, 127–33.

6. See Dale M. Bauer, *Feminist Dialogics*, for her discussion concerning women and other outcasts, from a Bakhtinian perspective.

7. For a discussion of women's use of and by language, see Robin Lakoff, *Language and Woman's Place*.

8. Aside from its fame for the well-known sculpture, *La Dama de Elche* (*The Lady of Elche*), this locale is also known for its ancient stand of palm trees, located in the "Huerto del Cura" ("Garden of the Priest"), a National Artistic Garden. The ancestors of the present-day palm trees are reputed to have been planted by the Phoenicians. In her poetic text, Fuertes weaves together through oblique reference the many strands of Elche's past, and how they relate to women, and women to them.

9. In his *Five Faces of Modernity*, Matei Calinescu discusses how (post)-modern architecture makes reference to the past. See his chapter entitled "The Novelty of the Past: The View from Architecture," 279–87.

10. See Vincent Scully, "The Great Goddess and the Palace Architecture of Crete." It is interesting to note that preclassical architecture based itself not

upon regular and mathematical forms but rather upon the irregularities of the natural world. In their introduction to *Feminism and Art History*, Norma Broude and Mary D. Garrard remark that "in the siting and design of the palaces of Bronze Age Crete [there is] a persistent and deliberate use of other modes of spatial organization, which relate to the imagery and the symbols of the Stone Age Great Goddess. These include labyrinthine and serpentine paths of movement, and architectural forms that are open, hollow, non-monumental, and responsive to the sculptural forms of nature. . . . This is architecture based on . . . a reciprocity between architecture and nature" (Broude and Garrard 1982, 3). This reciprocity is precisely what Fuertes evokes in her "primera columna" ("first Column").

11. I am indebted to Jaime Siles for having pointed out to me the presence/absence of Hera in the Fuertes poem.

12. Scully views the reciprocity of architecture and nature as an underlying factor in the Minoan and classical Greek traditions.

13. John Berger, in his *Ways of Seeing*, offers a fine discussion of the mute art object as typically female. He comments that female nudity is most often frontal, for the pleasure of the male viewer (Berger 1972, 47–64).

14. Svetlana Alpers, "Art History and Its Exclusions: The Example of Dutch Art," contained in *Feminism and Art History*.

15. Julia Kristeva would view this enriching void as an indication of the semiotic.

16. Debra A. Castillo discusses the fluid concept of the "I" in Martín Gaite's *Cuarto de atrás* (*Back Room*).

17. Autobiography is a genre that traditionally has been permitted to women. See the excellent studies by Shari Benstock, Bella Brodski, Northrup Frye, Sandra M. Gilbert, Susan Gubar, Estelle C. Jelinek, Celeste Schenck, and Domna Stanton.

18. Calinescu posits that a characteristic of postmodernist literature is a subversion of the text by the text itself. This strategy is an integral part of the work of Martín Gaite, both in her poetry and her novels.

19. This would be a very apt example of a "retroactive" reading, based on textual "ungrammaticalities," as proposed by Michael Riffaterre in his *Semiotics of Poetry*.

20. This technique will be studied more fully in chapter 7, in reference to the poetry of Pere Gimferrer and Jenaro Talens.

21. The gaze is incorporated into the text through the metaphor of the eye, sight, and vision, and is similar to the strategy employed by Rafael Alberti in his *Los 8 nombres de Picasso*. It seems to me that Martín Gaite here is questioning vision and the visual image, and whether one can ever perceive that which is "real," simply because of the intervention and/or barrier of vision, with its physiological and neurological imperfections. Her questioning stance is communicated via her destabilizing, decentering, and delimiting "vision of vision" and its focus, or lack of focus.

22. The poet uses the verb "revelar," which can mean "to reveal" or in a filmic or cinematic sense, "to develop."

23. My use of this last metaphor, "blind alley," is premeditated: it mimics the type of "visual" metaphors favored by the poet, and evokes them in an inverted manner, namely, "blind" being the absence of sight. Presence is once again defined by absence.

24. Studies that I found to be particularly helpful on Martín Gaite's *Cuarto*

de atrás are those by Castillo, Linda Gould Levine, Elizabeth Ordóñez, and Marcia L. Welles.

25. Martín Gaite foregrounds the element of ludic play at various levels of her text. I myself continued the "play" by playing out her poem's story, both by entering into the frame of her text, and by allowing her text to enter the frame of my own text(s), both my life and this manuscript.

26. Subsequently I did visit the Thyssen-Bornemisza Museum in Madrid, and viewed Hopper's painting, thus extending yet further the dazzling, dizzying reflection (on), and refraction of, Martín Gaite's text, and my own as well. With this inversion of the "life into art" experience, I "play"-ed out into another dimension the subversion of texts of all kinds, celebrating and rupturing the limits between reality and the artistic text, I myself acting out that reality is merely a different type of text, with a different set of conventions.

CHAPTER 5. (SELF-) PORTRAITS, (DIS)GUISES, AND FRAMES: THE (DIS)FIGURING GAZE OF JAIME GIL DE BIEDMA AND JOSÉ ANGEL VALENTE

1. Heffernan's *Museum of Words* "treats the history of ekphrasis as a history of struggle between rival systems of representation" (Heffernan 1993, book jacket). See also Krieger's *Ekphrasis: The Illusion of the Natural Sign* for a comprehensive and critical overview of how *ekphrasis* enacts ideological and aesthetic standards from Homer to the postmodern age.

2. In the preparation of this study I used Jaime Gil de Biedma, *Las personas del verbo*.

3. This poem is dedicated to the painting of Paco Todó, a contemporary Catalan painter (b. 1921, Tarragona). Todó's painting does not itself include works of "trompe d'oeil" tendency, but does demonstrate the influence of Paul Klee, Georges Braque, and Paul Cezanne.

4. The inherent and systematic ambiguities of negation are a language universal. See the study by Paul and Carol Kiparsky.

5. James Smith Pierce defines the vanishing point in the following manner: "In pictures constructed according to the principles of linear perspective, the point or points of convergence for all lines forming an angle with the picture plane" (Pierce 1968, 64).

6. This possible reading is supported by a similar image taken from another poem from this same collection entitled "Pandémica y celeste." In it, the poetic speaker states "Imagínatelo, / en una de esas noches memorables / de rara comunión, *con la botella / medio vacía*, los ceniceros sucios, / y después de agotado el tema de la vida" (Gil de Biedma 1966, 134. (Italics mine.)

7. Hypallage: A change in the relation of words whereby a word, instead of agreeing with the word it logically qualifies, is made to agree grammatically with another word. (*Princeton Encyclopedia of Poetry and Poetics* [1974, 358]).

8. It seems to me that Gil de Biedma represents the act of (pro)creative possession through the metaphor of the sexual encounter of Self and Other.

9. Gil de Biedma offered his own comments on the genesis of both "Contra Jaime Gil de Biedma" and "Después de la muerte de Jaime Gil de Biedma": "En realidad, de lo que se trate es de la crisis del fin de la juventud. Cuando uno termina con una neurosis, es decir, que uno en parte se muere. Hay toda una parte de uno que se muere" (Campbell 1971, 247).

10. In the preparation of this study I used José Angel Valente, *Punto cero: Poesía 1953–1979* (*Point Zero: Poetry 1953–1979*) .

11. Germane to this discussion is the fact that Webster's *New World Dictionary* includes in its definition of the fairy tale the concept of untruth: (1) a story about fairies, giants, magic deeds, (2) an unbelievable or untrue story, a lie (Webster, 503).

12. See the excellent study by Linda Hutcheon, *Narcissistic Narrative: The Metafictional Paradox* (1980), who discusses the relationship among the mirror, metatextuality, and narcissism.

13. See Steiner's chapter 5, "A Renaissance-Modernist Dalliance: Joyce and Picasso" in her *Pictures of Romance.*

14. Valente utilizes this same discursive strategy in other poetic texts. See my book *Recent Spanish Poetry and the Role of the Reader* (Persin 1987, 26–44).

15. The author chose her wording carefully so as to take full advantage of the puns possible with "terms," "literally," and "artful."

16. The verse line "Mon semblable, mon frère" also appears in the poem by Gil de Biedma entitled "Pandémica y celeste" ("Pandémica and Celestial) from his collection *Moralidades* (*Moralities*) (1966). It reads "hipócrita lector—*mon semblable,—mon frère!"* ("hypocritical reader—*my likeness,—my brother!"*). This is the same line of verse that ends "Au lecteur" ("To the Reader"), Baudelaire's opening poem of *Les fleurs du mal* ([The] *Flowers of Evil*). In the Valente text taken from his book *El inocente* (*The Innocent* [One] (1970), the speaker anthropomorphizes the dog into his reader—or "caninizes" the reader into his dog. This metamorphosis may be based on T. S. Eliot's intertextual allusion to the Baudelarian line of verse. The closing lines of verse of the American/English poet's opening section of *The Waste Land* entitled "The Burial of the Dead" read thus:

Oh keep the Dog far hence, that's friend to men,
Or with his nails he'll dig it up again!
You! hypocrite lecteur!—mon semblable—mon frère!

Either Baudelaire or Eliot—or both—could be the source(s) of the intertext for Gil de Biedma and Valente. Many thanks to John C. Wilcox for having helped me to pinpoint these sources.

17. Code-switching also comes into play in the poetry of Gil de Biedma. See my article on "Self as Other."

18. It is evident that this poem was of some import to the poet, since another with the title of "A Pancho, mi muñeco: aniversario" ("To Pancho, My Doll: Anniversary") appeared in his *Treinta y siete fragmentos* (*Thirty-Seven Fragments*) (Barcelona: Ambit Serveis Editorials, S.A., 1989).

19. I espouse a broad definition of ekphrasis that includes the verbal representation of a visually perceptible art object, whether real or imagined. See my first chapter, and also that of Krieger's *Ekphrasis.*

20. The twentieth-century artist who created the art form of soft sculpture is Claes Oldenberg. The other art form that comes easily to mind in this context is that of "photo-realism" sculpture, created by Duane Hanson. In this medium, the artist took body casts of his middle-aged and overweight models, then dressed them in everyday clothing at its most garish.

21. See, for example, "Muñecas" ("Dolls") by María Victoria Atencia in chapter 6.

22. In his "Changes in the Study of the Lyric" Jonathan Culler suggests that

the rhetorical device of apostrophe be studied further, in order to reveal how it puts into play the presence of absence, and problematizes the positionality of the speaking subject. (*Lyric Poetry: Beyond New Criticism*,) eds. Chaviva Hošek and Patricia Parker, [1985, 38–54]..

23. Valente avails himself of this particular verbal strategy in many of his poetic texts, whereby the reader is encouraged to go back and read a poem a second time, based on the experience of the last few lines of verse. His texts entitled "El cántaro" ("The Pitcher") or "La rosa necesaria" ("The Necessary Rose") come easily to mind.

24. Two prose texts by Valente which are accompanied by drawings are *Los ojos deseados* (*The Desired Eyes*) and *Nueve enunciaciones* (*Nine Enunciations*). The former contains illustrations by Guillermo Pérez Villalta, and the latter, drawings by Brinkmann.

CHAPTER 6. POP GOES THE (W)EASEL: PORTRAITS BY AND OF MARÍA VICTORIA ATENCIA AND ANA ROSSETTI

1. An outstanding example of the male gaze and of its pervasiveness is to be found in a "Frank and Ernest" cartoon (Thaves). The two characters are pictured in a library, standing close to a sign that reads Medieval History and Legend. One asks the other, "This "Lady Godiva" tale. . . . Can you sum it up for me?" And the other replies, "Sure. Lady on dare / rides mare through square while bare, / long hair only wear." The silent, naked body of a woman as the object of the male gaze underlies history, legend, art, poetry—any written or visual text—, whether it be manifested in literature, painting, cinema, advertising campaigns, or the popular comic strip.

2. For a discussion of the contrast between the male and female gaze, see especially the studies by Dale Bauer, John Berger, Erika Bornay, Mary Ann Caws, W. J. T. Mitchell, and Griselda Pollock.

3. The cover of the June 1993 number of the literary magazine *Zurgai* is a case in point. It was a special issue dedicated to women poets. The cover is of a female cartoon character, modeled on those of the comic strip "Dick Tracy." She is in an enclosed room, backed by a closed shutter. The character is speaking on the telephone, and the balloon showing her words contains the names ". . . Angela Figuera, Blanca Andreu. . . ." The patriarchal cloistering and silencing of women underlies the representation, but the female gaze allows the woman to have contact with the outside world via the telephone and her own naming of women poets. Since Figuera and Andreu are of different generations, this image also makes oblique reference to a separate tradition of poetry written by women. The female gaze breaks the frame of patriarchal representation in another manner, since the cartoon and the telephone are postmodern manifestations of the elision between art forms of various types.

4. Other contemporary Spanish women poets who have an abiding interest in the visual arts are Blanca Andreu, Amparo Amorós, Juana J. Marín Saura, and María del Carmen Pallarés, to name only a few.

5. A second edition of *Marta & María* appeared in 1984.

6. See Sharon Keefe Ugalde's *Conversaciones y poemas* (1991, 3–17).

7. Vanishing point: In pictures constructed according to the principles of linear perspective, the point or points of convergence for all lines forming an

angle with the picture plane. (James Smith Pierce, *From Abacus to Zeus: A Handbook of Art History* [Pierre 1968, 64]).

8. In her overview of Atencia's poetry published in *Spanish Women Writers*, Ugalde identifies the issue of female identity as a unifying characteristic in Atencia's poetry.

9. Atencia, *El mundo de M.V.* The version of the poem that I used appeared in Atencia's *Ex Libris,* 79. This latter collection is a compendium of Atencia's verse to date.

10. See Griselda Pollock's chapter 4, "Modernity and the Spaces of Femininity" in *Vision and Difference-Femininity, Feminism, and Histories of Art* for a discussion of women's place and space within the modern context.

11. Suzanne Juhasz views this division as a characteristic of poetry by women. See chapter 1, "The Double Bind of the Woman Poet," in *Naked and Fiery Forms.* Alicia Suskin Ostriker, in her book *Stealing the Language. The Emergence of Women's Poetry in America* expresses a similar view in chapter 2, "Divided Selves: The Quest for Identity."

12. I am much indebted to Ugalde for her careful reading of an earlier draft of this chapter. She suggested to me the idea of simultaneous models.

13. Characteristics of the postmodern include self-referentiality, the questioning of genre definitions, the inclusion of various "art" forms, and the simultaneous celebration and rupture of frames of all types. For a discussion of the postmodern in art and literature, see studies by Calinescu, Silvio Gaggi, and Linda Hutcheon.

14. I am much indebted to Victoria León, a daughter of María Victoria Atencia, who very generously forwarded to me a copy of her doctoral thesis, "María Victoria Atencia: Poesía completa (1955–1990). Edición, notas y traducción inglesa" ("María Victoria Atencia: Complete Poetry (1955–1990). Edition, Notes, and Translation to English"). In regard to the poem "Mujeres de la casa" (Women of the House") she notes that what her mother cites in her poetic text, "(. . . 28 de noviembre, Calle del Angel, 1)" (. . . 28 November, Angel Street, number 1") are "Fecha y casa natal de M.V. (La primera edición del poema indicaba el número de la casa de enfrente, el 2 (el 6 entonces), que era la de sus abuelos paternos. Para evitar desviaciones la autora decidió luego ceñirse a la casa de su nacimiento" (Leon, 28) ("Date and birth place of M. V. ‹The first edition of the poem indicated the number of the house in front, number 2 (number 6 then),› that was of [the house of] her paternal grandparents. In order to avoid detours, the author since decided to gird herself to the house of her birth"). Thus, it seems to me that the poet with this reference to her own life creates for the reader yet another frame within the text, which both closes in and closes out by the very nature of its meaning.

15. This conflict in "womanly" values reminded me of the baroque painting by Jan Vermeer van Delft entitled *The Letter.* A scullery maid has just handed a bejeweled, seated noblewoman a note. They are exchanging a duplicitous glance. The scene is framed by an open doorway as well as by a pulled-back curtain. The workaday world of broom, laundry basket, scattered clothing, and crumpled papers contextualizes another atemporal one, suggested by the look of eternal love in the lady's eyes.

16. J. Hillis Miller discusses the conflation of the two distinct mythological stories of Arachne and Ariadne through a deconstructive reading in his article "Ariachne's Broken Woof."

17. An apt example of women's exaltation and imprisonment by patriar-

chally imposed standards is the image of women and female/feminine beauty projected in commercial advertising campaigns.

18. I am much indebted to Martha LaFollette Miller for her careful reading of an earlier draft of this chapter. She suggested to me the idea of projection onto the museum object.

19. See Ostriker, *Stealing the Language,* chapter 6 "Thieves of Language: Women Poets and Revisionist Mythology." Ostriker demonstrates how women poets revise and rewrite many patriarchally created myths from a female perspective. Catherine Jaffe, in her article "Gender, Intersubjectivity. . . ." demonstrates how Atencia's "Eva" elicits a "feminine reading" response based on the revision of the biblical myth of the Garden of Eden.

20. In regard to Rossetti's subversive strategies, see in particular the studies by Mary Makris, Yolanda Rosas and Hilde Cramsie, and Mirella Servodidio.

21. In his book *Las diosas blancas: antologiá de la joven poesía española escrita por mujeres (The White Goddesses:* Authology of Spanish Poetry Written by Young Women) the anthologist Ramón Buenaventura noted in his brief introduction to the poetry of Rossetti her propensity for the visual. He states: "Es la gran *voyeuse* de la poetambre universal. No conozco ninguna otra poeta, en ninguna lengua, que posea su capacidad de acecho visual del sexo, su capacidad para encandilarnos con lo que ve. Le pueden ganar en arrebato y pasión, en revolcón y cuenta nueva, hasta en caricia y roce; pero no en cómo nos transmite las delicadas sutilezas de la penetración por la mirada" ("She is the grande *voyeuse* of universal poetdom. I do not know any other poet, in any other language, who possesses her capacity for [the] visual ambush of sex, her capacity to dazzle us with what she sees. They can beat her on ecstacy and passion, on rolling about and new reckoning, even on caress and rubbing [intercourse]; but not on how she transmits to us the delicate subtleties of penetration by means of the gaze") (Buenaventura 1985, 60).

22. See also the studies by Makris, Servodidio, and John C. Wilcox.

23. Makris, Servodidio and Ugalde make note of Rossetti's propensity toward scopophilia, or the "gaze as a structuring, organizational and subversive device" (Makris 1993, 239).

24. In collaboration with Fernando Rubio, Rossetti staged an exhibition entitled *Imago Pasionis, (1990)* which is comprised of his visual and her verbal texts. The visual images (acrylic paint on canvas) are portraits of contemporary archangels, dressed in modern clothing such as blue jeans, polo shirts, and running shoes. The paintings are accompanied by Rossetti's poetic texts. These portraits evoke paintings by Murillo or Zurburán, for example, but also allude to the contemporary context by way of their props and design. These visual/verbal texts are "bipolar" and celebrate/subvert various modes of discourse. I am indebted to Ugalde for having acquired for me a color copy of the exhibit and of Rossetti's verbal text.

25. Rossetti, *Los devaneos de Erato.* The version of the poem that I used is from Rossetti's *Indicios vehementes (Poesía 1979–1984) (Vehement Indications,)* 38.

26. Servodidio already has noted the importance of touch in Rossetti's poetry.

27. The baroque is a principal topos in Rossetti's poetry, and is represented most clearly in her *Devocionario (Prayer Book.)* See especially the study by Carmela Ferradáns, as well as the interviews with Ugalde and Jesús Fernández Palacios. In the latter, Rossetti comments that she would have preferred to live

in the seventeenth century, in a convent, and specifically names Santa Teresa. In an article by Téllez Rubio, the poet comments on her attraction to the transgression of limits of any kind. The idea of transgression is a hallmark of the baroque.

28. Rossetti's deliciously wicked poem on Saint Sebastian recalls that of Jorge Guillén from the latter poet's *Homenaje* (*Homage*) (*Aire Nuestro, Homesaje*), where the generation of '27 poet uses apostrophe in order to allow the saintly youth's portrait to "speak out" by means of the poem's salacious, irreverent speaker, who poses a question to the silent martyr. The reader's response to the outrageous question gives voice to the supposedly mute art object. Like Rossetti, Guillén also utilizes an ungendered speaker, who suggests sadomasochism, homosexuality, and the eroticization of death:

> ¿Quién te pone en peor estado,
> San Sebastián desventurado:
>
> El cruel que arroja su flecha
> Contra un mozo que Dios acecha,
>
> O ese pintor que como efebo
> Te imagina, ya Adonis nuevo,
>
> Y mezclando hermosura y muerte
> Desea en tu martirio verte
>
> Suave y sangriento sin un grito,
> Repugnantemente exquisito?

(Who puts you in a worse state, / unlucky Saint Sebastian: // The cruel [one] who hurls his arrow / Against a lad for whom God lies in wait , // Or that painter who as ephebus / Imagines you [fam. sing.], already [a] new Adonis, // And mixing beauty and death / Desires in your martyrdom to see you [fam. sing.] // Soft and bloody without a shout, / Repugnantly exquisite?)

29. See especially the studies by Ferradáns, Makris, Rosas and Cramsie, and Ugalde. In the preparation of this study I used the version of "Chico Wrangler" ("Wrangler Boy") that appears in Rossetti's *Indicios vehementes* (*Vehement Indications*) (1985), 99. "Calvin Klein, underdrawers" first appeared in Buenaventura's *Diosas blancas*, 68, and then in Rossetti's *Yesterday*, 54. There are slight variations of indentation, capitalization, and punctuation between the earlier and later version of the second poem. In the preparation of this study, I used the earlier version of the "Calvin Klein" text.

30. For a revision of the erotic gaze from a female perspective see Ostriker, *Stealing the Language*, chapter 5, "The Imperative of Intimacy: Female Erotics, Female Poets".

31. Many thanks to Ugalde for having forwarded to me a color copy of the visual/verbal text of Rossetti's "Calvin Klein Underwear." Her thoughtfulness and generosity are very much appreciated. This mixed-media version appeared in *Poemas autógrafos* (*Poems by the Author's Hand*) [Madrid: Círculo de Bellas Artes, 1987]).

32. See the 1981 essay by Ann Rosalind Jones, "Writing the Body: Toward an Understanding of *L'écriture Féminine*," in Judith Newton and Deborah Rosenfelt, eds., *Feminist Criticism and Social Change*, 86–101. See also Liz Yorke,

Impertinent Voices: Subversive Strategies in Contemporary Women's Poetry, part 3 "Writing the Body: Desire and the M/Other-Text."

CHAPTER 7. PERE GIMFERRER AND JENARO TALENS OR (THE) CAMERA, OR THE LENS AND THE I'S/EYE'S OBSCURE OBJECT OF DESIRE

1. See Susan Buck-Morss, *The Dialectics of Seeing* concerning Walter Benjamin's dependence on the sense of sight.

2. The relationship of poetry to cinema is not new. As Timothy Rogers and others have already noted, Rafael Alberti and other poets of the generation of '27, as well as surrealists and Dadaists, expressed their fascination with the filmic media. See also Steven Kovács, *From Enchantment to Rage. The Story of Surrealist Cinema.*

In regard to the intersection of literature and the filmic arts, the author was reminded of the short story "Las babas del diablo" ("The Devil's Drivel") by Julio Cortázar, in which the narrator realizes only later that he unwittingly saved a young boy from disaster merely by taking a photo of him. This story later was the basis for a full-length feature film entitled *Blow-up.*

3. The editions that I use in this study are listed as follows. Pere Gimferrer *Cine y literatura* ; *La muerte en Beverly Hills* in *Poemas 1963–1969* (Poems 1963-1969) (1979); *Los espejos/(Els miralls)* in *Poesía 1970–1977* (Poetry 1970–1977) (1978); *El vendeval* (The Gale), bilingual edition, 1989.

Jenaro Talens

The Branded Eye: Buñuel's Un chien andalou (1993); *La mirada extranjera* (The Foreign Gaze) with Michaël Nerlich (1985); *Tabula rasa* (1985); *Purgatori/ Purgatorio* (Purgatory) (1986).

After completing this study, I learned of a new poetry collection by Talens entitled *Orfeo filmado en el campo de batalla.* Because of its date of publication, it was not considered here.

4. For an excellent theoretical study on the art of the cinema, see Gilles Deleuze, *L'image/Mouvement.*

5. See John Tagg for a fine overview of the history of photography. In his study he uses a Marxist approach.

6. See Mitchell's discussion of the camera obscura in chapter 1, "What Is an Image?" of his *Iconology: Image, Text, Ideology.* Roland Barthes, for his part, holds that in photography the hand on the shutter button is more important than the eye. See his *Camera lucida* (Barthes 1981, 15). For a discussion of Barthes's views, see Martin Jay, *Downcast Eyes: The Denigration of Vision in Twentieth-Century French Thought.*

7. Barthes views the photograph as "dangerous": "Yes, indeed: the Photograph is *dangerous* by endowing it with *functions*, which are, for the Photographer, so many alibis. These functions are: to inform, to represent, to surprise, to cause to signify, to provoke desire" (Barthes 1981, 28).

8. The common housefly is an anthropod, which has mosaic eyes, composed of thousands of visual units termed *omnatidia.* Each omnatidium has a clear outer cornea under which is a lens that focuses the light on the end of the light sensitive element made of eight or so retinal cells. These are believed to respond as a unit. Each omnatidium is separated from the adjacent cells by

rings of pigment cells. Many thanks to Cecilia P. Murnighan for having provided me with this information.

9. Barthes's study originally appeared in a French edition, *La chambre claire* (1980). I used the English edition, *Camera lucida* (1981).

10. In his study Barthes does not separate photography from cinema: "I decided I liked Photography in *opposition* to the Cinema, from which I nonetheless failed to separate it" (Barthes 1981, 3).

11. Barthes also utilizes the concept of the *studium*, "which doesn't mean, at least not immediately, "study," but application to a thing, taste for someone, a kind of general, enthusiastic commitment, of course, but without special acuity" (Barthes 1981, 26).

12. For a feminist reading of the "blank page," see Gubar's ""Blank Page" and the Issues of Female Creativity." Also, the author was reminded of the poem "Octubre" ("October") by Juan Ramón Jiménez, where a plow's furrow is equated with the act of writing.

13. Both oral poetry and oral drama as performance are language-based, but neither are written. My apologies to Mess. Marcel Marceau, for his performances are also excluded.

14. See the short but suggestive article by Wright Morris, "The Camera Eye," in which the author discusses the relationship between photography and literature.

15. For the "novísimos" and beyond, see especially José María Castellet, *Nueve novísimos poetas españoles (Barcelona: Barral, 1970.)* Biruté Ciplijauskaité, (ed.), *Novísimos, postnovísimos, clásicos: La poesía de los 80 en España; Studies in 20th Century Literature* 16, no.1 (1992); and *Anales de la literatura española contemporánea* 18, no.1 (1993). The latter two are journal numbers dedicated to recent Spanish poetry.

Two other poets of the "novísimos" generation who use various forms of ekphrasis as a discursive strategy are Guillermo Carnero and Jaime Siles. See Carnero's *Dibujo de la muerte (Drawing of Death)* (Barcelona: Ocnos, 1971) and his *Ensayo de una teoría de la visión (Poesía 1966–1977) (Essay on a Theory of Vision [Poetry 1966–1977])* (Madrid: Visor, 1989). For Jaime Siles, see especially his *Alegoría (Allegory)* (Barcelona: Anthropos, 1971) *Columnae (Columns)* (Madrid: Visor, 1989), and his *Semáforos, semáforos (Semaphores, Semaphores)*, (Madrid: Visor, 1990).

The contemporary debate in regard to the modern/postmodern dialectic will not be dealt with here. See the studies by Calinescu and Silvio Gaggi. I tend to agree with those that posit that postmodernism is a continuation of modernism, rather than a complete rupture and antithesis.

16. Gimferrer has recourse to many other art forms, especially pop art, in his poetry. See the study by Timothy Rogers.

17. Gimferrer's *Cine y literatura*, (1985) in itself is a hybrid text that rests on complementarity, since his prose text on cinema is accompanied by a series of photographs or still shots taken from the films that he discusses. Thus, this text in and of itself is ekphrastic in nature, since by means of the still photos the writer acknowledges the impotence of writing to capture cinema's essence. Photographic discourse wounds and also cures this penetration, absence, or lack.

18. I am well aware of the fact that Gimferrer's theorization of film appeared in print well after the books of poetry under consideration. Nonetheless, my opinion is that his particular views on film inspired the structuring and focus

of his poetry, and only later did he get around to publishing his text on film theory.

19. In the survey conducted by José Batlló, Gimferrer himself makes reference to the influence of the surrealist era upon his work. See Batlló's *Antología de la nueva poesía española*.

20. "The figure in the carpet / the tapestry drawing" is an ambiguous image. In the Henry James story entitled "The Figure in the Carpet," a young critic seeks to find the unifying factor in a writer's work, which he refers to as "the figure in the carpet," the shadowy existence present, but also absent if one is not aware. He attempts to identify this figure, and even seeks out an interview with the author himself, who refuses to reveal it, but who encourages the budding critic to continue with the search. Ultimately, at the end of the story, everyone who could have aided his search is dead, and the sadder but wiser critic is left with the knowledge that there is indeed a figure in the carpet, but its identification is forever beyond his grasp. The Oneness of the text is inhabited by an Other, whose presence is supplemental yet intrinsic to the text's very nature. It is for each reader to decipher in unique fashion the nature of "the figure in the carpet." Each reading will acknowledge the presence of the Other, but will also be incomplete.

For this reader, "the figure in the carpet / the tapestry drawing" brought to mind several distinct readings, all of which may apply to, and are consistent with, the concepts studied here. First, I thought of a visit that I made to the Royal Tapestry Factory in Madrid, where the weavers demonstrated how the design of the tapestry is sketched onto a series of vertical cords already in place on the loom, cords which will serve as the basis for the final product. The chalk marks are significant only if one is aware of the fact that there is indeed a design on those cords; otherwise, they appear to be random smudges. Secondly, one must remember that the tapestry, as a final product, has two sides. Each is a mirror image of the other; but each is hidden from the other in the viewing process. And finally, before each tapestry design is handed over to the weavers, a printing or cartoon is produced, so that all of the details of composition and color may be worked out (the drawings of Goya come easily to mind). Once again, printing and tapestry are inextricably "interwoven" in a subversive relationship of text and supplement. Each is and is not the Other. The One is both present and absent in the Other. Each reflects as well as subverts the Otherness that is art, representation, and ultimately, all forms of discourse.

See also Barthes in regard to mirrored art forms (Barthes 1991, 6).

21. I have deliberately chosen the term *veridical* because of its Latin origin, namely, "to say the truth," rather than the word truthful, which comes from an Old English root.

22. For an extensive bibliography on the work of Jenaro Talens, see the monographic issue of *Quervo poesía* 8 (1986) [Valencia, Spain]. See also the prologue by Juan M. Company to Talens's *Proximidad del silencio (Proximity of Silence [1980–1981])*.

23. See Claus Clüver's "On Intersemiotic Transpositions" for a discussion of the various combinatorial possibilities between verbal and visual texts, Mitchell's *Picture Theory* chapter 9 "The Photographic Essay," and Jefferson Hunter, *Image and Text*.

24. Louis Aragón was a French poet and novelist, onetime Dadaist and surrealist, and later an ardent Communist.

25. Although it rests outside the scope of this study, Talens implicitly questions the connection between surrealism and postmodernism.

26. For a discussion concerning postmodernism and cinema, see Anne Friedberg, "Les Flaneurs du Mal(l): Cinema and the Postmodern Condition."

27. The collection ends with a series of moves that decenter the text's authority even more. There is an appendix by Vicente Ponce, who explains the origin of the collection's title, "tabula rasa."

28. See also Talens's *Proximidad del silencio (1980–81)* (*Proximity of Silence [1980–81]*).

Bibliography

LITERARY THEORY

Adams, Hazard, and Leroy Searle, eds. *Critical Theory Since 1965*. Tallahassee: University Presses of Florida, 1986.

Auerbach, Eric. *Mimesis: The Representation of Reality in Western Literature*. 1946. Reprint, Princeton: Princeton University Press, 1974.

Bakhtin, Mikhail M. *The Dialogic Imagination*. Edited by Michael Holquist. Translated by Caryl Emerson and Michael Holquist. Austin: University of Texas Press, 1981.

————. *Speech Genres and Other Late Essays*. Edited by Caryl Emerson and Michael Holquist. Translated by Vern W. McGee. Austin: University of Texas Press, 1986.

Barthes, Roland. "Authors and Writers." In his *Critical Essays*, translated by Richard Howard, 143–50. Evanston, Ill.: Northwestern University Press, 1972.

————. "From Work to Text." In *Textual Strategies: Perspectives in Post-Structuralist Criticism*, Edited and translated by Josué V. Harari, 73–81. Ithaca: Cornell University Press, 1979.

Bauer, Dale M. *Feminist Dialogics: A Theory of Failed Community*. Albany: State University of New York Press, 1988.

Bloom, Harold. *The Anxiety of Influence*. New York: Oxford University Press, 1973.

Booth, Wayne C. "Freedom of Interpretation: Bakhtin and the Challenge of Feminist Criticism." In *The Politics of Interpretation*, edited by W. J. T. Mitchell, 51–82. Chicago: University of Chicago Press, 1983.

Bornay, Erika. *Las hijas de Lilith*. Madrid: Cátedra, 1990.

Calinescu, Matei. *Five Faces of Modernity*. Durham, N.C.: Duke University Press, 1987.

Conte, Joseph M. *Unending Design: The Forms of Postmodern Poetry*. Ithaca: Cornell University Press, 1991.

Culler, Jonathan. "Changes in the Study of the Lyric." Hošek and Parker, 38–54.

————. *On Deconstruction: Theory and Criticism after Structuralism*. Ithaca: Cornell University Press, 1982.

————. *The Pursuit of Signs*. Ithaca: Cornell University Press, 1981.

————. *Structuralist Poetics*. Ithaca: Cornell University Press, 1975.

Debicki, Andrew P. "New Poetics, New Works, New Approaches; Recent Spanish Poetry." *Siglo XX/20th Century* 8.1–2 (1990–91): 41–53.

De Lauretis, Teresa. *Alice Doesn't: Feminism, Semiotics, Cinema*. Bloomington: Indiana University Press, 1984.

Derrida, Jacques "Living On. Border lines." In *Deconstruction and Criticism,* edited by Harold Bloom et al., 75–176. New York: Seabury Press, 1979.

Gaggi, Silvio. *Modern/Postmodern. A Study in Twentieth-Century Arts and Ideas.* Philadelphia: University of Pennsylvania Press, 1989.

Gubar, Susan. "'The Blank Page' and the Issues of Female Creativity." *Critical Inquiry* 8, no.1 (1981): 243–263.

Guillén, Claudio. "On the Concept and Metaphor of Perspective." In *Literature as System: Essays Toward a Theory of Literary History,* 283–371. Princeton: Princeton University Press, 1971. Originally published in *Comparatists at Work.* Edited by S. G. Nichols, Jr. and R. B. Vowles. Waltham, Mass.: Blaisdell, 1968.

Harpham, Geoffrey Galt. *On the Grotesque: Strategies of Contradiction in Art and Literature.* Princeton: Princeton University Press, 1987.

Holland, Norman. *The Dynamics of Literary Response.* New York: Oxford University Press, 1968.

Hollander, John. "Breaking into Song: Some Notes on Refrain." Hošek and Parker, 73–89.

Holquist, Michael. "Answering as Authoring: Mikhail Bakhtin's Trans-Linguistics." Morson, 59–71.

Hošek, Chaviva, and Patricia Parker. *Lyric Poetry: Beyond New Criticism.* Ithaca: Cornell University Press, 1985.

Hutcheon, Linda. *Narcissistic Narrative: The Metafictional Paradox.* Waterloo, Ont.: Wilfred Laurier University, 1980.

———. *A Theory of Parody: The Teachings of Twentieth-Century Art Forms.* New York: Methuen, 1985.

Jones, Ann Rosalind. "Writing the Body: Toward an Understanding of *l'écriture féminine.*" Newton and Rosenfelt, 86–101.

Juhasz, Suzanne. *Naked and Fiery Forms.* New York: Harper Colophon Books, 1976.

Kayser, Wolfgang. *The Grotesque in Art and Literature.* Translated by Ulrich Weisstein. 1957. Reprints, Bloomington: Indiana University Press, 1964.

Kiparsky, Paul and Carol Kiparsky. "Fact." In *Semantics,* edited by Danny D. Steinberg and Leon A. Jakobovitz, 345–69. Cambridge: Cambridge University Press, 1971.

La Belle, Jenijoy. *Herself Beheld: The Literature of the Looking Glass.* Ithaca: Cornell University Press, 1988.

Lakoff, Robin. *Language and Woman's Place.* New York: Harper & Row, Publishers, 1975.

Markale, Jean. *Women of the Celts.* Translated by A. Mygind, C. Hauch, and P. Henry. Rochester, Vt: Inner Traditions International, 1986.

Miller, J. Hillis. "Ariachne's Broken Woof." *Georgia Review* 31 (1977): 44–60.

———. "The Critic as Host." In *Deconstruction and Criticism,* edited by Harold Bloom et al., 217–253. New York: Seabury Press, 1979.

Montefiore, Jan. *Feminism and Poetry. Language, Experience, Identity in Women's Writing.* New York: Pandora, 1987.

Morson, Gary Saul, ed. *Bakhtin: Essays and Dialogues on His Work.* Chicago: University of Chicago Press, 1986.

Newton, Judith, and Deborah Rosenfelt, eds. *Feminist Criticism and Social Change*. New York: Methuen, 1985.

Ostriker, Alicia Suskin. *Stealing the Language. The Emergence of Women's Poetry in America*. Boston: Beacon Press, 1986.

Patterson, David. *Literature and Spirit*. Lexington: University Press of Kentucky, 1988.

Pérez Firmat, Gustavo. *Literature and Liminality: Festive Readings in the Hispanic Tradition*. Durham, N.C.: Duke University Press, 1986.

Perloff, Marjorie. *The Futurist Moment: Avant-Garde, Avant Guerre, and the Language of Rupture*. Chicago: University of Chicago Press, 1986.

————. *Poetic License. Essays on Modernist and Postmodernist Lyric*. Evanston, Ill.: Northwestern University Press, 1990.

————. *The Poetics of Indeterminacy. Rimbaud to Cage*. Princeton: Princeton University Press, 1981.

Princeton Encyclopedia of Poetry and Poetics. Edited by Alex Preminger. Princeton: Princeton University Press, 1974.

Riffaterre, Michael. *Semiotics of Poetry*. Bloomington: Indiana University Press, 1978.

Schneiderman, Leo. *The Literary Mind: Portraits in Pain and Creativity*. New York: Insight Books, 1988.

Scholes, Robert. *Protocols of Reading*. New Haven: Yale University Press, 1989.

————. *Textual Power*. New Haven: Yale University Press, 1985.

Spires, Robert. *Beyond the Metafictional Mode*. Lexington: University Press of Kentucky, 1985.

Stewart, Susan. *Nonsense: Aspects of Intertextuality in Folklore and Literature*. Baltimore: Johns Hopkins University Press, 1978, 1979.

Sturrock, John, ed. *Structuralism and Since*. New York: Oxford University Press, 1981.

Waugh, Patricia. *Metafiction: The Theory and Practice of Self-Conscious Fiction*. New York: Methuen, 1984.

Yorke, Liz. *Impertinent Voices: Subversive Strategies in Contemporary Women's Poetry*. New York: Routledge, 1991.

VISUAL ARTS AND LITERATURE

Alpers, Svetlana. "Art History and Its Exclusions: The Example of Dutch Art." Broude and Garrard, 183–199.

Alpers, Svetlana, and Paul Alpers. "Ut pictura noesis?: Criticism in Literary Studies and Art History." *New Literary History* 3 (1972): 437–58.

Barthes, Roland. *Camera lucida*. New York: Farrar, Straus & Giroux, 1981. Originally published as *La chambre claire*. Paris: Editions du Seuil, 1980.

————. "Rhétorique de l'image." *Communications* 4 (1964): 40–51.

Baxandall, Michael. *Patterns of Intention*. New Haven: Yale University Press, 1985.

Benjamin, Walter. "The Work of Art in the Age of Mechanical Reproduction."

In *Illuminations*, edited by Hannah Arendt, 217–51. New York: Schocken Books, 1969.

Bergmann, Emilie L. *Art Inscribed: Essays on Ekphrasis in Spanish Golden Age Poetry.* Cambridge: Harvard University Press, l979.

Bernheimer, Charles. "Manet's *Olympia*: The Figuration of Scandal." *Poetics Today* 10, no.2 (1989): 255–77.

Bly, Peter A. *Vision and the Visual Arts in Galdós: A Study of Novels and Newspaper Articles.* Liverpool: Francis Cairns, 1986.

Braider, Christopher S. "The Denuded Muse: The Unmasking of Point of View in the Cartesian *Cogito* and Vermeer's *The Art of Painting.*" *Poetics Today* 10, no.1 (1989): 173–203.

Brooks, Cleanth. *The Well-Wrought Urn: Studies in the Structure of Poetry.* 1947. Reprints, New York: Harcourt, Brace & World, 1975.

Broude, Norma, and Mary D. Garrard, eds. *Feminism and Art History.* Icon Editions. New York: Harper & Row, Publishers; 1982.

Buck-Morss, Susan. *The Dialectics of Seeing.* Cambridge: MIT Press, 1989.

Bryson, Norman. *Vision and Painting.* New Haven: Yale University Press, 1983.

Butor, Michel. *Les mots dans la peinture.* Genève: Skira, 1969.

Caws, Mary Ann. *The Art of Interference: Stressed Readings in Verbal and Visual Texts.* Princeton: Princeton University Press, 1989.

Chaffee, Diane. "Visual Art in Literature: The Role of Time and Space in Ekphrastic Creation." *Revista Canadiense de Estudios Hispánicos* 8. no.3 (1984): 311–20.

Clüver, Claus. "On Intersemiotic Transposition." *Poetics Today* 10, no.1 (1989): 55–90.

Cook, Albert. *Changing the Signs: The Fifteenth-Century Breakthrough.* Lincoln: University of Nebraska Press, 1985.

Darst, David H. *Imitatio (Polémica sobre la imitación en el Siglo de Oro).* Madrid: Editorial Orígenes, 1985.

Deleuze, Gilles. *L'image/Mouvement.* Paris: Les Editions de Minuit, 1983.

Derrida, Jacques. *The Truth in Painting.* Translated by Geoff Bennington and Ian McLeod. Chicago: University of Chicago Press, 1987.

D'haen, Theo. "Frames and Boundaries." *Poetics Today* 10, no.2 (1989): 429–37.

Diggory, Terence. "Painting the Speaking Subject." *Diacritics* 15, no.3 (1985): 15–22.

Dotterer, Ronald, and Susan Bowers, eds. *Sexuality, the Female Gaze, and the Arts: Women, the Arts, and Society.* Selinsgrove, Pa.: Susquehanna University Press, 1992.

Estudios sobre Literatura y Arte. Dedicados al profesor Emilio Orozco Díaz. A. Gallego Morells, Andrés Soria, and Nicolás Marín, compilers. 3 vols. Granada: Universidad de Granada, 1979.

Foley, Leo Albert. *Art, Wisdom and the Pursuit of Excellence.* Lincoln: University of Nebraska Press, 1986.

Frank, Joseph. "Spatial Form in Modern Literature." *Sewanee Review* 53 (1945): 221–41, 433–56, and 643–53. Later appeared as *The Idea of Spatial Form.* New Brunswick, N.J.: Rutgers University Press, 1991.

Friedberg, Anne. "Les Flaneurs du Mal(l): Cinema and Postmodernism." *PMLA* 106, no.3 (1991): 419–31.

Gaite, Carmen Martín. *El Cuarto de atrás*. Barcelona: Ediciones Destino, 1978.

Garvin, Harry R., and James M. Heath, eds. *The Arts, Society, Literature*. Lewisburg, Pa.: Bucknell University Press, 1984.

Gilman, Ernest B. "Interart Studies and the "Imperialism" of Language." *Poetics Today* 10.1 (1989): 5–30.

Gombrich, Ernest H. *Art and Illusion*. Bollingen Series, no. 35. Princeton: Princeton University Press, 1969.

———. *Art, Perception and Reality*. Baltimore: Johns Hopkins University Press, 1972.

Grojnowski, Daniel. "Poésie et Photographie: *Kodak* de b. B. Cendrars." *Poetique* 75 (1988): 313–23.

Hagstrum, Jean H. *The Sister Arts: The Tradition of Literary Pictorialism and English Poetry from Dryden to Gray*. Chicago: University of Chicago Press, 1958.

Heffernan, James A. W. *Museum of Words: The Poetics of Ekphrasis from Homer to Ashbery*. Chicago: University of Chicago Press, 1993.

Herméren, Göran. *Influence in Art and Literature*. Princeton: Princeton University Press, 1975.

Hunt, John Dixon, ed. *Encounters: Essays on Literature and the Visual Arts*. New York: W. W. Norton & Company, 1971.

Hunter, Jefferson. *Image and Word: The Interaction of Twentieth-Century Photographs and Texts*. Cambridge: Harvard University Press, 1987.

La iconografía en el arte contemporáneo (Coloquio Internacional de Xalapa). México: Universidad Nacional Autónoma de México, 1982.

Jakobson, Roman. "On the Verbal Art of William Blake and Other Poet Painters." *Linguistic Inquiry* I, no.1 (1970): 1–23.

Janson, H. W. *History of Art*. New York: Harry N. Abrams, 1962.

Jay, Martin. *Downcast Eyes: The Denigration of Vision in Twentieth-Century French Thought*. Berkeley: University of California Press, 1994.

Kristeva, Julia. *Desire in Language. A Semiotic Approach to Literature and Art*. New York: Columbia University Press, 1980.

Klonsky, Milton, ed. *Speaking Pictures: A Gallery of Pictorial Poetry from the Sixteenth Century to the Present*. New York: Harmony Books, 1975.

Kováks, Steven. *From Enchantment to Rage. The Story of Surrealist Cinema*. Cranbury, N.J.: Associated University Presses, 1980.

Krieger, Murray. *Ekphrasis: The Illusion of the Natural Sign*. Baltimore: Johns Hopkins University Press, 1992.

———. "The Ekphrastic Principle and the Still Movement of Poetry; or Laokoön Revisited." In his book *The Play and Place of Criticism*, 105–28. Baltimore: Johns Hopkins University Press, 1967.

Kurman, George. "Ecphrasis in Epic Poetry," *Comparative Literature* 26 (1974): 1–14.

Langer, Susanne K. *Feeling and Form: A Theory of Art Developed from "Philosophy in a New Key."* New York: Charles Scribner's Sons, 1953.

———, ed. *A Source Book of Writings by Artists, Critics, and Philosophers.* 1958. Reprint, New York: Oxford University Press, 1961.

Laude, Jean. "On the Analysis of Poems and Paintings." *New Literary History* 3 (spring 1972): 471–86.

Lessing, Gotthold Ephrain. *Laokoön: An Essay on the Limits of Painting and Poetry.* Translated with an introduction and notes by Edward Allen McCormick. 1962. Reprint, Baltimore: Johns Hopkins University Press, 1984.

Livermore, Ann. *Artists and Aesthetics in Spain.* London: Tamesis, 1988.

Markiewicz, Henryk. "Ut Pictura Poesis . . . A History of the Topos and the Problem." *New Literary History* 18, no.3 (1987): 535–58.

McClathy, J. D., ed. *Poets on Painters: Essays on the Art of Painting by Twentieth-Century Poets.* Berkeley: University of California Press, 1988.

Meltzer, Françoise. *Salome and the Dance of Writing; Portraits of Mimesis in Literature.* Chicago: University of Chicago Press, 1987.

Meyers, Jeffrey. *Painting and the Novel.* Manchester England: Manchester University Press, 1975.

Mitchell, W. J. T. *Iconology: Image, Text, Ideology.* Chicago: University of Chicago Press, 1986.

———. *Picture Theory.* Chicago: University of Chicago Press, 1994.

———. "Space, Ideology, and Literary Representation." *Poetics Today* 10, no.1 (1989): 91–102.

Morris, Wright. "The Camera Eye." *Critical Inquiry* 8, no.2 (1981): 1–15.

Munro, Thomas. *The Arts and Their Interrelations.* New York: Liberal Arts Press, 1951.

Pérez Firmat, Gustavo. *Literature and Liminality: Festive Readings in the Hispanic Tradition.* Durham, N.C.: Duke University Press, 1986.

Pierce, James Smith. *From Abacus to Zeus: A Handbook of Art History.* Englewood Cliffs, N.J.: Prentice Hall, 1968.

Pleynet, Marcelin. *Painting and System.* Chicago: University of Chicago Press, 1984.

Poetics Today. Special issue. "Literature and Art," edited by Wendy Steiner. 10, nos.1 and 2 (1989).

Pollock, Griselda. *Vision and Difference: Femininity, Feminism and Histories of Art.* New York: Routledge, 1988.

Praz, Mario. *Mnemosyne: The Parallel Between Literature and the Visual Arts.* Bollingen Series, no. 16. Princeton: Princeton University Press, 1970.

Pring-Mill, R. D. F. "Some Techniques of Representation in the *Sueños* and the *Criticón*." *Bulletin of Hispanic Studies* 45 (1968): 270–84.

Rivkin, Laura. "Seeing, Painting, and Picturing in *La Regenta*." *Hispanic Review* 55 (1987): 301–22.

Schapiro, Meyer. "On Some Problems in the Semiotics of Visual Art: Field and Vehicle in Image–Signs." *Janua linguarum*, 487–503. The Hague: Mouton et Cie., 1970.

Scully, Vincent. "The Great Goddess and the Palace Architecture of Crete." Broude and Garrard, 33–43.

Seznec, Jean. "Art and Literature: A Plea for Humility." *New Literary History* 3 (1972): 569–74.

Spitzer, Leo. "The "Ode on a Grecian Urn," or Content vs. Metagrammar." *Essays on English and American Literature*. Edited by Anna Hatcher. Princeton: Princeton University Press, 1962. First appeared in *Contemporary Literature* 7 (1955): 203–26.

Steiner, Wendy. "The Causes of Effect: Edith Wharton and the Economics of Ekphrasis." *Poetics Today* 10, no.2 (1989): 279–97.

———. *The Colors of Rhetoric*. Chicago: University of Chicago Press, 1984.

———. Introduction to *Poetics Today* 10, no.1 (1989): 1–3. Special issue. "Literature and Art."

———. *Pictures of Romance. Form against Context in Literature and Painting*. Chicago: University of Chicago Press, 1988.

Sutton, Walter. "The Literary Image and the Reader: A Consideration of the Theory of Spatial Form." *Journal of Aesthetics and Art Criticism* 16 (1957–58): 112–23.

Tagg, John. *The Burden of Representation: Essays on Photographies and Histories*. Minneapolis: University of Minnesota Press, 1988.

de Torre, Guillermo. "Ut Pictura Poesis." In his *Minorías y masas en la cultura y el arte contemporáneos*, 161–86. Barcelona: EDHASA, 1963.

Weisstein, Ulrich. "Collage, Montage and Related Terms: Their Literal and Figurative Use in and Application to Techniques and Forms in Various Arts." *Comparative Literary Studies* 15 (1978): 124–39.

———. "Literature and the Visual Arts." In *Interrelations of Literature*. edited by Jean-Pierre Barricelli and Joseph Gibaldi. New York: Modern Language Association of America, 1980.

SPANISH LITERATURE

General

Anales de la literatura española contemporánea. Special Issue. "Twentieth-Century Spanish Poetry." 18, no.1 (1993).

Baehr, Rudolf. *Manual de versificación española*. Translated by K. Wagner and F. López Estrada. Madrid: Gredos, 1981.

Batlló, José. *Antología de la nueva poesía española*. Madrid: El Bardo, 1968.

Bergmann, Emilie L. *Art Inscribed: Essays on Ekphrasis in Spanish Golden Age Poetry*. Cambridge: Harvard University Press, 1979.

Bou, Enric. "El poeta en el museo: pasajes y paisajes (A propósito de Pedro Salinas y Marià Manent)." *Revista de Estudios Hispánicos* 22. no.2 (1988): 63–79.

Bretz, Mary Lee. "Espronceda's *El diablo mundo* and Romantic Irony." *Revista de Estudios Hispánicos* 16 (1982): 257–74.

Buenaventura, Ramón, ed. *Las diosas blancas: antología de la joven poesía española escrita por mujeres*. Madrid: Hiperión, 1985.

Cañas, Dionisio. "En lugar de la certeza: Poesía y percepción: tres poetas españoles de hoy: Francisco Brines, Claudio Rodríguez, y José Angel Valente." *DAI*, May, *Dissertation Abstracts International* 1983. 43 (ll): 3614A.

Castellet, José María. *Nueve novísimos poetas españoles.* Barcelona: Barral Editores, 1970.

Ciplijauskaité, Biruté, ed. *Novísimos, postnovísimos, clásicos: La poesía de los 80 en España.* Madrid: Orígenes, 1990.

Debicki, Andrew P. "Una poesía de la posmodernidad: Los novísimos." *Anales de la Literatura Española Contemporánea* 14 (1989): 33–50.

———. "Poesía española de la postmodernidad." *Anales de literatura española* (Alicante) 6 (1988): 165–80.

———. *Poetry of Discovery: The Spanish Generation of 1956–71.* Lexington: University Press of Kentucky, 1985.

———. *Spanish Poetry of the Twentieth Century: Modernity and Beyond.* Lexington: University Press of Kentucky, 1994.

———. "Three Moments of Post-Civil War Spanish Poetry." In *After the War: Essays on Recent Spanish Poetry and Spanish-American Studies,* edited by Salvador Jiménez Fajardo and John C. Wilcox, 29–45. Boulder: Society of Spanish, 1988.

de Torre, Guillermo. *Minorías y masas en la cultura y el arte contemporáneos,* chap. 6, "Ut pictura poesis," 161–86. Barcelona: EDHASA, 1963.

Díaz Plaja, Guillermo. *Ensayos sobre literatura y arte.* Prólogo de Manuel Cerezales. Madrid: Aguilar, 1973.

Havard, Robert G. *From Romanticism to Surrealism: Seven Spanish Poets.* Totowa, N.J.: Barnes & Noble Books, 1988.

Persin, Margaret H. *Recent Spanish Poetry and the Role of the Reader.* Lewisburg, Pa.: Bucknell University Press, 1987.

Pring-Mill, Robert. "The Redemption of Reality through Documentary Poetry." In *Ernesto Cardenal: Zero Hour and Other Documentary Poems,* Edited by Donald D. Walsh. New York: New Directions, 1980.

Quance, Roberta. "Entre líneas: posturas críticas ante la poesía escrita por mujeres." *La balsa de la medusa* 4 (1987): 73–96.

Roske, Joachim L. "Hacia un nuevo lenguaje artístico colectivo." *Revista de Occidente* 95 (1971): 196–204.

Rubio, Fanny, and José Luis Falcó. *Poesía española contemporánea (1939–1980).* Madrid: Alhambra, 1982.

Siebenmann, Gustav. *Los estilos poéticos en España desde 1900.* Madrid: Gredos, 1973.

Soufas, C. Christopher. *Conflict of Light and Wind: The Spanish Generation of 1927 and the Ideology of Poetic Form.* Middletown, Conn.: Wesleyan University Press, 1989.

Spanish Women Writers. Edited by Linda Gould Levine, Ellen Engelson, and Gloria Feiman Waldman. Westport, Conn.: Greenwood Press, 1993.

Spires, Robert. *Beyond the Metafictional Mode.* Lexington: University Press of Kentucky, 1985.

Studies in 20th-Century Literature. Special Issue. "Contemporary Spanish Poetry." Edited by Andrew P. Debicki. 16, no.1 (1992).

Ugalde, Sharon Keefe. *Conversaciones y poemas: La nueva poesía femenina española en castellano.* Madrid: Siglo Veintiuno, 1991.

Zurgai: poetas por su pueblo. Special issue. "Mujeres poetas." [Bilbao, Spain] June 1993.

Individual Poets

Rafael Alberti

Primary Sources

———. *A la pintura*. Buenos Aires: Losada, 1948.

———. *La arboleda perdida: Libro primero*. México: Séneca, 1942.

———. *La arboleda perdida: Libros primero y segundo*. Buenos Aires: Compañia General Fabril Editora, 1959.

———. *La arboleda perdida: Libros tercero y cuarto*. Barcelona: Seix Barral, 1987.

———. *Lo que canté y dije de Picasso*. Barcelona: Editorial Bruguera, 1981.

———. *Los 8 nombres de Picasso y no digo más que lo que no digo*. 1970. Reprints, Barcelona: Kairós, 1978.

———. *Picasso en Avignon*. Paris: Le Cercle d'Art: 1970.

———. *Picasso, le rayon ininterrompu/Picasso, o el rayo gve no cesa*. Paris: Le Cercle d'Art: 1972.

———. *Poemas escenicos*; Buenos Aires: Losada, 1962.

Secondary Sources

Areán, Carlos. "La imagen pictórica en la poesía de Alberti." *Cuadernos hispanoamericanos* 288–90 (1974): 198–209.

———. "Rafael Alberti en la poesía de la pintura." *Arbor* 461 (1984): 91–105.

Benson, Douglas K. "La mar y el Prado: Compenetración y hablante en la poesía de Alberti." *Siglo XX/20th Century* 3, nos.1–2 (1985–86): 5–11.

Caparrós Esperante, Luis. "Los Picasso de Rafael Alberti (Equivalencias de Poesía y Pintura en *Los 8 nombres de Picasso*)." *Castilla* 2–3 (1981): 7–21.

Cerdán, Francis. "Rafael Alberty y la pintura de Antonio Saura: *Visión memorable*." In *Dr. Rafael Alberti: Poeta en Toulouse*, 225–238. Université de Toulouse—Le Mirail: Service de Publications, 1984.

Crespo, Angel. "Realismo y pitagorismo en el libro de Alberti *A la pintura*." *Papeles de son armadans* 30 (1963): 93–126.

Jiménez Fajardo, Salvador. *Multiple Spaces: The Poetry of Rafael Alberti*. London: Tamesis Books, 1985. Reviewed by Roberto Manteiga in *Hispania* 70, no.2 (1987): 271–72.

———. "Rafael Alberti's Pictorial Memory." *Siglo XX/20th Century.* 3, nos.1–2 (1985–86): 2–5.

———. "Words Painting Words: Rafael Alberti's "Tiziano'." *Revista Hispánica Moderna* 2 (1989): 151–62.

González, Bernardo Antonio. "Ekphrasis and Autobiography: The Case of Rafael Alberti." *Anales de la literatura española contemporánea* 15, nos.1–3 (1990): 29–49.

González Martín, Jerónimo P. "Alberti y la pintura." *Insula* 305 (1972): 1, 12–13.

———. *Rafael Alberti*. Barcelona: Ediciones Júcar, 1978.

Lorenzo-Rivero, Luis. "Rafael Alberti: Pintura, poesía y política." *Letras de Deusto* 15, no.31 (1985): 5–25.

Manteiga, Roberto C. "Color Synthesis and Antithesis: The Parallel Construction of Color Images in Rafael Alberti's Early Works." *Crítica Hispánica* 3, no.1 (1981): 21–35.

———. *The Poetry of Rafael Alberti: A Visual Approach.* London: Tamesis, 1978.

———. "Rafael Alberti's "Poesía Taurina': A Visual Perspective." *Hispanic Journal* 1, no.2 (1980): 73–87.

Monguió, Luis. "Rafael Alberti: Poetry and Painting." *Crítica Hispánica* 1 (1979): 75–85.

Morris, C. Brian. "Forgotten Idols: Miss X and Charley Bowers." *Siglo XX/20th Century* 3, nos.1–2 (1985–86): 15–23.

Pauls, Marcia Lou. "Outspoken Texts: Ekphrasis in Rafael Alberti's Early Poems."

Risco, Antonio. "Notas sobre *A la pintura* de Rafael Alberti." *Hispanic Review* 55 (1987): 475–89.

Sieber, Harry. "Alberti's Boticelli." *Kentucky Romance Quarterly* 16 (1969): 329–37.

Soufas, C. Christopher. "Alberti's Post-Albertian Epistemological 'Velázquez' as Self-Consuming Artifact and Art-Historical Criticism." *Siglo XX/20th Century* 3, nos.1–2 (1985–86): 23–27.

———. "Rafael Alberti." *Conflict* 201–38.

Wesseling, Pieter. *Revolution and Tradition: The Poetry of Rafael Alberti.* Valencia-Chapel Hill: Albatross/Ediciones Hispanófila, 1981.

Winkelmann, Ana María. "Pintura y poesía en Rafael Alberti." *Papeles de son armadans* 30 (1963): 148–62.

Zardoya, Concha. "La técnica metafórica albertiana (en *Marinero en tierra*). Cromatismo." *Poesía española del siglo XX.* 3: 425–42. Gredos: Madrid, 1974.

María Victoria Atencia

Primary Sources

———. *Ex Libris.* Madrid: Visor, 1984.

———. *Marta & María.* 1976. Reprints, Madrid: Caballo Griego para la Poesía, 1984.

———. *El mundo de M.V..* Madrid: Insula, 1978.

———. *La pared contigua.* Madrid: Hiperión, 1989.

Secondary Sources

Ciplijauskaité, Biruté. "Recent Poetry and the Essential Word." *Studies in 20th Century Literature* 16, nos.1 (1992): 149–63.

———. "La serena plenitud de María Victoria Atencia." *Alaluz* 22 (1990): 7–12.

Jaffe, Catherine. "Gender, Intersubjectivity, and the Author/Reader Exchange in the Poetry of María Victoria Atencia." *Letras Peninsulares*, 5, no.2 (1992): 291–302.

León, Victoria. "María Victoria Atencia: Poesía completa (1955–1990). Edición, notas y traducción inglesa." Ph.D. diss., University of Málaga, 1993.

Metzler, Linda D. "Images of the Body in the Poetry of María Victoria Atencia." *Anales de la literatura española contemporánea* 18, no.1 (1993): 173–81.

Ugalde, Sharon Keefe. *Conversaciones y poemas: La nueva poesía femenina española en castellano*, 3–20.

———. "María Victoria Atencia," In *Spanish Women Writers*, edited by Levine, Marson, Starcevic, and Waldman, 28–32. Westport, Conn.: Greenwood Press, 1992.

———. "La sujetividad desde "lo otro" en la poesía de María Sanz, María Victoria Atencia, y Clara Janés." *Revista Canadiense de Estudios Hispánicos* 14, no.3 (1990): 511–23.

———. "Time and Ekphrasis in the Poetry of María Victoria Atencia." *Confluencia* 3, no.1 (1987): 7–12.

Gloria Fuertes

Primary Sources

———. *Historia de Gloria: amor, humor y desamor* Madrid: Cátedra, 1981.
———. *Obras incompletas*. Madrid: Cátedra, 1978.

Secondary Sources

Debicki, Andrew P. "Gloria Fuertes: Intertextuality and Reversal of Expectations." *Poetry of Discovery*, 81–101.

Persin, Margaret H. "Humor as Semiosis in the Poetry of Gloria Fuertes." *Recent Spanish Poetry*, 119–136.

Jaime Gil de Biedma

Primary Sources

———. *Moralidades, 1959–1964*. Mexico City: Joaquín Mortiz, 1966.
———. *Las personas del verbo*. 1975. Reprint, Barcelona: Editorial Seix Barral, 1982.
———. *Poemas póstumos*. 1968. Reprint, Madrid: Poesía para Todos, 1970.

Secondary Sources

Campbell, Federico. *Infame turba*. Barcelona: Lumen, 1971.

Cañas, Dionisio. "Gil de Biedma y su paseo solitario entre las ruinas." *Revista de Occidente* 110–11 (1990): 101–10.

Persin, Margaret H. "Intertextual Strategies in the Poetry of Jaime Gil de

Biedma." *Revista Canadiense de Estudios Hispánicos* 11. no.3 (1987): 573–90.

———. "Self as Other in Jaime Gil de Biedma's *Poemas póstumos*." *Anales de la literatura española contemporánea* 12 (1987): 273–90.

Quance, Roberta. "Writing Posthumously: Jaime Gil de Biedma." *Anales de la literatura española contemporánea* 12 (1987): 291–309.

Pere Gimferrer

Primary Sources

———. *Cine y literatura*. Barcelona: Planeta, S. A., 1985.

———. *Poemas 1963–1969*. Madrid: Visor, 1979.

———. *Poesía 1970–1977*. Madrid: Visor, 1978.

———. *El vendeval*. Barcelona: Ediciones Península, 1989.

Secondary Sources

Debicki, Andrew P. "Una poesía de la postmodernidad: los novísimos." *Anales de la literatura española contemporánea* 14 (1989): 33–50.

Rogers, Timothy. "Verbal Collage in Pere Gimferrer's *Poemas 1963–1969*." *Hispania* 67, no.2 (1984): 207–13.

Talens, Jenaro. "Reflexiones en torno a la poesía última de Pere Gimferrer." *Insula* 304 (1972): 15.

Manuel Machado

Primary Sources

———. *Alma. Apolo*. Introduction by Alfredo Carballo Picazo. Madrid: Ediciones Alcalá, 1967.

———. *Apolo. Teatro pictórico*. Madrid: V. Prieto y Cía., 1911.

———. *Ars moriendi*. Madrid: Ediciones Mundo Latino, 1921.

———. *Canciones y dedicatorias*. Madrid: Imprenta Hispano-America, 1915.

———. *Cante hondo*. Madrid: Imprenta Helénica, 1912. 2d ed. Madrid: Renacimiento, 1916.

———. *La guerra literaria*. Edited by María Pilar Celma Valero and Francisco J. Blasco Pascual. Madrid Larceu Narcea, 1981.

———. *El mal poema*. Madrid: Castro y Cía., 1909.

———. *Obras completas*. Vols. 1–4. Madrid: Editorial Mundo Latino, 1923.

———. *Phoenix. Nuevas canciones*. Madrid: Ediciones Héroe, 1935.

———. *Sevilla y otros poemas*. Madrid: Editorial América, 1918.

Secondary Sources

Agrait, Gustavo. "A propósito de Manuel Machado." *La Torre* 3, no.10 (1989): 281–95.

Alonso, Dámaso. "Ligereza y gravedad en la poesía de Manual Machado." In his *Poetas españoles contemporáneos*. Madrid: Gredos, 1952.

Bou, Enric. "Decadencia e imperio: la poesía pictórica de Manuel Machado."
I, *Divergencias y unidad: perspectivas sobre la generación del 98 y Antonio
Machado.* Edited by John P. Gabriele, 125–40. Madrid: Discurso Orígenes,
1990.

Brotherston, Gordon. *Manuel Machado: A Reevaluation.* Cambridge: Cambridge University Press, 1968.

Carballo Picazo, Alfredo. Introduction to *Alma. Apolo* by Manuel Machado.
Madrid: Ediciones Alcalá, 1967.

Celma Valero, María Pilar, and Francisco J. Blasco Pascual. Introduction and
notes to *La guerra literaria* by Manuel Machado. Madrid: Narcea, 1981.

Díaz-Plaja, Guillermo. "El autorretrato en los Machado." *Boletín de la Real
Academia* 55 (1975): 219–26.

Diego, Gerardo. *Manuel Machado, poeta.* Madrid: Nacional, 1974.

D'Ors, Miguel. "Manuel Machado: "Ciertas inexactitudes . . ." In *Estudios sobre
literatura y arte dedicados al profesor Emilio Orozco,* Edited by A. Gallego
Morell, Andrés Soria y Nicolás Marín, 437–53. Granada: Universidad de
Granada, 1979.

Gayton, Gillian. *Manuel Machado y los poetas simbolistas franceses.* Valencia:
Editorial Bello, 1975.

López Estrada, Francisco. *Los "primitivos" de Manuel y Antonio Machado.*
Madrid: Cupsa Editorial, 1977.

Navas Ruiz, Ricardo. "Felipe IV: Notas a un poema." *Papeles de son armadans*
49, no.145 (1968): 87–94.

Phillips, Allen W. "Decadent Elements in the Poetry of Manuel Machado." In
*Waiting for Pegasus: Studies on the Presence of Symbolism and Decadence
in Hispanic Letters,* Edited by Roland Grass and William R. Risley, 65–76.
Macomb: West Illinois University Essays in Literature, 1979.

———. "Manuel Machado y el Modernismo." *Cuadernos Hispanoamericanos*
407 (1984): 77–92.

Romero Luque, Manuel. *Las ideas poéticas de Manuel Machado.* Seville, Spain:
Diputación Provincial de Sevilla, 1992.

Sánchez Canton, F. J. *The Prado.* 1959. Reprint, London: Thames and Hudson, 1966.

Villena, Luis Antonio de. "Recapitulación y decadencia." *Cuadernos Hispanoamericanos* 428 (1986): 125–30.

Carmen Martín Gaite

Primary Source

———. *A rachas.* 1976; Madrid: Hiperión, 1986.

Secondary Sources

Castillo, Debra A. "Never-ending Story: Carmen Martín Gaite's *The Back
Room.*" *PMLA* 102 (1987): 814–28.

Levine, Linda Gould. "Carmen Martín Gaite's *El cuarto de atrás:* A Portrait of
the Artist as Woman." Servodidio and Welles, 161–72.

Ordóñez, Elizabeth. "Reading, Telling and the Text of Carmen Martín Gaite's *El cuarto de atrás.*" Servodidio and Welles, 173–84.

Servodidio, Mirella, and Marcia L. Welles, eds. *From Fiction to Metafiction: Essays in Honor of Carmen Martín Gaite.* Lincoln, Nebr.: Society of Spanish and Spanish American Studies, 1983.

Welles, Marcia L. "Carmen Martín Gaite: Fiction as Desire." Servodidio and Welles, 197–207.

Ana Rossetti

Primary sources

———. "Calvin Klein Underwear." In her. *Poemas autógrafos.* Madrid: Círculo de Bellas Artes, 1987.

———. *Devocionario.* Madrid: Visor, 1986.

———. *Los devaneos de Erato.* Valencia: Prometeo, 1980.

———. *Indicios vehementes (Poesía 1979–1984).* Madrid: Hiperión, 1985.

———. *Yesterday.* Madrid: Torremozas, 1988.

Rossetti, Ana, and Fernando Rubio. *Imago Pasionis.* Palacio Municipal San Fernando. 16–31 March 1990.

Secondary Sources

Ciplijauskaité, Biruté. "Los diferentes lenguajes del amor." *Monographic Review /Revista Monográfica* 6 (1990): 113–27.

Fernández Palacios, Jesús. "Entrevista con Ana Rossetti." Prologue to Rossetti's *Indicios vehementes.* Madrid: Hiperión, 1985.

Ferradáns, Carmela. "La (re)velación del significante: Erótica textual y retórica barroca en "Calvin Klein, Underdrawers" de Ana Rossetti." *Monographic Review/Revista Monográfica* 6 (1990): 183–91.

Makris, Mary. "Mass Media and the "New" Ekphrasis: Ana Rossetti's "Chico Wrangler" and "Calvin Klein, Underdrawers." *Journal of Interdisciplinary Literary Studies* 5, no.2 (1993): 237–49.

Rosas, Yolanda, and Hilde Cramsie. "La apropiación del lenguaje y la desmitificación de los códigos sexuales de la cultura en la poesía de Ana Rossetti." *Explicación de Textos Literarios* 20. no.1 (1991–92): 1–11.

Servodidio, Mirella. "Ana Rossetti's Double-Voiced Discourse of Desire." *Revista Hispánica Moderna* 45 (1992): 318–27.

Téllez, J. José. "Está sola y busca: Aproximaciones a la poesía de Ana Rossetti." *Zurgai* (June 1993): 82–87.

Ugalde, Sharon Keefe. *Conversaciones y poemas.* 147–66.

———. "Erotismo y revisionismo en la poesía de Ana Rossetti." *Siglo XX/20th Century* 7, nos.1–2 (1989–90): 24–29.

Wilcox, John C. "Ana Rossetti y sus cuatro musas poéticas." *Revista Canadiense de Estudios Hispánicos* 14, no.3 (1990): 525–40.

Jenaro Talens

Primary Sources

———. *The Branded Eye: Buñuel's Un chien andalou.* Minneapolis: University of Minnesota Press, 1993. Originally published as *El ojo tachado.* Madrid: Ediciones Cátedra, 1986.

———. *Orfeo filmado en el campo de batalla.* Madrid: Hiperión, 1994.

———. *Proximidad del silencio (1980–81).* Madrid: Hiperión, 1981.

———. *Purgatori/Purgatorio.* Madrid: Hiperión, 1986.

———. *Tabula rasa.* Madrid: Hiperión, 1985.

Talens, Jenaro, and Michaël Nerlich. *La mirada extranjera.* Madrid: Hiperión, 1985.

Secondary Sources

Company, Juan M. Prologue to *Proximidad del silencio (1980–81)* by Jenaro Talens. Madrid: Hiperión, 1981.

Quervo Poesía 8 (1986) [Valencia, Spain].

José Angel Valente

Primary Sources

———. *A modo de esperanza.* Madrid: Adonais, 1955.

———. *El inocente.* Mexico City: Joaquín Mortiz, 1970.

———. *La memoria y los signos.* Madrid: Revista de Occidente, 1966.

———. *Nueve enunciaciones.* Málaga: Sur, Hoy Dardo, 1982.

———. *Los ojos deseados.* Madrid: El Instituto de Estética y Teoría de las Artes, 1990.

———. *Poemas a Lázaro.* Madrid: Indice, 1960.

———. *Punto cero (Poesía 1953–1979).* 1972. Reprint, Barcelona: Ed. Seix Barral, 1980.

Secondary Sources

Debicki, Andrew P. "José Angel Valente: Reading and Rereading." *Poetry of Discovery: The Spanish Generation of 1956–71*, 102–22.

Marson, Ellen Engelson. *Poesía y poética de José Angel Valente.* New York: Eliseo Torres, 1978.

Miscellaneous

Buñuel, Luis. *My Last Sigh: The Autobiography of Luis Buñuel.* Translated by Abigail Israel. New York: Vintage Books, 1984.

Cirlot, Joan E. *A Dictionary of Symbols*. Translated by Jack Sage. New York: Philosophical Library, 1962.

The Columbia Viking Desk Encyclopedia. 1953. Reprint, New York: Viking Press, 1960.

Costa, René de. "Juan Gris and Poetry: From Illustration to Creation." *The Art Bulletin* 71 (1989): 674–692.

Kamber, Gerald. *Max Jacob and the Poetics of Cubism*. Baltimore: Johns Hopkins University Press, 1971.

Index

251